# INVOLUNTARY CONSENT

# INVOLUNTARY CONSENT

## THE ILLUSION OF CHOICE

## IN JAPAN'S

## ADULT VIDEO INDUSTRY

### AKIKO TAKEYAMA

STANFORD UNIVERSITY PRESS • STANFORD, CALIFORNIA

Stanford University Press
Stanford, California

Printed in the United States of America on acid-free, archival-quality paper

Library of Congress Cataloging-in-Publication Data
Names: Takeyama, Akiko, 1970– author.
Title: Involuntary consent : the illusion of choice in Japan's adult video industry / Akiko Takeyama.
Description: Stanford, California : Stanford University Press, 2023. | Includes bibliographical references and index.
Identifiers: LCCN 2022049266 (print) | LCCN 2022049267 (ebook) | ISBN 9781503628762 (cloth) | ISBN 9781503633780 (paperback) | ISBN 9781503633797 (ebook)
Subjects: LCSH: Pornographic film industry—Japan. | Sex Workers—Japan—Social conditions. | Motion picture actors and actresses—Japan—Social conditions. | Sexual consent—Japan. | Free choice of employment—Japan.
Classification: LCC PN1995.9.S45 I68 2023 (print) | LCC PN1995.9.S45 (ebook) | DDC 392.60952/135—dc23
LC record available at https://lccn.loc.gov/2022049266
LC ebook record available at https://lccn.loc.gov/2022049267

Cover design: Susan Zucker
Cover photograph: Shutterstock
Typeset by Elliott Beard in Minion Pro 10/14

# CONTENTS

# NOTE ON JAPANESE TERMS
## AND CURRENCY

In this book, Japanese names are written in the Japanese order with family names first. An exception is made for authors and performers whose names have been published using the Western name order. All names are given pseudonyms to maintain confidentiality with the exception of Amatsuka Moe, Kozai Saki, and Fujiwara Hitomi, all of whom go by their model names. Some of the identifiable information concerning my informants is also modified for the same reason.

This text uses the modified Hepburn system of romanization. Long vowels are denoted by macrons (ā, ē, ī, ō, ū), with the exception of places or terms that are well known in English (Tokyo, for example).

Currency exchange has been calculated using a rate of 100 yen per US dollar, although the exchange rate has fluctuated during the period of my field-work, follow-up research, and book writing phase over the last seven years.

# INVOLUNTARY CONSENT

# INTRODUCTION

It was a bit after 7:30 p.m. on a chilly spring evening in Tokyo. I didn't know what to expect on my way to a meet-and-greet celebration for Japanese porn star Amatsuka Moe. All I knew was that she had recently won SKY PerfecTV!'s 2018 Adult Female Performer of the Year, one of the most prestigious awards in Japan's adult video (AV) industry. Using my smartphone for directions, I walked down a narrow side street, entered a nondescript seven-story multi-tenant building, and took a tiny elevator to the third floor. When the door opened, I was surprised. About 200 Japanese white-collar workers in dark business suits—many being nonregular employees, as I later learned—were crammed into a roughly 1,000 square-foot room with a makeshift stage and portable chairs. The room was a packed with middle-aged male fans obsessed with a young porn star.

I was surprised by both the turnout and the timing. Held in Tokyo's famous Akihabara district, the largest electronics retail marketplace in the world, the party took place on March 28—a few days before the end of Japan's fiscal year, one of the busiest times of the year for office workers of any stripe. The party-goers did not simply show up for the event, either. To gain admission, they had to purchase at least one of Amatsuka's DVD titles for about US$30 at M's Aki-habara, a nearby adult retail store, by 7 p.m. on the same day. M's Akihabara is about a minute away by foot from the Akihabara train station, a major Tokyo railway and subway transit point. To purchase the DVDs and walk to the event on time, most of the attendees had to leave their offices right after work; this is unusual for Japanese men, especially during such a hectic time of the year, when most would be inclined to put in overtime hours.

Sugimoto, Amatsuka's manager, greeted me at the front desk. I had met him earlier at a meeting of the Japan Production Guild (JPG), a nonprofit organization established in 2017 that consists of forty-three AV modeling agencies.[1] Sugimoto directs the organization and is president of B-Star, one of Japan's largest and most established AV modeling agencies, which Amatsuka belongs to. Sugimoto led me through the crowd to the stage in back, where I saw Amatsuka cheerfully interacting one-on-one with a long line of men eager to meet her.

The scene reminded me of Japanese mainstream *aidoru* (idol) events, where fans line up to shake hands and get a photo—like a book signing on steroids. *Aidoru* is a general term to refer to a type of entertainer and celebrity known for their personality, talent, and image.[2] Their images are manufactured and commodified primarily as singers, but also as actors, models, and dancers. Amatsuka, an AV idol known among male aficionados for her slender body and perfectly round D-cup breasts, was wearing a short pastel-pink dress with flower stitching around her tastefully exposed cleavage. Her soft, smooth shoulders were exposed, her naked legs teetering on top of white 5.5-inch platform heels. Her color-matching makeup with pastel-pink cheek powder and lip gloss made her pale, pretty face shine. With her makeup and hairdo—medium-long silky brown hair layered and curled inwardly like a Disney princess—she looked like a radiant flower against a sea of dark-suited salarymen.

Amatsuka's interactions with her fans are a model of production line efficiency. She spends only about thirty seconds with each fan. Those who purchased one DVD are allowed to shake hands and take a photo of her in two different poses. With two DVDs, they are allowed to have a photo taken with her. For her fan photos, Amatsuka endlessly repeats several different feminine poses: a heart shape formed by her long thin fingers at her chest; resting her chin on her well-maintained hands; flashing a peace sign with her French-manicured fingernails; big smiling face with index fingers on her cheeks; an exaggerated, wide-eyed "I'm-in-trouble" expression, with her index finger on her lower lip. Despite the long queue, fans patiently wait their turn. Some hang out with other fans or kill time on their phones. Others enjoy watching Amatsuka on stage. Once a fan gets on stage, he enjoys a brief conversation with

Amatsuka while holding hands. He might present a gift he brought and receive special thanks or simply focus his limited time on speaking to her. No matter how he spends the time, a nearby attendant soon gives a verbal cue, *jikan desu* ("It's time"), to ready them for a two-shot. Once the shot is taken, Amatsuka clutches the fan's head above the ears, playfully shaking his hair like a puppy dog. (Her way of showing appreciation and saying goodbye, she told me later.) Making eye contact with the attendant, Amatsuka lets the fan go, and the attendant gives his camera or phone back. Rinse and repeat.

Most of the men are in their forties. As a group, they look fatigued from their long workday. Most have loosened or removed their ties to relax. Their shirts, which were probably stiff with starch in the morning, have become rumpled. They wear comfortable fake leather shoes and carry nylon backpacks or messenger bags. Other fans are wearing casual khaki pants, hoodies, walking shoes, and sun hats. (They might have had a day off or may be unemployed.) Many of the men have a middle-aged paunch and hairline. By stark contrast, Sugimoto, who is around the same age, wears a simple white T-shirt and gray cotton jacket paired with rolled-up blue jeans, his ankles exposed in a pair of white leather sneakers in mint condition. His hair is slicked back with gel, eyebrows trimmed and face freshly shaven. His workday is just getting going. Even fully clothed, his well-toned body is noticeable, with his intensive focus embodied in his straightened back and brisk walk: he's clearly a supervisor, sitting at the top of a pecking order in terms of wealth, influence, and access to the idol.

Sugimoto's focus is a matter of necessity. Sales events like this have become increasingly necessary in the AV industry to stem the tide of online streaming, which is threatening the market for DVD sales in Japan. In 2000, nearly all adult videos in Japan were released on DVD; today they comprise only 60 percent of overall AV sales. Yet DVDs are twice as profitable as on-demand streaming video, and in the AV industry, selling at least 1,000 DVD copies of most titles is a crucial milestone to cover production costs.[3] (Sugimoto told me that Amatsuka, who is a top-selling actress and whose production budget is much larger than usual, has a sales goal of 2,500 DVD copies per title.) To put this in historical context, a typical adult content DVD title, whose retail price is usually set at 2,980 yen (US$30), on average barely sells more than 1,000 copies. This contrasts with VHS titles, which were typically priced around 9,000 yen (US$90) and sold at least 6,000 copies to video rental shops and individual consumers throughout Japan. Simple math shows that an AV maker today must produce eighteen more titles to maintain the same level of sales profit once enjoyed three decades ago.

To increase sales of DVDs, video makers in Japan typically use *taimen hanbai* (a face-to-face, personal selling method) inspired by the wildly successful female idol group AKB48. The group, which has a rotating cast of forty-eight members, launched in 2005 and has sold more than 40 million CDs, the most by a single Japanese artist or group.[4] Modeling themselves after AKB's sales strategy, AV video makers rent cheap event spaces, sparsely decorate them, and entice fans to buy DVDs to get modest pleasure through a brief brush with an AV idol. And as these male fans know—most came of age during Japan's Employment Ice Age and are financially struggling—going to hostess clubs or other sex-related services would cost more than the price of a DVD or two. So, it's a win-win situation for the video producers and the fans. At tonight's event, the video producers sold more than 400 copies from Amatsuka's oeuvre—catchy titles (translated into English) like *Give Me a Peek of Your Panties with a Scornful Look*, *My Girlfriend's Sister Never Stops Seducing Me for 28 Days*, and *Princess of Otaku: I Am in Charge of Sexually Satisfying Disgusting Nerds*. They met about one-fifth of their sales goal.

The AKB48 sales method also benefits AV actresses like Amatsuka, whose longevity as an AV idol relies on her popularity and sales output. Most AV actresses disappear from the market after performing in their debut videos unless they cultivate and maintain a loyal fan base. Knowing that, Amatsuka treats each fan as if he were a VIP. She memorizes many of her repeat customers' names and tries to remember and write down conversations she's had with them for their next meeting. Fans I spoke with told me unanimously that she treats them like royalty. Easy to say but hard to execute, I thought. At this event, Amatsuka stood on the stage and connected with hundreds of her fans for more than two hours without once sitting down. I could only imagine how tired, even pained, her legs and toes felt inside her super high heels, and how stiff her cheek muscles must be with her unfailingly big smiles. The mental effort to correctly remember names and prior conversations, yet never showing any signs of fatigue or weariness, was also remarkable. This is all part of the promotion work required by her production company, S1, with whom she has an exclusive contract to release all of her titles and yield to copyrights. In other words, Amatsuka's labor-intensive job is unpaid work, subsumed broadly under a performance guarantee that remains scant on labor details.

For the entire evening, Amatsuka took only one ten-minute break, retreating to a greenroom where one of S1's female directors, Takano, waited.

With Sugimoto's permission, I joined them. As soon as I sat down on a sofa, I noticed how tired my feet were in a pair of Dansko shoes, known for their comfort, from just standing and observing Amatsuka on the stage for an hour and a half. Meanwhile, Amatsuka sat in a plastic chair at a table, meticulously autographing stacks of Polaroids with her signature flourish: "Moe" drawn in round English alphabet letters with two cute wings on both sides, garnished with a smiling face in a big heart above the right wing. The symbolic wings represent her stage name, Amatsuka, which means "angel" in Chinese characters. Her cute-girl branding is consistently communicated throughout her performances, both within and outside her videos, even though she claims that she used to be a tomboy and cultivated her pronounced femininity only after becoming an AV actress.

Amatsuka has put an immense amount of effort into sustaining her top-selling performer status. Since her debut in 2014, she has won two adult awards for Best New Actress;[5] joined a music unit, Ebisu Muscat, and an idol group, Sexy-J, both of which consist of other adult video actresses; and released a solo CD. In 2017, her talent activities extended to a protagonist role in two non-AV video features.

"You must be so worn out," I said. Amatsuka smiled at me and shook her head.

"Don't you want to relax for a while?" I asked.

"It is easier for me to keep going without a break. It's harder to go back once I sit down to relax and lose momentum," she answered with a smile.

Takano turned toward me and confirmed, "It's true. She never takes a break once she turns on her switch to be in work mode."

"On my days off," Amatsuka said, "I sometimes stay in pajamas all day long, just relaxing in bed and playing with my phone." She continued, "To be honest, I oftentimes get sick from overwork and suffer from a high fever on my off days. So, I try to recover myself when I am off."

Indeed, her exposed body—shoulders, back, and legs—did not seem well protected from catching a cold, especially when most of the people at the event still wore long-sleeve shirts and jackets.

At the end of her break, Amatsuka looked into her hand mirror to fix her hair and perfect her smile. Standing up, she straightened her shoulders. Once Sugimoto opened the greenroom door, she walked back to the stage and merrily restarted her routine—posing for her fans, shaking hands, chatting, posing for two-shots, and massaging fans' heads—over and over for the next hour and a half.

The crowd gradually got smaller. By 10:30 p.m. only about two dozen of her die-hard fans remained, hanging out near the elevator to say goodbye to her one last time. These men seemed to know each other well, as they see one another at almost all her events. Once the last fan left the stage, Amatsuka came down to join the small crowd, where the men lined up to give her a high five before they took the elevator down. One said to her, "Thank you. It was fun!" Another commented, "You were so pretty tonight." Amatsuka smiled, "You make me so happy!" Others said, "I'll see you at the next event." She waved back, "See you soon!" None of these men appeared to be trying to get ahead in the pecking order to monopolize her attention; rather, they seemed to enjoy the male-male friendships that she facilitated, like a magnet drawing them all together. The friendly atmosphere made me feel I could easily hang out with them too. I followed the men to the elevator after thanking Sugimoto and Amatsuka for allowing me to attend. Just as she had done for her fans, Amatsuka held my hand in both her hands and looked into my eyes to say, "It was so nice having you around. Thank you for coming today!" I immediately felt as if I were connected to her, even though I didn't know much about her.

Heading outside, I was surprised to see that the street was filled with a few dozen of the fans who had left earlier. They knew where to wait for Amatsuka to see her off, keeping away from the front of the building to avoid trouble with the tenant owners. They instead lined up around the corner where, one fan explained to me, the car Amatsuka takes always makes a left turn. After a half hour or so, a black SUV driven by Sugimoto pulled up to the front of the building as Amatsuka emerged, hopping into the backseat. As the car rounded the corner, she rolled down her window and waved, "Thank you all. Have a good night!" One fan remarked, "The 'president' drives a nice car. It's the latest model of the Maserati GTS. The model was displayed at Narita airport with a price tag of 15,000,000 yen (US$150,000)." Our blurred faces gleamed off the tinted windows.

---

While Amatsuka's "face-to-face" promotion event appeared no different from mainstream idol events I have witnessed, like AKB48's, below the surface were significant differences. AV idols are often wracked by fear, anxiety, and self-doubt—feelings that lie just behind their cheerful façade. They grapple with multilayered, contradictory dilemmas: relishing the publicity and attention paid to them as AV idols while living in constant fear of having their identities revealed; experiencing a newfound sense of self-empowerment in tandem with a steadily declining commodity value following their AV debut; and receiving marginal to no labor or sexual exploitation protection by law.

The multiple dilemmas AV actresses experience are like a Russian nesting doll of paradoxes that the AV industry manifests: enjoying the image of a thriving business while also facing declining sales and piracy issues due to advanced digital technology; an ever-increasing supply of aspiring AV idols that has led to a buyer's market but also fierce public scrutiny; and perhaps most paradoxical, the legality of producing pornographic images under the constitutional protection of free expression while sex work itself is not protected by the country's labor laws. While Japan's AV industry—what many business insiders refer to as *kocchi no sekai* (this world)—has rapidly expanded since its establishment in the early 1980s, it continues to be marginalized and stigmatized as a sleazy business in Japanese law and society.

As a result, the pendulum continues to swing back and forth between pro- and anti-pornography advocates in the context of political economy, popular culture, and legal systems. Since the mid-2010s, the pendulum has swung decidedly into the anti-porn camp. Amid the increasing popularity of AV idols and declining video sales, the AV establishment has become pilloried and mired in what is known today as *Shutsuen Kyōyō Mondai*, the issue of forced performance. As I detail in the next chapter, a 2015 high-profile Tokyo district court case triggered the issue, which has led to intense public scrutiny and legal and moral debate. Human rights activists, women's support groups, and some Diet members contend that a significant number of young, ordinary women are coerced into performing in adult videos against their will or are enticed into becoming AV performers. Specifically, they claim, young, ordinary women are forced to sign illegitimate performance contracts and are strictly bound to them. More broadly, violence against and exploitation of women, these groups argue, go unseen in both actual AV content and the greater cultural context in which AV stars become commodities. Morally polarized views on pornography—liberation versus oppression—have been projected on prospective AV idols and potential victims, teetering between the rapidly growing digital economy and the mainstream conservative moral economy.

Ultimately, Amatsuka's event offers only a glimpse of one dimension of the AV industry and one top-level layer of AV talent. Her work takes place in an ecosystem inhabited by the major players and stakeholders in Japan's AV industry: talent agencies, video makers, actors and craftspeople, video stores, and end users; her life is imbricated with mainstream Japanese society and its moral economy. Like Amatsuka's events, AV performers' public appearances are carefully crafted for commodification, objectification, and realistic fiction—what I call pornographic illusions. Behind their façade—which is often a deep fake of their real selves, with made-up names, backgrounds, and surgically enhanced body parts—their experiences remain largely unknown, and their voices clouded by the illusions. Thus, AV actresses' experiences offer unique insights into larger sociohistorical contexts of gender and sexual labor, technology and creative industries, and law and liberal democracy.

The equivocal nature of AV work, surrounded by contesting views and ambivalent legality regarding consensual sex on camera, has become the focus of my scholarly inquiry into sexual labor in Japan's gendered economy, especially regarding issues of consent. While making sense of how women involuntarily consent to precarious sexual labor *and* contend with cultural pressures, I guide a reader through a journey to understand the nuanced ways that consent giving is staged within and outside Japan's AV industry. In so doing, I problematize principles of autonomy, freedom, and equality that justify pornography and labor submission alike in the name of free expression and free choice in a liberal democratic society. I take aim particularly at the principles underlying liberal contractualism, which bundle consent and freedom to promote self-governing subjectivity, on the one hand, while forbidding coercion and enslavement, on the other.

Involuntary consent, which is ubiquitous in everyday life, falls through the cracks created by this fundamentally dualistic view of consent and coercion. As a result, a consent giver's subjection to various forms of exploitation or harm typical of gendered, precarious labor is reduced to an individual experience rather than a structural problem. I argue that liberal contractualism renders involuntary consent illegible and perpetuates structural violence—a form of violence that puts consent givers, who tend to be socioeconomically vulnerable, at risk of submission and exploitation *by choice.*

## OF INVOLUNTARY CONSENT

This book examines *involuntary consent* in the Japanese adult video industry—and, by extension, within other precarious forms of employment, which have become the norm in Japan over the last thirty-five years.[6] I refer to involuntary consent, workwise, as an agreement a worker gives to a potential employer when faced with the condition of having no better option but to take a job being offered—whether to survive, to serve as a stepping stone toward better opportunities, or for another "lesser of two evils" type of reason. This is different from being "forced" or "coerced" to do something against one's will by another person or government entity. Neither overtly forced nor completely voluntary, the concept of involuntary consent guides us toward a deeper understanding of how "independent contractor" status and the like obscures the structural vulnerability of marginalized people to precarious labor and exploitative working conditions.

Women's consent to sexual labor in AV renders them of ambivalent legal status: they are not prostitutes, wage workers, or independent contractors, though their experiences share elements with all three of these forms of work. Their status provides a unique window into critically exploring liberal notions of free speech and the free market that justify sexual entertainment, while structural inequalities leave women especially vulnerable to exploitation in sex-based occupations like AV. What does it say about "free choice" when the marginalized feel that consenting to precarious labor is their best option? How do women make sense of their "consent" to stigmatized sex work that nevertheless comes with monetary and other opportunities? How do they handle the abuse, exploitation, and mental distress they experience at work and in society?

AV performers exist at the margins of legal protection in both the AV community and mainstream Japanese society. Characterized by a lack of policy and laws beyond the protection of children from sexual commerce,[7] AV performance work is permitted by multiple legal loopholes. There is, to start with, an ambivalent juridical line between legal pornography and illegal prostitution. Japan's Anti-Prostitution Law criminalizes the act of committing sexual intercourse in exchange for money. However, in the name of free speech, having commercial sex on camera for the production of pornographic images is not illegal. (Indeed, the 2015 Tokyo district ruling, which banned nonconsensual sexual acts in AV, implies consensual sex on camera *is* permitted.) The existence and perpetuation of rape culture also undermines Anti-Rape Law. The law protects innocent victims of sexual assault but not prostitutes or sex workers who experience sexual violence at work. AV performers' consent to sexual performance on camera is taken as tacit agreement to the "whole package," including the externalities of identity reveal, stigma, and discrimination that come with the job. Otherwise, pornography involving adults is largely perceived as a "victimless crime." Finally, employment and labor laws exclude sex work as a form of wage labor due to its "harmful" nature: it is legally defined as *yūgai gyōmu* (harmful work) that disturbs public order and moral decency. As a result, sex work can only be provided as contract-based freelancing, not wage labor. Sex workers' independence is therefore technically a must-have condition in the production of adult videos. At the same time, as independent contractors, these workers are deprived of labor rights. Thus, four bodies of laws—free speech, anti-prostitution, anti-rape, and labor employment—protect sexual entertainment and victims of sexual violence but not *sexual labor* and *sex workers*. This is the juridical context wherein AV performers are asked to consent to sexual labor.

Contract making, which is necessary for sound business practices in the AV industry, is destined to exploit the consent giver's precarity. Under the current legal system, they may be eligible for legal protections only when they can prove that they are victims of forced performance in adult videos. For this, a woman needs to make a report to law enforcement and show evidence that she was coerced into having sex against her will or forced to engage in "harmful work." This move poses risks, however; even if she simply wants to improve her working conditions by filing a report, she risks losing her job or being raped or abused again if she continues with the work. Indeed, a sex worker who encounters trouble on the job and turns to the law for help may have to accept victim status in exchange for legal aid—a status that, among other concessions, necessitates quitting AV work. In this way, she loses both her bargaining power as a worker and her source of livelihood. At the same time, abandoning victim status reinforces the legal premise that sex workers are independent contractors whose work is consensual and contractual. This catch-22 situation effectively silences AV performers about what systematically goes on behind the scenes. The end result is the (re)production of pornographic illusions (of a "victimless crime") and legal fictions of free choice.

Despite the vulnerability of consent-giving women due to the illegality of sex work, the legality of sexual commerce has leveraged the Japanese AV industry's swift transformation into a cutting-edge creative enterprise in today's burgeoning digital economy. Far from seedy "underground" stereotypes about where and how pornography is produced, the AV industry has aligned with Japan's strategic effort to remake itself into an information technology-driven nation, a country committed to providing economic incentives for those working in the so-called *kontentsu sangyō* (content or "creative" industry).[8] This business concept, *content*, emerged in the mid-1990s, along with revolutionary advancements in information technology. Within a decade, it was taken to another level: the Japanese government made the content industry the heart of its political slogan—"a technology-driven nation, a nation built on intellectual property"—to tap into and monetize human creativity to revitalize the national economy.[9] As such, the content industry was envisioned as the nation's future.[10] Aligning with this national move toward a "copyright regime," the AV industry established its own advocacy group, the IPPA (Intellectual Property Promotion Association), and promoted adult videos as intellectual property.[11] The AV industry has also increasingly adopted such business practices as contract making and copyright protection, evolving into a seemingly innovative business enterprise.

The rapid development of Japan's new economy coincided with the massive flexibilization of employment to improve labor efficiency. A series of amendments to the Worker Dispatch Law paved the road. When established in 1986, the Worker Dispatch Law permitted employment agencies to dispatch temporary workers in only sixteen emerging sectors such as office automation, software development, and computer engineering. This limitation met the intention of the law, which was to mobilize highly skilled professionals more flexibly while protecting wage workers. Ten years later, however, the eligible sectors expanded to include ten more sectors such as market surveys, advertising, and telemarketing, among others. By 1999, the law permitted all sectors except construction, port operations, security, medicine, and manufacturing. Among these five exceptions, manufacturing had long been controversial due to great concerns about chipping away at the original intention of the law. Despite the controversy, however, manufacturing was removed from the negative list in 2004.

These changes took place amid the so-called *Shūshoku Hyōga Ki* (Employment Ice Age, 1993–2005), when many young Japanese had to accept precarious labor, hopping from one nonregular employment job to another, without job security or full benefits.[12] Japanese corporations began hiring increasing numbers of flexible, nonregular workers amid these policy-driven reforms, to cut labor costs.[13] Thanks to labor deregulation and financial capitalism, the "Izanami boom" (2002–2008) resulted in the longest economic expansion in Japan's postwar history. However, it failed to trickle down compared to earlier booms, through which citizens actually benefited and income increased.[14] This "cheerless boom" was welcomed with ambivalence. Meanwhile, the nonregular employment rate in the entire workforce increased from 16.6 percent in 1986 to 21.5 percent in 1996, to 33.2 percent in 2006, and to 37.6 percent in 2016.[15] Nearly 40 percent of the entire workforce are nonregular employees today.[16] Such changes, leading to both market volatility and disgruntled workers, were not due to a collective decision made by workers themselves.[17]

Ironically, amid these conditions, the Japanese government highlighted the collective volition of "self-governing citizens" as a matter of "supreme importance" in the building of a twenty-first-century Japanese society. The gap between top-down policy making and bottom-up nation building was then, as I discuss further in chapter 1, supposed to be overcome through the creation of the "self-governing subject." Although Japanese citizens were already sovereign subjects under the country's post-WWII constitution, the Council of Judicial Reform identified the self-governing subject (in contrast to the object to be governed) as a new model needed in "building a society of freedom and justice and bringing creative energy to the nation."[18] In this way, the Council has performatively (re)constituted self-governing citizens as the producers of a liberal democratic society. In this kind of political rhetoric, the cart (those who are governed) is put ahead of the horse (policy), wherein the causality between political goals and their driving forces becomes blurred. Indeed, the political goal—the creation of self-governing subjectivity—implies a lack of such subjectivity. At the same time, the rhetoric suggests that such subjectivity always already exists as the driving force of liberal democracy and ongoing social changes, including the flexibilization of employment. Just as AV actresses are hired as independent contractors, feeding the pornographic illusion of their involvement in the industry as being a victimless entertainment, Japanese workers more generally are contracted as self-governing citizens according to the government's political fiction.

Japan's new high-growth industries, on the cutting edge of technology, have indeed created new job opportunities for "independent" and creative citizens. But these conditions have also produced tens of thousands of non-regular employees and working poor. Most content-based freelancers and part-time workers struggle with scant job security and minimal wages. The average annual income for animation creators, for example, was 33,280,000 yen (US$33,280) before taxes in 2013; nearly 30 percent of animators make less than 2,000,000 yen (US$20,000) a year, which is right at the country's poverty line.[19] The new economy initiative, which prioritized economic effects, has given little attention to labor processes or rights. Likewise, the AV industry primarily focuses on sales growth over labor protections for its content creators. Such profit supremacy has only accelerated since the widespread use of mobile devices, high-speed internet access, and digital platforms have enabled free access to content in the 2010s and 2020s. Online business has transformed the creative industry across film, television, music, gaming, and animation, among other industries. The digital economy has intensified labor processes, creeping further into workers' personal lives and requiring them to work harder to improve cost efficiency.[20]

In the AV industry, as Amatsuka Moe's event exemplifies, unpaid, extra work is incorporated into performers' job requirements as face-to-face personalized sales, self-promotion through social media platforms, and emotional labor for fans. The AV production process itself has also been intensified. To cut back on production costs such as studio, transportation, and labor expenses, video shooting, which used to be spread out over a few days, mostly has become a one-day job. Everything—commuting to a studio, makeup, video shooting, and package photo shooting—is squeezed into a day by extending work hours from early morning to midnight. The AV performer's job has thus become much more demanding for less pay—although such labor issues remain in the shadow of AV's image as a "thriving" industry.

Even more demanding, AV performance work has increasingly gained currency. This makes sense, within this specific context of historically challenging working conditions for women. Japanese women, who entered the general workforce in record high numbers at the height of the late-1980s bubble economy, soon found that they were expected to quit their jobs after marriage and childbirth. They were often hired as general office staff and paid far less than their male counterparts, who were hired as regular full-time employees with prospects for promotion. For example, 36 percent of the entire female workforce were nonregular workers in 1989, steadily increasing to 45.1 percent in 1999 and 53.7 percent in 2009. Today, three out of five female workers are nonregular employees.[21] Due to the intensified labor processes in recent years, seemingly lucky regular employees work at so-called *burakku kigyō* (black companies, meaning sweatshop-like workplaces) and face serious labor issues such as *karōshi* (death by overwork). In the mid-2010s, the mainstream media sensationalized the shocking *karōshi* of two young, elite Japanese women in their twenties and early thirties who worked for Dentsu Inc., the world's largest advertising agency, and NHK, the national broadcasting corporation.[22] These tragedies alarmed many Japanese to how excessive labor exploitation has been normalized not only in small start-up companies and black companies, but also by the most reputable Japanese corporations. Furthermore, "death by overwork" no longer applies only to men. AV job opportunities, which appear to offer better pay, more leisure and downtime, and greater chance for self-empowerment, have therefore become a better option according to a growing number of young Japanese women.

If some women are attracted to AV jobs under these circumstances, the majority of enthusiastic AV fans I met are their counterparts in terms of holding nonregular employment jobs with little to no prospects for promotion to regular employee status. These men, who came of age during Japan's Employment Ice Age, have remained nonregular workers since starting their first jobs.[23] The male AV fans I interviewed self-identified as lower-middle (or lower) class in comparison to peers who successfully landed at major firms as regular employees. Some fans have even experienced working at a black company. To me, their livelihoods sounded only slightly more secure than those of Japan's "underclass," or nonregular workers other than housewives who work part-time and make 1,860,000 yen (roughly US$18,600) yearly on average.[24] It is estimated that nearly 9,300,000 Japanese are classified as underclass, almost 15 percent of the entire workforce. Along with the alarming statistics, these relatively new terms—Employment Ice Age, nonregular employment, black company, and underclass—have drawn greater public attention to precarious labor conditions in twenty-first-century Japan.

Labor and life precarity is gendered, though this gendering is often rendered invisible. Studying how online content platforms have been promoted as a new job site in contemporary Japan, Gabriella Lukács (2020) reveals that young Japanese women, who are marginalized from full-time employment with benefits, find certain job opportunities attractive. They can express themselves as net idols, bloggers, and cell-phone novelists, to name a few new career paths. Despite their contribution to the country's digital economy, Lukacs points out that their willingness to provide unpaid yet personally fulfilling labor is exploited by platform owners and also rendered invisible by technological design. Such gendered, flexible labor parallels that provided by aspiring AV idols in Japan's adult video industry. Sexual labor in the AV industry and gig labor in the information technology sector are a continuum of precarious labor that increasing numbers of women, who find no better opportunities, give consent to. Furthermore, AV users, especially enthusiastic male fans, often share the same labor insecurities. The AV fans I interviewed often felt their masculinity challenged because of financial struggles; they cannot afford to get married or do not feel comfortable socializing with men higher up the socioeconomic food chain. Thus, many men with nonregular employment status, as I highlight in chapter 5, rely on their female counterparts—those who provide sexual and emotional labor under similar work conditions—to bring a measure of fulfillment to their lives.

How and why do women performers consent to having explicit sex on camera? The women I interviewed provided various reasons for giving consent, including "The job seemed interesting,"[25] "I had no reason to decline [the offer],"[26] "It just occurred to me to give it a try for no specific reason,"[27] "I wanted money,"[28] "I wanted to become famous,"[29] and "I was self-destructive out of heartbreak."[30] Few women told me that enjoying sex attracted them to a career in AV. "If a woman likes sex," a thirty-seven-year-old former AV actress and current owner of a talent agency said to me, "there are many other places to enjoy herself, and if a woman simply wants money in exchange for sex, there are plenty of other jobs available behind a closed door." She stressed the higher risk of exposure to stigma and discrimination that comes with AV. In this sense, AV performance is a unique job that combines decent earnings with the chance of stardom through sexual labor. With this combination in mind, I realized that the women I interviewed all have one thing in common: they have no other, better choice but to perform in AV.

My inquiry into involuntary consent lifts a veil created by AV actresses' silence, and sheds light on social injustices that lurk in the liberal assumptions undergirding infrastructures of contract making. Like online platform owners who leave net idols and bloggers with little room to negotiate their service standards, adult video makers leave AV performers with few options for contractual negotiations. Such circumstances limit the control of individuals over their labor, a major disadvantage for the party with less power. The situation of AV actresses could be paralleled with that of "guest workers" who make the seemingly irrational choice of subjecting themselves to unfree labor in Japan. In her book *Illicit Flirtations*, Rhacel Parreñas argued that Filipina entertainers decided to go to Japan and work as hostesses, even though many were identified as trafficked victims, because they chose indentured mobility for a chance at a better life abroad rather than endure poverty in their home country. Instead of interrogating these women's decision as "false consciousness," Parreñas has questioned the principle of freedom in liberal traditions that preclude individuals from choosing *not* to be free—to agree to indentured servitude or enslavement. The principle safeguards only consent and freedom, justifying what cultural anthropologist Talal Asad calls "liberal violence." Intertwined with a project of bourgeois, masculinist nation building, liberal violence "universaliz[es] reason itself" in the name of expanding freedom, free markets, and the rule of law while simultaneously "conquering" illiberal things such as coercion, enslavement, the informal economy, and corruption.[31] Nonvoluntary consent to sexual labor, gig labor, and guest work alike then falls through the cracks created by this fundamentally dualistic view of consent and coercion.

Although precarious labor conditions are ubiquitous within today's profit-seeking capitalist system, consent that is not voluntary remains essentially nonexistent in liberal contractualism. To be more specific, consent perceived as *voluntary* is granted focal awareness within this system, while the involuntary aspects of exploitative working conditions are relegated to the margins. In the AV industry, job insecurity, sexual violence, and mental illness are considered personal problems rather than structural issues. The inequalities and exploitation typical of gendered, precarious labor are reduced to an individual woman's problem with "risk management," as I discuss in chapter 3. Furthermore, violence is normalized as "bad luck" befalling individuals and as part of everyday life in AV.[32] *Involuntary Consent* brings legal systems, political economy, and gendered precarious labor together to rethink liberal assumptions of autonomy, freedom, and equality under the law that condone labor exploitation in the name of individual choice.

## LIBERAL REASONING

Why focus on the AV industry to explore the liberal assumptions that lead to the giving of involuntary consent? Simply put, the very existence of pornography hinges on notions of personal liberty, free expression, and the free market. Similarly, liberal reasoning has continued to protect pornography, even though the meaning of "porn" has changed over time. Pornography has long been justified as a form of free speech and protected from state censorship. Within a decidedly neoliberal "content industry" framework that stresses individual pleasures over cultural and artistic value,[33] adult videos have increasingly become "adult goods" and "masturbatory tools."[34] The liberal rationale for pornography as a constitutionally protected form of free speech has then yielded to its *neoliberal* value, as a marketable commodity in twenty-first-century Japan. In this market-driven context, the porn industry can more easily elide the feminist question about pornography: "Whose free speech?" The industry's answer to this question, consequently, relies almost exclusively on the assumption that those participating have freely given their consent—an assumption that becomes the "clearance" for AV makers to produce and circulate adult videos legitimately. In this business model, consent and contract,[35] rather than fealty to free speech per se, has become the industry standard.

Scholars have long written about consent and contracts, asking a wide range of legal, political, and philosophical questions: What makes an agreement to a contract legally enforceable? Why do rational individuals, in order to live in societies, make social contracts and give up much of their freedom, submitting to laws and political order? How are person, property, and contract intertwined with law and justice?[36] These questions, however, neither focus on nor address *who* is presumed to be a consenting subject in terms of gender, race, class, and other factors, nor delve into sociohistorically specific contexts wherein individual freedom and submission are defined.

AV performers' lack of fully voluntary and free consent to sexual labor is grounded in a particular kind of gendered, systemic vulnerability within the specific politico-legal context of the content industry in Japan. In this book, I focus on women as a discursive identity category for empirical and theoretical reasons. Empirically, most AV performers are women, whose consent is a must-have condition in the adult video industry. Male performers are in the minority, and often exempted from signing contracts.[37] Indeed, labor exploitation and human rights violations of male performers are another issue in need of further investigation that goes beyond the scope of this project. Theoretically, I draw from postcolonial feminist scholar Gayatri Spivak's notion of "strategic essentialism," a tactic through which minority groups embrace a simplified version of their identity as a means of coming together to achieve political goals, such as equal rights.[38] By "women," I mainly refer to cisgender AV actresses and, by extension, precarious women workers and other feminized gig-economy workers. Acknowledging heterogeneity within "women" and their sex work, I strategically deploy gender and labor as analytical categories through which to examine bourgeois, masculinist infrastructures of contract making and reveal structural violence against women.

Gender and class are significant aspects of contract making. Consent givers, who are usually in vulnerable positions vis-à-vis consent seekers, are subject to the seekers' vested interest in the protection of their privileges—status, reputation, and property rights. Feminist political theorist Carole Pateman points out that the employment contract entitles the capitalist owner to not only buy the worker's property—labor power—in exchange for a wage, but also to subordinate the worker to his will while the labor is being extracted. Citing Karl Marx, Pateman reiterates that "the system of wage labour is a system of slavery," with the only difference between these two systems lying in the worker's consent.[39] In other words, this consent legitimates the capitalist owner's ability to seek underpaid, precarious labor in the name of profit seeking. The principle of consent similarly trumps consent givers' sexual experiences, even if the consented-to sex turns out to be violent. In his book *Screw Consent*, political scientist Joseph Fischel argues that it is consent, not the actual quality of sexual intercourse, that determines what is "good," consensual sex in contrast with "bad," nonconsensual sex (i.e., rape).[40] Consent is essentially a politico-legal device used to premise liberal individualism and flatten structural inequalities between two parties. It can justify violence against the consent giver.

Gender and class-sensitive perspectives allow us to see how everyday interactions on the ground impact the ability of socially marginalized people to contract on "equal terms." In his book *Contract as Promise*, legal scholar Charles Fried writes, "Legal obligation can be imposed only by the community, and so in imposing it the community must be pursuing its goals and imposing its standards, rather than neutrally endorsing those of the contracting parties."[41] The contract-signing process is therefore by no means neutral in terms of who comes to the table first, who sets contractual terms, and whose property rights are protected, particularly with contracts between a corporation and an individual. Feminist scholars have revealed how phallocentric legal concepts are disadvantageous to women.[42] Just as an employment contract enables the capitalist owner to be a master over his wage workers' on-the-clock time, a sexual contract allows men to dominate women by creating the appearance that women have willfully subordinated *themselves* within such institutions as marriage and, in this case, sexual commerce. Women employees must "act like men," that is, be autonomous subjects who contract their consent to "sell" their property, such as labor power and sexuality. By the same token, they are expected to subordinate themselves to their "bosses." The bourgeois, masculinist logic of the "reasonable man" standard, as Pateman famously argues, protects men's freedom at the cost of women's subordination *as if by choice*.[43]

The existence of involuntary consent—which, I argue, lies at the heart of subordination by choice—complicates long-standing "anti-porn versus sex-positive" feminist debates about the relationship between gender, sexual labor, and human agency in liberal democratic societies. Anti-porn feminists have claimed that a woman's choice is never made freely, as the choice to become a "respectable" housewife or "promiscuous" whore is, for example, two sides of the same coin of patriarchal control over women's sexuality.[44] This group envisions that abolishing all forms of sexual oppression, including pornography and sex work, is the only way to dismantle sexism and free women from false consciousness.[45] By contrast, sex-positive feminists have reclaimed women's agency and call into question abolitionist approaches to sex work.[46] For them, any sexual activity among consenting adults, including pornography and sex work, can become feminist projects to critique masculinist institutions and liberate female sexuality from within.[47] While such debates have addressed women's consent—whether it's given out of "false consciousness" or for the sake of "sexual liberation"—little room is left for nonvoluntary consent that cuts across both a morally conservative abolitionist regime and politically progressive liberal regime. Nor have these debates systematically investigated the lived experience of sex workers' contract making in specific sociolegal contexts. The result is that the abstract voluntary-versus-forced dichotomy overlooks nuanced power dynamics in lived experiences of consent giving and contract making.

Consent is not always what liberal individualism assumes. Coercion is not always so obvious either. Studying porn work in the US, feminist studies scholar Heather Berg has found that porn workers' motivations for sex include social pressures and self-imposed competitiveness, especially when a buyer's market gives an impression that there is a "seemingly endless supply of willing workers."[48] Berg writes, "They can say no to any number of things, but in so doing risk damaged reputations, strained relationships, and lost work."[49] The power dynamics in the wage relationship thus "shape what consent means in practice."[50] Furthermore, as Jo Doezema points out, the assumption that sex workers embrace their work by choice creates the "wrong theoretical framework [through which] to analyze the experience of sex workers"; this risks, she writes, condoning the "abuse of human rights of sex workers who were not 'forced.'"[51] Once consent is given, voluntarily or involuntarily, any ambiguity or ambivalence in the consent giving is erased by the abstract binarism of the contract. As such, the lived experience of sex work is buried under layers of often-invisible power dynamics and concealed contracts. Contract making is, after all, a private practice, remaining confidential throughout negotiation, signing, and performance.

Due to this confidentiality, contract making is not an easy subject for anthropological inquiry. Signed and kept private, a contract remains invisible. An investigation of the ethnographically traceable effects of contracts helps us see what the process is like in action and understand its infrastructure. For example, cultural anthropologist Hannah Appel's study of oil contracts between US-based transnational corporations and Equatorial Guinea, an African sovereign state, shows how these contracts are bent into legal and political singularities;[52] the consenting "State" fuses citizens into a singular "juridical individual with a unitary will,"[53] just as an actress juridically transforms into an autonomous subject with a unitary will in Japan's AV industry. Appel argues that the "freedom" to sign contracts is an "always-already compromised freedom that is at the heart of liberalism."[54] Despite nominal autonomy and compromised freedom, however, a contract sounds "just" and "transparent" under the rule of law, in contrast to unethical acts or corruption in "uncivilized" societies.[55] This perception itself is an effect of liberal reasoning's politico-legal fictions. My anthropological study not only depicts the effect of liberal reasoning on the contract-making process but also offers an ethnographic point of departure for examining a grounded, rather than abstract, political theory of contract making.

---

Based on eighteen months of fieldwork between 2015 and 2018 in Japan, this book ethnographically investigates Japan's AV industry as a window into women's involuntary consent, and accounts for the infrastructures of contract making within and beyond Japan's AV industry. To bring fragmented pieces of information into a comprehensive picture, I listened to an array of social actors tell their stories, not only AV actresses but also other business insiders and end users.[56] I also interviewed people who engaged in public discourse on "forced performance in AV," such as anti-porn activists, women's support group case workers, newspaper reporters, human rights attorneys, and AV Human Rights and Ethics Committee members. Along with in-depth interviews, my fieldwork included discourse analyses surrounding forced AV performance and archival research of the Japanese government's policy records.

A latecomer to the Western liberal paradigm, Japan has consistently struggled to "catch up" and maintain pace with the West throughout its modern political and economic history. Shaping a new national consciousness—self-governing subjectivity—has been Japan's twenty-first-century attempt to reimagine a society of freedom and justice.[57] Developing an information

technology-driven economy is yet another attempt to rebuild national prosperity. Women's voicing of their systemic oppression, perceived as "getting in
the way" of these nation-building projects, is largely dismissed and silenced.
Such liberal violence, I argue, is a double-edged sword. "Universaliz[ing]
reason itself,"[58] as Asad reminds us, it allows subordination to social injustice *by choice* while simultaneously blaming the subordinated for their "bad"
choices. Moreover, handpicked victims are deemed deserving of humanitarian aid through which what anthropologist and sociologist Didier Fassin calls
"humanitarian reason"—compassion is distributed from "the more powerful
to the weaker, the more fragile, the more vulnerable."[59] The powerful set the
rules, governing the powerless indirectly while legally leveraging their interests at the nexus of political economy, social governance, and rule of law.

*Involuntary Consent* explores how not only liberty but also violence is experienced in the space between consent and coercion, freedom and slavery,
and justice and injustice. Consent that is not completely voluntary manifests
in this in-between space; it is, I argue, the primary way consent is exchanged
in everyday life. Japanese courts, the mass media, and public discourse have
essentially reduced the issue of liberal violence to a matter of individual consent—as if putting one's sexual labor on the free market is an act of autonomy, unless that autonomy is overtly violated. Such a public view, coupled with
actresses' silence, only perpetuates the political premise underlying contractualism: a willful subject freely sells a piece of property—talents, services, or
other forms of labor power—to an equal counterpart in exchange for a fair
price. This premise, in turn, renders structural violence seemingly inevitable.
By illuminating how such a premise is safeguarded, abused, and negotiated by
different social actors—AV actresses, talent agencies, video makers, AV fans,
and the Japanese general public alike—*Involuntary Consent* strips liberal reasoning and infrastructures naked.

## A BRIEF HISTORY OF THE JAPANESE
## ADULT VIDEO INDUSTRY

The adult video industry, as I refer to it, is a set of economic activities involving the production and distribution of authorized adult videos (*adaruto
bideo*). There are the so-called *ura bideo* (underground, uncensored videos)
or unauthorized DIY videos that circulate unofficially. These nonregulated
videos are increasingly problematized from the standpoint of criminal jus-

tice: obscenity, piracy, and digitally facilitated sexual violence. More research needs to be done in these areas. For this book, however, I primarily focus on the mainstream AV industry, where business is self-regulated to comply with the law. In the mainstream domain, women's consent to sexual labor is also more officially processed—contracts, in other words, are a bigger part of the exchange of labor for money—than in underground syndicates. Even so, the public-facing component of Japan's AV industry has always been embedded within a series of tensions: from official versus unofficial videos, decency versus indecency, to what's shown on the screen versus what's behind the scenes. These tensions waver between changing notions of what's proper and what's technologically possible. Throughout the relatively brief history of the Japanese AV industry, pornographic and legal illusions have depended primarily on such unseen things—media technologies, obscenity protocols, distribution formats, industry profitability, and the trend of women performing in adult videos.

The Japanese AV business has historically been one of the only forms of sex commerce to pay close attention to new media technologies as well as obscenity law. The birth of the Japanese adult video industry is rooted in the adoption of video recording technology for pornographic production in the late 1970s.[60] This production quickly met increasing demand due to the rapid spread of home video players in the 1980s.[61] Meanwhile, the industry adopted its own obscenity protocols for feature films—blurring out genitals on screen, for example—to comply with the country's obscenity regulations.[62] Strict measures, however, have given way to more relaxed ones over time. Through the early 1990s, no private parts (including genitals, pubic hair, and anus) could be shown without "thick" *mozaiku* (literally mosaic, meaning fuzzing out), whereas by the mid-1990s only "thin" *mozaiku* was required over genitals and pubic hair, and the anus could be exposed in some videos. These standards continue to evolve according to ever-changing codes based on what law enforcement deems a disturbance of *kōjo ryōzoku* (public order and moral decency). Even in the era of digital technology, where exposed genitals in foreign pornographic videos circulate widely in cyberspace, it is still illegal to produce such explicit videos within Japan and sell them on the domestic market, whether in-store or online.[63]

Over the last half century, the industry has evolved in tandem with technological changes in video formats, from VHS to DVD to today's on-demand streaming. The video distribution system has changed accordingly, from "rental" in the 1980s to "sales" in the 1990s to "streaming" in the new millennium. Interestingly, the industry's thriving moments—called *Ēbui būmu* (or "AV boom"), occurring in the late 1980s[64] and mid-1990s through mid-2000s—aligned with new formats in distribution and the relaxation of obscenity regulations. However, like other culture industries such as film, television, music, and publishing, the AV industry has been facing declining sales since the early 2010s. Consumers spend far less on DVDs today due to the existence of adult streaming content, much of which is free or available for a cheap subscription fee.[65] Still, Japan's AV industry relies heavily on DVD sales for profitability. This is because the industry, which did not anticipate the speed of the streaming takeover, made licensing contracts with online distribution companies.[66] The industry makes only about 30 percent of its profits from licensing its content online, compared to roughly 60 percent selling DVDs.[67] On top of the sales decline, the industry faces illegal reproduction and distribution of their products, mainly through mobile devices and online platforms. Despite the prosperous image of the AV industry in light of copious online pornographic content, the business is suffering.[68]

Despite the challenges the industry faces, AV work attracts a seemingly inexhaustible supply of young women. A new breed of AV actresses has emerged that makes the career trajectories of earlier performers seem quaint in comparison. In the 1980s, Kuroki Kaoru, an art student attending a national university, first broke into the mainstream. She had a wholly different style and personality for adult video: highly intelligent, upper-class noble-style speech, posture, and demeanor. Known for her chic dresses, long silky black hair, and unshaven armpits, she became a sensation soon after making her AV debut in 1986. She frequently appeared in Japanese television and magazine interviews, speaking frankly on a wide range of topics, from her own sexual desires to the concept of eroticism and women's sexual liberation. Kuroki's stardom fueled the early popularity of adult videos, playing a significant role within the booming industry and bringing AV to the attention of the Japanese public.

The leading figure in the 1990s AV boom was Iijima Ai, who established nationwide popularity among both male AV fans and mainstream television viewers, including women. She made her debut in 1992, soon becoming an AV idol, and gained great popularity; from there, she transitioned away from adult videos to daytime TV talk shows as a regular guest.[69] In contrast with Kuroki Kaoru, who spoke intelligently about politics, art, and eroticism, Iijima was a down-to-earth, girl-next-door type. While Kuroki maintained an upper-class façade through her distinctive fashion and excessively polite mannerisms, Iijima was frank about her middle-class family background, dressing casually and sporting long, bleached, softly curled hair. She was also known for her forthright personality. In her 2000 autobiography, *Platonic Sex*, she openly discussed her upbringing in a very strict family and the hardships she endured, including running away from home at fourteen, bullying at school, working at a night club, plastic surgery, adult video performance, sexually transmitted diseases, and an abortion. Iijima's honesty and resilience inspired young Japanese women who shared similar experiences. Although she died tragically in 2008 at age thirty-six in her Tokyo apartment for an unknown reason, her popularity helped change the prevailing perception of AV performance as a dead-end career and AV actresses as "defective women."

While AV stars before the 1990s tended to silently exit their careers and hide their pasts, new AV idols did not shy away from the limelight—at least under their model names.[70] They not only remained public figures after "retirement from AV" but also used their "exit-from-AV" narratives as stepping stones to meaningful second careers. Despite the variations in style of AV idols in the 1980s and 1990s, actresses generally had short careers in the industry.[71] Kuroki appeared in only three adult videos within a three-month period in 1986. Iijima performed in a total of twenty videos between 1992 and 1994.

By contrast, AV idols in the new millennium have extended their career longevity significantly and gained international fame. Sola Aoi (Aoi Sora in Japanese), a pioneering figure in Japan's adult content industry, came on the scene in 2002 and performed for nearly ten years, appearing in eighty-seven adult videos but also in numerous magazines, films, and television dramas. In China, where adult videos are banned, underground file sharing enabled fans to access Aoi's videos. She became an iconic representative of the "sexy modern girl" in the country's expanding consumer economy.[72] Marica Hase, a photogravure model, is another influential figure who made her AV debut in 2009 and established international fame. After performing in Japan for a few years, she moved to the US in 2012, where in 2013 she became the first Japanese woman chosen as *Penthouse* magazine's Pet of the Month; in 2020, she garnered a Hall of Fame by Urban X Award, given to honor achievement in ethnic pornography in the US. As of this writing, Hase still performs in adult entertainment videos at the age of forty-one. As such, AV work has appeared to provide opportunities for ambitious women to dream of success and fame that would be hard to realize in other male-dominated workplaces and stages in Japan and abroad.

Since the late 1990s, a few dozen AV idols, including Iijima, Aoi, and Amat-suka, among others, have contributed to casualizing the image of AV actresses in the eyes of the public.[73] As a result, increasing numbers of young women today long for the job, seeking a pathway that potentially leads toward future stardom.[74] Even though the actual pay for their performances has dropped in comparison to the industry's boom years, an AV gig is still an attractive option to women who need supplementary income and can find no better, more meaningful work in Japan's precarious labor market.[75] Some women dream of the kind of instant fame and fortune that a handful of AV idols have achieved in Japan and abroad by becoming celebrities, appearing in mainstream tele-vision shows and feature films, forming music idol groups,[76] and publishing best-selling novels.

The job market for AV performance has become increasingly competitive. Observing this new trend, Nakamura Atsuhiko, who has followed adult video performers since the early 2000s, argues that AV is now a buyer's market in which women cannot find jobs; it's no longer good enough for AV performers to simply engage in sexual conduct on camera. According to Nakamura, perform-ers are increasingly expected to be good looking by default; women's beauty alone no longer guarantees them the prestigious status of a *tantai* top-ranking performer as today's video makers seek perfect body proportions, flawless skin, the most prestigious degrees, and even celebrity status. These traits are high-lighted in performers' video packaging to promote them as part of a new crop of AV performers. Without the name value of *tantai*, other women are pres-sured to find ways to dramatize their performances and appeal to viewership by performing *shiofuki* (vaginal squirting), engaging in deep throat oral sex, and accepting gang rape and *bukkake* (multiple men's ejaculation on a performer's face). Whether for their beauty or the willingness to be sexually degraded on camera, AV actresses have come to be perceived increasingly as "selected women."[77] The highly competitive and demanding labor market situation is symptomatic of challenges the industry faces in the digital age.

For AV actresses, digital technology serves as a double-edged sword: a new possibility to cultivate their fan base and empower themselves but, at the same time, a high risk of being quickly and widely exposed to the public and vulner-able to social discrimination. This was especially true in the early 2000s when few understood what internet technology would do. Despite the popularity of AV jobs, the stigma attached to sex work is still strong, as *kōjo ryōzoku* (public order and moral decency) and obscenity protocols are still being enforced.

Suzuki Suzumi, a thirty-six-year-old former AV performer and University of Tokyo postgraduate, laments the harsh reality that she faces ten years after leaving the AV industry. In her 2020 essay "The Price of 10,000,000 Yen—the Performance Guarantee—for My Debut Video," Suzuki writes, "I will never be able to live any other life but the one that I used to have as an AV performer."[78] When her employer, Nikkei Newspaper Inc., Japan's *Wall Street Journal*, found out that Suzuki had appeared in adult videos in 2014, she resigned from her job as a journalist and became a freelance writer. Despite her hardships, however, Suzuki claims that she is not exactly a victim of "forced performance" since *nobody coerced* her. She simply holds a grudge against her careless nineteen-year-old self.[79] But she is also bitter about an unforgiving society that, she claims, never pardons women for a one-time "careless act" in youth. Kawana Mariko, a popular mystery writer who is open about her past and marriage to a famous AV director, also confesses that the more she focuses on her success in her second career, the more she receives inconsiderate comments on Facebook such as, "You, AV actress, don't ever pretend as if you're a writer. Such a joke!"[80] Once they have made the choice to perform in AV, women are destined to an interminable fate—(re)living their past as (former) AV actresses—and remain forever susceptible to symbolic violence.[81]

This is the sociohistorical background within which the so-called *Shut-suen Kyōyō Mondai* (issue of forced performance) came to light. Some might wonder how female performers are "forced" into working in a field with such a labor surplus. The issue is rather complicated. While more women are seeking AV performance jobs than ever before, they might not be "good enough" to make the cut today. Meanwhile, agencies still rely on scouts to recruit women with *hai supekku* (high specifications) for their most profitable *tantai* status. Furthermore, it is not physical or other forms of overt force that lead women to perform in adult videos against their will. Rather, the covert interplay between dishonest recruitment processes, legal loopholes, and lack of labor protections sets the stage for women's involuntary consent to sexual performance on camera. Recent technological advancements further complicate this insidious orchestration. With technologies proliferating pornography immediately and eternally in cyberspace, it has become impossible for performers to control the circulation of their images and personal information. Social media have made performers vulnerable to rude comments, cyberbullying, and sextortion. Within such a mélange, women's lack of voluntary assent puts them at high risk of labor exploitation, sexual violence, and mental distress.

*Involuntary Consent* is not a book about Japan's AV industry per se. Rather,

I use ethnographic inquiry to analyze consent and question liberal premises at the heart of the AV industry. I urge the importance of examining things that exist but not overtly so—involuntary consent, submission to unfreedom, and structural inequality—within sociolegal frameworks that incentivize profit over labor protections.

## CHAPTER OUTLINES

Within the Japanese AV industry, adult videos are simply thought of as intellectual property; copyright protection is prioritized. For women performers, however, adult videos are not simply copyrighted products but are *their* embodied images—their sexuality, persona, and intimate moments, captured by and for the camera. As such, the decision to work in AV is much more complex for these women than it is for others working in the industry. Performing in AV can present a lifelong problem that potentially undermines women's dignity, self-worth, and well-being. Adult videos are commodities that are deeply embedded in precarious labor processes. On-the-job exploitation and gender-based violence are normalized as part of the work.

The polarizing view of AV as empowering for "selected women" yet disempowering for "victims" of forced performance is an entry point into examining changing yet still pervasive stigmas attached to sexual labor, gendered precarity in labor markets, and the sexual moral economy—all factors that feed structural and symbolic violence against women and silence them regarding their lived experiences. *Involuntary Consent* asks: How do women who nominally give consent to sex on camera—as well as emotional labor on and off the set—make sense of the lines between consent and coercion, euphoria and suffering, and agency and subordination? To what extent are bourgeois, masculinist sociolegal logics capable of addressing how the socially vulnerable become susceptible to *self-subordination by choice*?

Beginning with an examination of public discourse on the issue of "forced performance" in AV, chapter 1, "Involuntary Consent," exposes and defines the parameters of nonvoluntary consent to critically explore how contracts are made and practiced in temporospatially gray areas; nonetheless, political discourses of "forced performance in AV" and economic discourses of sex work as self-determination overlook what's behind the scenes. Chapter 2, "The Actress," zooms in on AV actresses' lived experiences with contract making, sexual performance, interactions with fans, and their private lives, arenas in which they encounter both everyday violence and empowerment.

Zooming out from performers' voices and experiences, the next two chapters consider both structural aspects of and class dynamics within the Japanese AV industry. Chapter 3, "The Management of Girls," looks into the "invisible hand" manifested in infrastructures that enable talent agencies to recruit, patronize, and exploit women in the name of "management of girls" within male-centered business schemes. Chapter 4, "The Industry," illustrates what I call "infrastructures of contract," where the production process—shooting, marketing, and distribution—is compartmentalized, rendering AV actresses' holistic work experience largely invisible to other workers in the industry.

Expanding further outward, chapter 5, "The Male Fan," completes the book's examination of the AV industry ecosystem by examining the lives of enthusiastic male AV fans, who still purchase DVDs to support their favorite actresses while struggling with job security, health issues, and social marginalization due to their own depreciated voluntary consent to precarious work in mainstream Japanese society. These men watch adult videos and attend fan events not simply for sexual pleasure but for life fulfillment. Socially marginalized men and women, I contend, support one another mutually yet asymmetrically, and the AV industry capitalizes on the process.

Finally, the epilogue revisits tensions that teeter between the legal definition and social practice of consent and highlights the ways that the industry has become an easy target of 2022 legal reforms and punitive measures to enhance liberal contractualism. Legal solutions to sexual contract, after all, police discrete acts of contract making but not structural problems of gender inequality, labor precarity, and always-already-compromised consent in Japan.

Throughout this book, I use involuntary consent as an analytical lens to cast light on liberal violence. I employ gender and labor as analytical categories to delineate bourgeois, masculinist ideologies of autonomy, property, and contract whereby AV actresses simultaneously (re)produce and submit to pornographic and legal illusions. Women's voices and experiences in AV, seemingly embodying the spirit of free speech and the free market, pry open what exists but remains unseen.

# 1

## INVOLUNTARY CONSENT

Japan's adult video industry, often described as "harmless" entertainment, has been under public scrutiny since the mid-2010s.[1] This is largely due to a series of arrests of former talent agency CEOs and employees. This scrutiny began with the first court trial of its kind: oddly, a talent agency sued a woman, not the other way around, opening a Pandora's box of legal problems. The talent agency sought 24.6 million yen in damages (US$246,000) when, according to the *Japan Times*, a woman in her twenties alleged that she was "forced" into performing in an adult video (AV) at the agency's behest and subsequently abandoned her two-year contract. In 2015, however, the Tokyo district court dismissed the lawsuit. In the court ruling, the judge stated that actors and actresses are inevitably involved in performing sex in the making of a porn film; yet such activity "must not be conducted against their will,"[2] even if one has signed an AV performance contract. The ruling has triggered much public discussion about the problem of young Japanese women, including minors, being scouted on the streets and coerced (or tricked) into legally bounded sex acts in adult videos.

Such discourse created a "moral panic" and gave rise to a vaguely named issue, described by the media in expressions like the "invisible harm of sexual violence in adult video industries," "coerced adult video filming," and "forced adult video contracts."[3] In Japan, this nameless problem is now known as *AV Shutsuen Kyōyō*, and it has been identified as a major issue of violence against women by the Gender Equity Bureau Cabinet Office.[4] The term *AV Shutsuen*

*Kyōyō* is often translated into English as "forced (or coerced) performance in AV."[5] But the Japanese word *kyōyō* is much more nuanced. *Kyōyō* connotes coercion or compulsion rather than force; another word, *kyōsei*, implies force—that is, "coercion or compulsion, especially with the use or threat of violence."[6] However, as the English translation suggests, the distinction between *kyōyō* coercion and *kyōsei* force becomes ambiguous when a wide range of physical and psychological tactics—threats, fraud, persuasion, manipulation, and future opportunity—are used to elicit consent.

As such, what counts as consent is also blurry. Consent is often presumed to be clearly communicated through a speech act: "I hereby consent," for instance. In other words, consent is assumed to derive from a volitional individual who anticipates and calculates a future, consummating one's promise making by saying "I will." The speech act binds one to delivering the promise. This causal thinking is based on Western logocentric premises—namely, individual autonomy, free will, and positivism.[7] In reality, consent giving in Japan is much more ambivalent, messy, and contradictory at times. In vernacular Japanese, the subject, "I," is often omitted. The frequent use of middle voice in everyday conversation—neither active nor passive, but a more reflexive and reciprocal modality—obscures the causal relationship among the subject, the object, and an action verb.[8] Many of the women I interviewed, for example, explained how and why they did what they did in the process of recruitment and contract making: "[I] followed [a scout to an office] in response to [an invitation like], 'why not just talk?,'"[9] and "[I] responded to [the request], as [I] was asked to 'sign [the document] for the time being.'"[10] In these sentences, there is ambivalence as to whether the speakers are subject or object; they have allowed themselves to be subject to others' influence, even though their signed contracts imply a willingness to declare "I hereby agree." They did, indeed, bring themselves (as much as they were brought) to the office and signed the contracts (in response to a request). Thus, they were not overtly forced, but they were not free of external influences, either.

To capture the ambivalent nature of consent giving, along with the broad spectrum of *kyōyō* coercion, this chapter employs what I call *involuntary consent* as an analytical category through which to examine "forced performance in AV" on the ground. Defining involuntary consent as a neither overtly forced nor completely voluntary agreement to do something, I delve into the ways that consent, a central component of sex work, is sought and given. In Japan's AV industry, however, consent quickly vanishes from focal awareness, even though it is a must-have condition for the work. The dominant public discourse on "forced performance" in Japanese adult videos focuses on coercion, not involuntary consent. As a result, those sex workers who have consented to their work fall between the discursive cracks.

The Japanese government's humanitarian approach to the issue, moreover, has grabbed the public's attention, casting forced performance as a political issue of violence against women. While the government's assumption that the victims of such violence are young, naïve, "deceived" women has succeeded in the politicization of sexual coercion, it has also left the needs of consenting female sex workers—the vast majority of sex workers in Japan—unaddressed. Beginning with a case study of involuntary consent, I introduce a well-known former AV actress who in 2016 went public with the claim that she was mentally abused into performing in adult videos. I share similar cases reported to the Diet Cabinet Office's 2017 survey on sexual violence against women, as well as stories from a women's support group in Japan, to demonstrate how AV models end up binding themselves to an agreement once they give consent. Even if they find the agreement detrimental to their own interests, there is only so much they can do to protect themselves within the existing sociolegal systems. Any abuse and exploitation they may experience becomes barely legible; their consent is assumed to extend beyond a discreet business transaction to include their subjection to sexual stigma, social discrimination, and moral dilemmas.

I am less concerned with contract law itself, however, than the contradictory manifestation of equality, autonomy, and freedom in the everyday practice of contract making. For this reason, I analyze three interrelated elements in the shaping of a contractual *relationship* that perpetuates structural inequality and symbolic violence against women: (1) pre- and extra-contractual contexts that play an important role in constituting a power dynamic and yet are ignored within the legal frame of the contract; (2) women's paradoxical autonomy in the political fiction of "possessive individualism"[11]—that an autonomous subject sells a piece of property, with "property" being talents, services, or labor power (*not* the selling of oneself into slavery); and (3) the liberal assumption grounding the notion of consent: that a person's subjection to others is by choice, unless one is overtly forced through threat of violence. Most AV actresses are not overtly forced into the business, but they do not feel completely free to leave or refuse compliance with aspects of the job either. Despite such ontological and phenomenological complexities, their signed contracts render involuntary consent and its consequences illegible within existing legal frameworks. The liberal assumption of "possessive individualism," moreover, makes no place for the structural inequalities and violence animating the lived experience of laboring under contract. Labor power is, after all, inseparable from human bodies; and once workers have sold this power, they become subject to their employers' right to use their bodies. Under such conditions, involuntary consent epistemologically disappears, obscuring the complex infrastructures involved in contracting for sexual labor, both in and beyond the AV industry.

## "FORCED PERFORMANCE IN AV"

The high-profile 2015 Tokyo district court case became the catalyst for the mainstream politicization of "forced performance in AV." Nonetheless, such politicization does not necessarily reflect the voices of victims themselves or speak to their needs. Victims, who are expected to live in the shadows, often remain silent. Indeed, this tension was manifested in the sharp contrast between the lawyer's and victim's responses to the court ruling. At a highly publicized news conference, Ito Kazuko, the defense lawyer and human rights activist, celebrated the court's dismissal of the case as a great victory, saying, "The court declaring that companies are not allowed to force people to engage in sex without their consent is a strong message against sexual exploitation of women, and will hopefully spark a move toward establishing legislation against such an industry."[12] Ito appeared very proud of the result and hopeful for necessary changes. By contrast, the defendant not only was absent from the news conference but also revealed neither her identity nor her face. She provided a more vigilant written statement:

> Even though the trial is over, there are many challenges ahead. Once distributed over the Internet, the films I appeared in are now hardly "deletable," no matter how desperately I want to forget about them. I'm fearful someone I know may come across them at any time. Living like this is painful and I will never forgive the industry.[13]

Though her case may contribute to structural changes in the industry, the victim has essentially gained nothing out of her "victory" besides a null and void contract. She instead anticipates lifelong consequences in the internet age: psychological pain, fear of identity reveal, and general animosity against the industry.

The woman was, according to Ito, initially recruited at one of the busiest train stations in Tokyo on her way home from high school. A "talent" scout, promising that she would become a TV star, took her to the plaintiff's office—where she unsuspectingly signed a service contract that would trap her into performing unpaid work in soft-core porn videos. From her perspective, she was interested and agreed to work as a photogravure bikini model as a pathway to her future career; at this point, *shiji sareru ga mama keiyakusho ni shōmē shita* (following the directions provided, [she] signed a [given] contract).[14] The contract was full of legal jargon that made it difficult for her to understand what she was signing. The agency never gave her a copy of the contract nor consulted her parents, despite the fact that she was a minor and could not enter into a contract without her parents' permission. Once she turned twenty and became a legal adult, her agency asked her to sign another service contract. It turned out to be an arrangement for her to appear in a total of ten pornographic videos. When she expressed reluctance to appear in the first video, the agency threatened that she must comply, otherwise she must pay a penalty of a million yen (US$10,000). To avoid the penalty, she completed the shooting. "Naked and terrified by the gazes of the shooting crew," reported the *Japan Times*, "[the defendant] was forced into sex with men she had never met—her complaint of severe vaginal pain being ignored—before she began to contemplate suicide."[15] At one point, she firmly expressed her wish to quit, but the agency further threatened to charge her for planned videos valued at an estimated 2.2 million yen (US$22,000) per movie and also to divulge her activities to her parents.

Desperate for help, in late summer of 2014 she reached out to the victim-support group PAPS (People Against Pornography and Sexual Violence).[16] The organization advocates for the voiceless and invisible victims of sexual exploitation, and fights against pornography and sexual violence broadly in the sex industry. Miyamoto Setsuko, a social worker and former director of the support group, acknowledged that while most young women are not necessarily coerced into signing exploitative contracts by physical force, they do not voluntarily agree to perform in pornographic videos either. In her 2016 article "The Harm of Adult Videos: Yet-to-Be-Revealed Sexual Violence in the Adult Video Industry and Poverty among Youth," Miyamoto lamented that female victims were apologetic about signing contracts and causing "trouble." Blaming themselves, they rarely felt they were entitled to report their experiences of sexual violence and exploitation to public authorities, or anybody else, for that matter. Miyamoto stressed that they were often initially hesitant to open up even to her case workers, despite their desperation. They simply wished to get out of their "mess" or figure out how to best endure their suffering—a well-known Japanese ethic of *gaman*, perseverance. Miyamoto details a wide range of fear, pain, and suffering resulting from defendants' coerced performance in AV: panic attacks, blackmail, and social discrimination in the job market, housing, and marriage, among other areas.

Building on these case workers' reports, Ito (the lawyer), who also serves as head of the Tokyo-based international NGO Human Rights Now, asserted that what these women have been experiencing is gender-based violence. In the organization's timely Spring 2016 report, "Japan: Coerced Filming of Adult Pornographic Videos," Ito elaborates:

> It is a grave human rights violation to take advantage of young women who are uninformed and/or in financial difficulties and coerce them into performing non-consensual sexual acts on camera and circulate the filmed images commercially. The use of threats such as penalty charges is similar to slavery because people are put in the position of debt bondage.[17]

Making an analogy between indentured sexual labor and slavery, Ito clearly considers sexual violence against women a human rights violation.

Immediately following the release of the Human Rights Now report in March 2016, a member of the Japanese Communist Party, Ikeuchi Saori, who served in the House of Representatives (2014–2017), politicized the issue of "coerced filming of AV" as a form of sexual violence. Bringing it to the Japanese Diet, she requested juridical invalidation of forced sexual acts induced in AV performance contracts.[18] At the Diet, Ikeuchi used the 2015 Tokyo district court ruling as precedent for her inquiry. In her narration of the woman's experience, Ikeuchi kept using passive sentences to stress her victimhood: she *was recruited by* a scout to become a talent; *being deceived into* thinking it was a talent agreement, she signed a contract; she *was forced by* her agency *to* engage in sexual acts on camera due to the enforceable agreement; furthermore, she *was forced to* sign her performance contract [with the video maker] after the shooting when she was in shock and absent-minded. Ikeuchi also used passive voice while sharing another woman's story: once declining an AV performance offer over the phone, she *was told to* pay a visit to the agency's office to discuss the cancellation of her contract; while visiting the office, she *was raped by* multiple men, and the horrific scene was videotaped; and she *was threatened with* having the video circulate widely as a commercial product if she declined her AV performance offer. Attracting the audience's sympathy,

Ikeuchi reminded Diet members that, when the defendant in the 2015 lawsuit initially asked for help, a police officer mocked her claim of coercion as nonsense since she gave her consent; the officer advised her to peacefully walk away after the completion of her contractual terms.[19] At the peak of narrating these women's helplessness, Ikeuchi urgently asked the state to intervene to put a stop to this new form of sexual violence. The reaction was swift. Diet members agreed that the service contract itself fundamentally enabled violence against women. Finally, the Ministry of Justice deemed that the issue must be dealt with as a "human rights violation," that is, a crime.

Ikeuchi's presentation persuasively employed what Kristin Bumiller refers to as "expressive justice" and provided the Diet with what Didier Fassin calls "humanitarian reason."[20] Bumiller defines "expressive justice" as a way to express anger and outrage over injustice while renarrating high-profile sexual crimes and stories about sexual violence. Such a presentation, she argues, fulfills the "purpose of locating the threat to society and justifying a punitive response."[21] In other words, expressive justice uses graphic depictions of sexual crime to evoke strong emotional reaction such as anger, fear, and disgust, mobilizing the masses to support preventive measures, criminal prosecution, and protection of the victims. Ikeuchi's speech, in which she not only used dramatic stories but also employed passive sentences effectively, provoked a strong audience reaction as she successfully made her point about young, helpless women. Such expressive justice has led to the conclusion that violence against women is a human rights violation; therefore, the state should intervene. This is, as Fassin points out, a particular kind of humanitarian reason that justifies state intervention in the name of humanity and promotes criminal justice for the protection of human rights. Though this approach might sound akin to universal protection of women's rights, it risks excluding those who do not fit a stereotypical "good victim" image—young, innocent women—as if these were the only kinds of people worthy of compassion, state aid, and even justice.[22] Women who have given consent to sex commerce and received compensation are left on their own, even if they are being sexually abused and exploited.

By the early summer of 2016, the "forced performance" issue had become public, largely thanks to the effective mass media employment of expressive justice and humanitarian reason. The *Asahi Shimbun*, one of the largest newspapers in Japan, carried a series of online reports between 2016 and 2018, titling the series "The Issue of Forced Performance in AV."[23] NHK, Japan's national public broadcasting service, aired a television documentary, "'I Was Coerced to Perform': Targeting Ordinary Girls," in July 2016.[24] With the nationwide coverage, along with social media attention, magazine articles, and relentless TV exposure, a poorly understood problem became a prominent social issue almost overnight—with standardized language, "forced performance in AV," and an emphasis on the possibility that any young woman could become a victim.[25]

Following this increased national concern, the US Department of State's *2017 Trafficking in Persons Report* problematized the issue further as a form of human trafficking.[26] The report also noted "forced performance in AV" as a pressing, and growing, problem in Japan:

> Sophisticated and organized prostitution networks target vulnerable Japanese women and girls—often in poverty or with mental disabilities—in public areas such as subways, popular youth hangouts, schools, and online; some of these women and girls become trafficking victims. Some model and actor placement agencies use fraudulent recruitment techniques to coerce Japanese women and men into signing vague contracts, and then force them through threats of breach of contract or other legal action to engage in sexual acts to produce pornographic materials.[27]

Unlike Japanese narratives about the issue, which rely on vague sentences and passive voice, the English account is straightforward and assertive. The above description is fully in active voice, specifying the subject and object while using strong action verbs such as "target," "coerce," and "force." Despite its linguistic force, however, the actual subject of the English report is as unclear as that of the Japanese report. "Sophisticated and organized prostitution networks" are the faceless subject, implying a criminal syndicate like *yakuza*. By the same token, "some model and actor placement agencies" is both too specific and narrow to be the causative subject of human trafficking per se. As I discuss in chapter 3, street scouts and talent agencies are not necessarily part of organized criminal networks, yet their sleazy image makes them an easier target for prosecution and political scapegoating than video directors and AV makers, who do not directly deal with managing labor.

If the Japanese public discourse on "forced performance in AV" emphasizes stereotypically vulnerable victims, the English description in *Trafficking in Persons Report* focuses on stereotypically harmful offenders. Despite these differences in linguistic expression and focus, however, both accounts align with a criminal justice framework, which mobilizes discrete individuals to identify "bad guys" and "poor victims."[28] In this framework, the structural problems that cause sexual and labor exploitation remain unaddressed. Furthermore, human rights violations experienced by the majority of sex workers, who were neither forcibly coerced nor enthusiastically consented to the work, are overlooked or dismissed. Thus, any discussion from this point of view fails to address the nuances and complex inner workings of the situation. Rather, it (re)constructs a stereotypical image of victims—young Japanese women— evoking the public's fear of notable crimes for the support of state-level intervention. Dominant discourse around "forced performance in AV," in turn, systematically overlooks the structural aspect of precarious sex work itself.

## POSSESSIVE INDIVIDUALISM

Individual-centered criminal justice is hardly concerned with the gendering of political economy and legal systems. As I discuss at length in the introduction, Japanese AV performers are not protected as laborers. Their sex work is not acknowledged as legitimate wage work, according to Japanese employment law, due to the "disturbing" nature of the work to kōjo ryōzoku—public order and moral decency. Only the product they create is protected as "free speech." In other words, sex work as labor is not protected, but sex work as entertainment is. Under such conditions, sex work is illicit for female performers who have sex on camera, but not for the rest of the male-dominated industry: video makers, distributors, and users of the "free speech" produced. Moreover, the supplier of such sexual labor, namely street scouts and talent agencies, often become a target of criminal justice, while the demand side—the capitalist owners, producers, and consumers—remain protected. Within this masculinist market logic and legal framework, AV performers do not quite count as workers who benefit from the Labor Standards Act; they exist as free agents or coerced victims only—with nothing more nuanced happening in between and beyond.

To function properly within this framework, AV actresses must therefore be designated as freelancers, represented as their own "bosses" who control their labor power—embodied in sexuality and talent—as an asset. This legal notion of being one's own boss (a.k.a. self-employed) is based on the liberal premise of what Canadian political theorist C. B. Macpherson calls "possessive individualism," which is rooted in the political theory of self-ownership—that one is a whole person who owns one's body and controls it.[29] In short, the person is conceptually separated into two: the volitional subject and the body object. This separation conveniently allows the subject to sell a *part* of one's body, including an aptitude for labor, in exchange for money. In reality, however, any one "part" is inseparable from the rest of one's *whole* body; the whole person is subject to an employer who "buys" the right to put the seller under the buyer's command and extract labor. Contracting one's own labor out to another essentially means that one "sells" the "command over the use" of one's body and oneself; therefore the contract, as Carole Pateman asserts, "creates a relation of subordination."[30] Nonetheless, the liberal premise that individuals are, by law, autonomous, free, and equal obscures such power dynamics, as if both sides are equally proprietors of the means of production. Possessive individualism is thus a political fiction through which a capitalist owner and a paid worker are juridically constituted as "equals" upon making a labor contract. In other words, no matter how much workers are subordinated to their employer in practice, they remain independent contractors nominally.[31] Moreover, as contract workers, they lose their labor protections—such as paid sick leave and unemployment insurance.

However, a pro-sex worker feminist stance—summarized, perhaps, by the expression "[I] decide whether or not to sell [my body]"[32]—stresses workers' sexual autonomy and self-determination over their bodies. Selling sexual labor is, therefore, conceived of as a choice that women make as proprietors of their own bodies. This view aligns with the liberal discourse underlying the labor contract. Just like other forms of wage labor and independent contractor work, sex work is assumed to be "based on [one's] free will."[33] As with women's reproductive rights, women in these pro-sex worker and liberal market discourses are cast as autonomous decision makers, where selling sexuality is reduced to a simple economic transaction. Yet these seemingly separate entities—the *whole* person and a *part* of one's body—are two sides of the same coin: possessive individualism that consists of two mutually constitutive elements of subjectivity.

The legal framework largely tolerates sex commerce unless sexual labor is coerced and sexual autonomy is violated. The 2015 lawsuit touched on political concerns about sexual coercion, calling it an " 'unjustifiable matter' to let [a person] perform in adult videos against the person's will."[34] Assuming that sexual interactions are involved in the making of adult videos, the judge ruled that such an activity "must not be non-consensual."[35] The ruling clearly bans a type of act—nonconsensual sex—while suggesting consensual sex will be tolerated. Making it clear that a signed contract is unenforceable in sex commerce, however, the narrow focus leaves the vast majority of areas open to multiple interpretations, including the legality of sex commerce itself, sexual abuse, and economic exploitation. Unless one can be proven to have been overtly coerced, such an equivocal legal stance upholds the (neo)liberal paradigm of free will—and the free market.

The result is the creation of a large, ambiguous, and often contradictory in-between area—neither consent nor coercion—in which everyday life is lived. Not only liberty but also violence and exploitation are experienced in this in-between. But such ambivalence largely remains unseen. The 2015 lawsuit was, after all, a rare, chance exception; it was not the woman coerced to perform who filed the suit but a talent agent suing her for business losses. The lawsuit has pried open the "no-win" situation sex workers find themselves in. However, it has only scratched the surface of the deeply embedded structural violence that renders the socioeconomically powerless susceptible to giving *nonforced* but also *nonvoluntary* consent to the powerful, due to their desire for better pay, recognition, and a future. Meanwhile, the powerful can take advantage of consenting subjects' structural vulnerability and, if they wish, exploit them with the full support of the law. How do women performers navigate the multilayered, often-invisible structural violence within and outside the AV industry?

## "BRAINWASHED" CONSENT

Kozai Saki, who felt lured into performing in pornographic videos by appeals to her dream of a glamorous life, illuminates her experience as a woman caught in the in-between area. A former top-tier AV actress, she found herself embedded in various behind-the-scenes vulnerabilities. Coerced into performing in her debut video and coming out as a victim years later, she initially remained in the AV business for hope of money and fame but ultimately realized that her participation in sex work was happening against her will. She was not physically forced into AV performance but did not voluntarily consent either. She claims that she was brainwashed. Kozai developed an extended relationship with her talent agency before officially signing an exclusive management contract to appear in what she was informed would be a sexy image video, not AV. At the shooting site, the director unexpectedly asked her to consent to appearing fully nude and then to having sex on camera. She cried a lot and tried to negotiate with the director, but ultimately acquiesced to doing what he had asked. The rest is history.

The following narrative is based on a series of in-depth interviews I conducted with Kozai in 2018. However, as an ethnographer, it has not always been easy to bring dispersed pieces of information together to present a coherent story about AV contract making. This is partly because anyone's remembrance of everyday life is messy and fades away, even if one keeps good records. Moreover, just like anyone else, Kozai selectively narrated her experience—eloquently but also vaguely at times. She was careful about what to say and not say, especially about the moment of contract signing—the moment that became *the exclusive focus* of a trial to juridically determine whether her case would be considered "forced performance." While Kozai did not go into detail about how she signed her contract and under what circumstances, she detailed what she'd already made public—the recruitment process, elaborate deceptions, and coerced performance on set.[36] As will become clear from her story, Kozai's case exemplifies how seemingly voluntary consent can be carefully orchestrated, shedding light on the limitations of possessive individualism in determining whether consent was or was not given.

Kozai's entry into modeling began in college with a stint as a "race queen," or a model hired to strut around at automobile promotion events. Studying economics at a prestigious private college in Tokyo, she dreamed of owning her own business one day—an adult goods store for women, she told me, since this was an underdeveloped market in Japan. After graduation, she worked full time for an information and communication technology company and continued to model on weekends. In the summer of 2010, after her modeling agency went out of business, she was in search of another agency when a street scout spoke to her at a train station in central Tokyo; she immediately recognized the famous talent agency on his business card and some of the clients he mentioned. Wanting to learn more, she set up a meeting with him. After several meetings, she filled out an application, only to receive a rejection letter a few days later. The scout apologized, explaining how difficult it was for any woman over twenty to succeed in modeling; Kozai was twenty-four at the time. However, the scout also told her that he knew a very influential man named Aoki who could possibly help her.

Aoki, apparently an extremely busy man, was initially unavailable. Kozai's first meeting with him took place a few weeks later at a conference room in Roppongi Hills, an upscale commercial and residential complex known for its prominent tenants that include IT companies, financial and consulting firms, and legal firms. According to Kozai, the setup for this meeting was very dramatic. A young man, professionally dressed in a high-end business suit, welcomed her politely on her arrival in the lobby and escorted her to an elevator. He told her how lucky she was to be able to meet Aoki, that he was a wealthy business owner and financial investor and highly selective about face-to-face meetings. Once guided into the meeting room, she received Aoki's welcome. Expecting him to share details about his business or recruit her to his agency, Kozai was caught by surprise when Aoki asked her abruptly, "What do you want to do? What's your dream?" Kozai was at a loss for words. "We don't need people who don't know that," Aoki exclaimed. Kozai managed to share her dream of opening an adult goods store and becoming a business owner. "It's interesting," Aoki said, and next he offered to give her a series of one-on-one lectures to help plan and implement her business ideas. She accepted. This was the beginning of her long journey toward becoming an AV actress.

Aoki, Kozai remembers, presented himself intensely and authoritatively during his ninety-minute lectures about "vision" and business management, one to three times a week. He was often late to the meetings, making her wait for him. Kozai, however, was highly motivated, studying adult goods markets and existing business models to envision her future while waiting. Her lecture notebook, entitled "Vision Notes," overflowed with writing; within a year she'd accumulated ten volumes. The first notebook opens with questions such as "Why do I want to open a shop? How do I possibly make the business super successful?" Based on Aoki's lectures, she jotted down answers to these questions. One answer read, "Become a Gem of Asia" (meaning an iconic feminine figure with radiant beauty and sexiness), suggesting her hope of self-branding her name and image as a human advertisement for her own business, which she could capitalize on. A couple of pages later she shared another possible answer, "The Development of a Shop with Annual Sales of 700 Million Yen (7 Million Dollars)." Being trained by Aoki to visualize her future as concretely as possible in order to execute it, Kozai transformed her original idea of opening a little shop in Tokyo into the far more ambitious goal of tapping into the Chinese sex toy market and, by extension, Asia at large. She recalls getting nervous and straightening her back whenever she interacted with Aoki, who, according to Kozai, got irritated so easily as to intimidate her; her relationship with him was like "a scary expert [in business success] and his pupil," she said.

Kozai told me that she was "brainwashed" through these intensive interactions with Aoki into constantly thinking about her future business success and devoting her wholehearted effort to it. Besides her regular diet, personal training, and spa treatment plans, her weekly schedule was filled with Aoki's vision lessons as well as preparation for and review of their meetings. Other days, she was assigned to hang out and have dinner or enjoy *karaoke* with her scout and two staff members who worked under Aoki. In addition to these interactions with male staff, a female manager cared for Kozai's personal matters and psychological needs. When Kozai became what Aoki would refer to as "mentally weak," this woman would drive her to visit a famous fortune teller known for her accurate predictions for Japanese celebrities and business executives. The fortune teller kept telling Kozai that she would succeed in the "adult world," which Kozai interpreted as meaning that she would become a success in her sex toy business, and that her talent name, Kozai Saki, was full of good luck. With a name like that, she would surely achieve breakout business success soon; her given name, however, would not help her. Paying at least 50,000 yen (US$500) a visit for the fortune telling and prayers, she started to believe in, or more accurately tried to believe in, the prospect of living as Kozai Saki. Aoki had also convinced her to do anything necessary to gain success as he repeated, "Win your dream at all costs" and "Try everything except criminal acts." She did anything he recommended and avoided all distractions, including family and close friends who would have possibly intervened.

Looking back, she said that becoming "Kozai Saki" was not just a superficial adaption of her model name but a profound transformation of who she was for her prosperous future. Kozai, who had yet to perform any paid work for Aoki, had to put what Joanne Entwistle and Elizabeth Wissinger call "aesthetic labor" into her self-creation—or the prework labor required to "get a job," as well as maintenance of ageless beauty once a job is secured in the so-called image industry (e.g., modeling, acting, and dancing).[37] Aesthetic labor, as Entwistle and Wissinger argue, goes beyond superficial beauty work to include the deep emotion work necessary to produce an attractive "personality" emanating both physical *and* inner beauty.[38] Women are expected to cultivate and use their beauty and sexiness in a business context where sex sells. In retrospect, Kozai admits she was living in the bubble Aoki created, bouncing back and forth between who she imagined herself to be in the future—a superwoman—and who she was at the moment—a nobody. There was no in-between. It seemed only natural, then, for Kozai to accept Aoki's advice to appear in a sexy photo album book and image videos as a pathway toward the next stage.

Kozai agreed to exclusive management by Aoki's agency, through which she modeled for her photo album, *SAKIRISE*. Until then, Kozai and Aoki were not in any contractual relationship. No payment was involved on either end. She sacrificed her free time and savings for her business plan, assuming that Aoki truly believed in her success and invested his time and energy for future returns. Kozai repeatedly told Aoki, however, that she did not wish to appear in pornographic videos when his agency booked her in a sexy image video shot by MUTEKI (literally meaning invincible), one of the most prestigious AV labels in Japan. (MUTEKI is where many former celebrities and idols make their sensational AV debuts.) She was told, she said, that the video would be like a "photo album in motion," showing only down to the naked lower back; nothing like an adult video. She believed in him since there were a few such image-only videos with celebrities. In June 2011, nine months after meeting Aoki, Kozai agreed to participate in the video.

Far away from Tokyo, however, the director at the film studio told her that there was going to be a completely naked scene. Kozai's mind went blank. But she could not say no due to her personality. She described her personality as hard working, competitive, and ambitious, while also credulous, noncontentious, and "nice." Instead of confronting the director and expressing her honest feelings, she escaped to the makeup room to cry for several hours in the hope that the shoot would be canceled. Despite her "calculation"—that a woman's tears would have the power to change men's minds—her manager, the director, and the producer pleaded with her to do the shoot. She realized everyone else was there to produce a video and make a living. She was alone. Nobody was on her side, including her makeup artist, who provided her with company but could do nothing further for her. The longer she waited, the more pressure she felt. In her words, "I knew that no one could go home unless I finished the job. At that point, *kakugo wo kimeta* ([I] resigned myself to [the given situation])."

Kozai insisted that this was a coercive situation in which she resigned herself to the request for full nudity. Her debut video, *RACE QUEEN* (2011), itself captured moments of her reluctance, confusion, and even tear-stained face in the process of giving involuntary consent. For our third interview, Kozai invited me to her Tokyo apartment to play the video's opening interview scene. The video starts with her in a light-green summer dress, shyly smiling and strolling through a lush forest as soft sunlight filters through the trees. The tone changes in the next scene. The camera shows her with eyes closed, her posture stiff as her makeup artist brushes powder over her face. The screen then goes black as captions appear, one after another to evoke the audience's affective reaction: "The real thing (with the dual meaning of acting before the camera and hardcore sex) is approaching,"[39] "[Her] decision swings back and forth," and "[She] becomes uncertain." The viewer meets Kozai in the next scene, a closeup profile shot of her sitting in a chair, wearing a black camisole. With drooping head, her long straight hair blocks a clear view of her face.

The director can be heard asking, "Are you alright?"

Kozai lifts her head slightly. Her face appears puffy, and her eyes look drained. Pausing for a few seconds, she responds, "Yes [I am okay])."

The director goes on, "There have been so many things [for you to overcome], haven't there? It must not always be easy. But what the audience wants is your smiling face."

Listening to him intently and nodding, Kozai is on the verge of tears. "Wait a minute please. [I] might have [my] facial expression so confused [on camera]. Does [my face look like I am] smiling [to you] now? [It's] so complicated," Kozai says. She seemed uncertain in the video, suggesting that she felt she could not hide her complex feelings on camera.

"All [of us] have complicated feelings," the director sympathetically but firmly replies. "It might sound cruel to you. Once you take off your clothes, however, [you] can never turn back."

At that moment, Kozai clearly says, "[I] don't intend to back out at all!"

The director confirms her intention: "Well, [does that mean you] will be fine?"

She continues, somewhat anxiously but with determination: "[I'm] fine!"

She pauses before slowly finishing her statement. "It took [me] a year to get to this day. [My] feelings won't change. [I'm] certain about [my] decision."

Kozai stopped the video here. According to her, the interview scene was edited to appear as if she gave consent to having sex on camera, although she only decided to accept the director's original request for full nudity. In behind-the-scenes dialogue, according to Kozai, the director provoked her by saying, "[You are] going to get cold feet halfway through and back out, aren't [you]?" In her mind, Kozai screamed back, "How dare [you] talk [to me] like that! [You] don't know anything about the turmoil [I] had to go through in the last nine months." But in the next moment, she found herself saying, "[I'm] certain about [my] decision."

According to Kozai, the director's rhetorical question was cut out, and, of course, her internal protest was silent in the video. This is another example of Japanese-language middle voice—neither active nor passive—in the ambiguous exchanges of consent seeking-and-giving between two parties. Nonetheless, Kozai's reflexive and reciprocal dialogue with the director remains largely invisible in the video, other than her final words: "[I'm] fine!" and "[I'm] certain about [my] decision."

How was Kozai's involuntary consent to full nudity extended to actually having sex on camera? The vague exchanges between Kozai and her director carried on throughout the video. After the nude scene, Kozai told me that the director asked her to perform sexually explicit scenes such as kissing, petting, and fellatio. At this point, she realized that it was an adult video after all. She showed her reluctance to perform these scenes with a frown on her face and an uncooperative attitude, and she delayed shooting for as long as possible. But her feelings were hurt whenever the staff rolled their eyes, sighed overtly, and threw their equipment on the floor to make a loud statement. By midnight she was too worn out to resist the director's final request. Throughout the filming, the director never forced her to perform in AV but rather employed a wide range of tactics—deceit, rhetorical questions, and psychological pressure—to induce her to make certain choices.

Neither Aoki's "brainwashing" nor the coerced filming was disclosed until Kozai and another performer, both of whom signed with Aoki, came out as victims to the best-selling weekly tabloid *Shūkan Bunshun* in the summer of 2016, at the peak of public discourse on forced performance in AV. Kozai and Sato (pseudonym given in the tabloid article) revealed very similar experiences: both were scouted on the street only to receive rejection letters from the same modeling agency due to their ages; they were then introduced to Aoki. They were trained to become a successful "businesswoman" and a popular "singer," respectively, as they wished, and convinced by Aoki to use their beauty and sexiness to get ahead in their fields and realize their dreams. And they signed with Aoki's agency to find a "proper" venue through which to develop their brands but soon found themselves coerced to perform in adult videos. *Shūkan Bunshun* comments that they ended up having their "dreams" preyed upon.[40] The whole process was, Kozai claims in the interview, carefully calculated and staged for women with ambition to be set up for brainwashing per Aoki's vision.[41] She thinks that she was forcibly pressured rather than simply deceived because the prolonged process gradually and effectively undermined her awareness of what was happening. She felt she was being well supported rather than manipulated.

Kozai's and Aoki's views on what Kozai refers to as brainwashing seem to never converge. In the same article, Aoki and the fortune teller Kozai visited defend themselves. Aoki briefly commented, "[I] have neither threatened [anyone] to perform [in AV] nor intended to hide [my] AV business [from anyone], either. [I] spent plenty of time discussing [their] performance over several months. There are hundreds [of girls] who quit before [they] make [AV] debuts. Is something wrong with what is, I believe, normal?"[42] In his comment, Aoki repeats the word "performance," without clarifying whether he's referring to AV performance—as if his "girls" always already understand what he really meant by "performance." This could be understood as simple miscommunication, but Kozai's claim suggests that she agreed on sexy image videos, not AV, and that an agency can take strategic advantage of such miscommunication. Due to the knowledge gap between the industry and an actress, as the next chapter addresses, "miscommunication" almost always disadvantages the socioeconomically vulnerable party (i.e., the actress). Deploying the same logic as Aoki, the fortune teller defended herself. "By way of my friend, Aoki, I have met several AV actresses, but all of them have already *kakugo wo kimete ita* (resigned themselves to [AV performance])," she said. "[I] have never pushed [them]. Nor have I intended be involved in brainwashing [them], ever."[43] The word she uses, *kakugo* (resignation), with unspecified content and present perfect tense, connotes that these women have already found themselves in circumstances where they anticipate something unfavorable, painful, and perhaps even fatal, and yet have made up their mind to proceed with a given mission. A more well-known use of this word might involve soldiers on a battlefield who, confronted by a fight to the death, resign themselves to their fate. Both Aoki and the fortune teller contend that these women's resignation is a form of self-determination, belittling the idea that their influence or other external factors have compromised the actresses' agency.

In this kind of "he said, she said" dispute, material evidence, like a signed contract, weighs in judging a chronology of events and shaping legal outcomes. Nonetheless, not only does what "she said" often go unheard, but existing evidence is unfavorable to the "she." Although the magazine article did not mention it, Kozai shared her detailed schedule book with me, pointing to more "evidence" that she was manipulated during the contract making itself. As she recalls it, she had not given consent to AV performance prior to the shooting; she signed a performance contract, provided by MUTEKI, the video maker, retroactively. More specifically, as asked, she backdated the contract as June 13, 2011, to account for the shooting that she "consented" to a week prior—though the contract was actually signed on June 23, 2011. From her perspective, she could do nothing at that point except sign the document to receive payment for her already completed work. In hindsight, she regrets having done that because her signed contract and received payment reinforces the view that the economic transaction was properly complete on paper. Such "evidence" is, in turn, gold for Aoki and the AV industry; with paper in hand, they can prove that she had consensual sex on camera in exchange for a fair price.[44]

Kozai's story drew Japanese mainstream media attention and curiosity. She was one of the first well-known AV actresses to go public, with her model name and face exposed. Despite the media attention, she drew much less public sympathy than victims of forced AV performance who kept their identities confidential and left the business quietly, including her co-accuser, "Sato." Kozai's case was controversial. After her debut video, she made an exclusive contract with S1 (an abbreviation of "No. 1 Style"), a prestigious AV label that most celebrities and idols who made debuts through MUTEKI transferred to. She went on to appear in more than two dozen adult videos, performing in some of the highest-grossing films for Aoki's agency. Once her contract with S1 reached its maturity in 2014, she became independent from Aoki, continuing to perform in pornographic videos on a freelance basis. When she came out as a victim, she was still in the business until she finally retired two years later.

Some questioned whether her victimhood was compromised by her decision to not quit her job immediately. Others suspected it was all a publicity stunt aimed at compensation money and boosts to her popularity out of sympathy. In response to these criticisms, Kozai told me that she had no other options but to continue to perform in adult videos, for two reasons. First, it was very difficult for a woman near thirty with little real-world experience to find a "decent" job or start a new business in Japan's male-centered, youth-oriented job market. She also needed a fairly large sum of money to sue Aoki. Second, she was afraid of losing who she was and becoming a "nobody" by stepping down from "Kozai Saki"—not only a brand she cultivated but also an entrepreneurial self she had become. She said, "I couldn't simply let go of what I had truly cared for and struggled to build up. It might not make sense to those who have never been trapped in this kind of desperation and exploitation." Kozai told me that she was never able to fully devote herself to what she felt ashamed of, nor withdraw from it, due to dreams for her future that she'd become deeply invested in.

Kozai's dilemma demonstrates how force and desire coexist and enable submission by choice.[45] Enacting her dreams in the midst of intense feelings of ambivalence, she silently dealt with externally invisible suffering, which man-ifested in severe depression, insomnia, a gastric ulcer, and sudden hair loss due to excessive stress. "[It was] an act of self-harm," Kozai said, to perform in adult videos. Indeed, Kozai's experience reinforces Catherine MacKinnon's point that unless what a woman has gone through can be objectively deter-mined to be rape, sexual violence "is only injury from [a woman's] point of view"—a form of violence, in other words, that she must reckon with alone.[46] Kozai is now frustrated that her victimhood cannot be easily proven within the legal system. Meanwhile, her physical and mental health has deteriorated to the point where she has been diagnosed as a person with disabilities. She feels she is owed compensation to cover her medical bills, if not all of the in-justices she suffered from. The psychic and affective dimensions of injury are further compounded when a "forced performance in AV" legal claim fails on a consent defense; as with failed rape claims, "the woman has not only failed to prove lack of consent, she is *not considered to have been injured at all*," as MacKinnon puts it.[47]

Kozai's case does not quite fit within the dominant discourse of "forced performance in AV" versus sexual self-determination. She was neither a naïve young woman—a total victim—nor a fully autonomous entrepreneur. Nor was she a willful subject who, as the legal terms define it, freely decided to enter a contractual relationship. Thus, none of the dominant discourses that I discuss above—political, economic, and legal—perfectly capture her situation. Nor do "anti-porn versus sex-positive" feminist debates about sexual labor encapsulate women's agency in resignation. Instead, possessive individualism traps her in a series of dilemmas. Once deeply engaged in the liberal economic process, she strived to become "Kozai Saki" with her entrepreneurial vision of strategically branding herself a valuable commodity. Later, she tried to use the political dis-course of violence against women and convince the public that Aoki's forcible pressures were a form of "forced performance." Nonetheless, her resignation—neither overtly by force nor completely by choice, but by "brainwashing"—left her in a kind of discursive limbo.

## THE RULE OF LAW

Of course, Kozai's case is not typical. She was a valuable *tantai* performer, one of only a handful of actresses in the entire AV industry who are featured ex-clusively in their own videos and whose performance guarantees are set much higher than those of other performers. Not only was her meteoric career trajectory unusual, but so was the intense and lengthy precontractual process that she went through with her talent agency. Aoki's seemingly selfless investment in Kozai before her debut, however, makes sense in the peculiar context of Japan's AV industry, wherein the commodity value of any woman performer peaks when she is still "fresh" and "untainted." In other words, maximizing the commodity value of an AV performer at her debut is the best sales strategy since her performance guarantee rarely goes up following her debut, no matter how popular she becomes or how much her acting skills have improved. A majority of talent agents, however, cannot afford to put their clients, especially non-*tantai* performers, through what Kozai went through—the months of grooming through personalized attention and business-oriented "lessons" that Aoki offered her to increase her commodity value. Most women I interviewed told me that they were recruited by street scouts and made to sign contracts as part of a well-coordinated sequence of events. Once a new performer signed an exclusive management agreement to work with an agency, her manager took her to video makers for interviews; if a job performing in a video was offered, another contract outlining the performance agreement was produced and signed. Thus, the flow is typically seamless and quick from recruitment to contract to actual performance.

There are commonalities between Kozai's and other actresses' cases, however. Most women neither watched adult videos regularly nor knew much about the business until they began working in the industry.[48] In other words, there was a huge knowledge gap about AV production between the industry and these women. As is obvious in Kozai's case, the deck is heavily stacked in favor of the talent agent who possesses the legal expertise, business negotiation skills, and persuasive tactics used in contract making.

Reinforcing the inequality between an inexperienced performer and a talent agency, the Diet Cabinet Office's 2017 report, "Internet Survey on Sexual Violence Targeting Young People," revealed rampant malpractice surrounding AV industry contracts and their enforcement. Of 5,248 women between the ages of 15 and 39 who were surveyed, 24.2 percent said they had been asked on the street or in another public space whether they would like to be a magazine model or television actress.[49] While the vast majority ignored recruiters or refused them, 7.7 percent nevertheless went on to sign contracts.[50] Of those, 42.6 percent responded that they understood their contracts on signing (including the content of their job, cancellation policy, and so forth), but the remaining 57.4 percent admitted neither reading carefully nor fully understanding what they were getting into. Breaking down the figures further, 35.4 percent assumed that what was written was the same as what was verbally explained (and therefore didn't read their contracts carefully); 29.2 percent assumed reliability even if they did not read their contracts; and 23.1 percent felt that reading the text was too cumbersome. Some (20 percent) reported that they were hustled into signing (with little time to read carefully and understand fully). Of those who could not confirm the content of their contracts, some commented that they didn't sign anything written in the first place (19.3 percent) or couldn't remember the moment of making a contract (12.7 percent).[51] These statistical data indicate a serious and widespread breakdown in communication between recruiters and signees that constitutes malpractice in the signing of these contracts.

Unequal power dynamics when the signing occurs play a major part. But deceitful contractual enforcement is another way this asymmetrical relationship plays out. Of those who signed contracts, 26.9 percent reported that they were asked to expose their (half-)naked bodies or perform sexual acts that they had not agreed to in writing.[52] One out of three complied because they were in need of money or afraid of negative consequences, such as upsetting others involved or jeopardizing their physical safety.[53] Their concerns about upsetting others seem closely intertwined with their anxieties about their loss of dignity and physical safety. Some reported that they were convinced they had no other choice but submission if they wanted to avoid "huge sums of penalty fees"; others faced threats of having their secret involvement in pornographic videos "revealed to their parents, schools, and workplaces" unless they obeyed; and still others who were not so overtly blackmailed were "afraid of repercussions for their physical safety and social reputation."[54] Their concerns and fears are often difficult to objectively prove since these warnings of "penalties" and threats are informally given.

Moreover, for women performers to sign an enforceable and binding contract means something quite different for those on the business side. As I detail in chapter 3, talent agents told me that they use the contract as an "empty threat" to manage their business and have no intention of using it for legal disputes. An owner of one talent agency, who has run a business for nearly two decades after a few years of AV actress experience, said to me, "We simply use the contract as a preventive measure to avoid performers' irresponsible behaviors such as no-show, last-minute cancellation, and tardiness." I could not believe this when I heard it initially, but learned later that it was standard practice among talent agencies (with the exception of the one that filed the case I introduced at the beginning of this chapter). Of course, the agency's true intention is kept unknown, especially to their talent. As with Kozai's case, lacking awareness of the agency's "hand," would-be performers acquiesced to their agencies' or directors' demands not necessarily because they were physically forced to but because they were mentally coerced, pressured, or otherwise persuaded into cooperating. Their compliance is therefore not voluntary. They felt *kakugo wo kimeru shika nai* ([they had] *no other choice but to resign* [themselves]) in a given circumstance.[55] Or they found *yaru shika nai* (*no other choice but to do*) in response to peer pressure or due to contractual obligations. As such, it is not so much about the contract's enforceability by law but its commonsensical (mis)understanding in practice that leads contractors to deliver a job that they feel compelled to do.

In Japanese society, where people are conventionally inclined to avoid conflict and prioritize social relationships over their own self-interest, the attitude that can lead to *unforced but involuntary* consent is ubiquitous. Japanese American anthropologist Dorinne Kondo has captured how Japanese people, especially women—herself included, as she became enmeshed in Japanese society as a "daughter" of her host family over the course of a two-year homestay in the 1980s—avoid saying no in their day-to-day lives. Similarly to the young Japanese women who become involved in AV, Kondo was not overtly coerced but nevertheless pressured to involuntarily agree to do things for others such as teaching English, fulfilling her duty as a filial "daughter," and taking on the role of a "proper" Japanese citizen. Her frustration grew as she felt herself becoming "trapped by societal convention." Kondo then realized that there was a profoundly different way of thinking about the self in Japan: individuality was valued only insofar as social relationships were not compromised.[56] Under such circumstances, she "*had no choice* but to comply."[57] Kondo's ethnographic moment vividly recaptures why Kozai could not say no or walk away when she faced her own dilemma. Her resistance would have deeply upset relational others at the filming site. Each time she convinced herself that everything would be fine if she would only yield to their demands.

Understanding Japanese—seemingly passive and relational—subjectivity is important here, rather than assuming these cases to be deviant from the Western model of discretely bounded subjectivity. In Japan, reflexive and reciprocal interactions obscure a clear sense of "I" and instead shape a context-specific sense of the relational self.[58] Such a self is never predetermined. Nor is one's volition fixed, even if subjective experience is still legally defined according to a discourse of willful individualism.

The discrepancy between the legal premise of the sovereign subject and the conventional practice of the relational self has, in turn, become the very reason for judicial system reforms in Japan. As I briefly discuss in the introduction, promoting a new national consciousness of *tōchi shutai*, the "self-governing subject," as ideal citizen has become a Japanese political goal. A 2001 Opinion Brief, "Judicial Systems that Sustain the Japan of the 21st Century," declared the Spirit of Law, the Rule of Law as the fundamental principle of governance in the new millennium, situating judicial restructuring as the "last and most fundamental" among a series of neoliberal political, administrative, and economic reforms. The brief stated:

> A common thread underlying various reforms is the collective volition that each individual citizen strives to transform one's consciousness from *the object to be governed* to *the self-governing subject*, so that one becomes an autonomous and socially accountable subject who actively participates in building a society of freedom and justice and bringing creative energy to the nation. Judicial system reform . . . unites all sorts of reforms organically under one of the basic principles of the Japanese Constitution, Rule of Law. It should be at the heart of determining the "shape of this country." Its success depends upon individual people's understanding of the current situation [of globalization and downturn in the national economy] and undertaking of the national project as self-governing subjects with courage and hope. Without it, reform fails. No success, no future in this country.[59]

The Japanese Cabinet made the Judicial Restructuring Plan official in the following year.

The language of reform for the sake of autonomy, freedom, and justice is disarming and persuasive. However, this is another example of innately paradoxical liberalism. Japanese citizens have been sovereign subjects since the 1947 Constitution of Japan, also known as the Postwar Constitution, which replaced the country's authoritarian monarchy with a form of liberal democracy. It featured Article 13, which protected the constitutional right to self-determination. What used to be plausibly liberatory—simply being a "sovereign subject"—is no longer good enough, if not exactly detrimental to the twenty-first-century liberal democracy of Japan. Citizens are now expected to be active *tōchi shutai* (the "self-governing subject"), not passive *tōchi kyaku-tai* (the "object to be governed"). This logic becomes possible when the political fiction of self-ownership—that individually separate and distinct citizens think rationally and act responsibly for the collective interest—conceptually breaks away from the conventionally prevailing ethics and values of relational selves. In short, liberalism consists of forcible pressure to replace what used to be plausibly liberatory with what is imagined to be *more liberatory*, endlessly, so that a nation can conceive of itself as moving forward, toward "progressive" teleological goals.

Liberalism rarely questions this inherently paradoxical premise. Rather, it is driven by a very forcible pressure whereby individuals are told to be self-governing yet are continuously pushed to get on the liberatory bandwagon, whether they like it or not. As observed via the issue of "forced performance in AV" in Japan, the conventional Japanese sense of the relational self, for instance, has been identified as an "illiberal thing" to conquer but has not been completely swept away. The new "autonomous" subjectivity advocated by the state has yet to be practiced widely. Furthermore, the promotion of such subjectivity has been compromised with the so-called *Shūshoku Hyōgaki* (Employment Ice Age), circa 1993–2005, when many had to accept precarious labor conditions and social disparity grew rapidly. (I discuss this issue further in chapter 5 through a male perspective on the gendering of involuntary consent.) In this milieu, pressing the politico-legal fiction of the "self-governing subject," who is responsible for "building a society of freedom and justice," functions as a form of *liberal violence*—violence that symbolically targets national consciousness, not structural inequality, as the object to be overcome by the self-governing subject's "creative" capacities. Meanwhile, deteriorating socioeconomic conditions render these same subjects ever-more precarious as workers.

Some might ask: can't Japanese people just respond yes or no more decisively so that contracts function properly? This question, however, overlooks some fundamental problems. First, a contract is ultimately a promise about future events; you have yet to know what exactly will happen or how things will go upon deciding whether to give consent. "For a decision to be made," as Jacques Derrida puts it, "you have to go beyond knowledge."[60] Rational choice, then, simply relies on inferences, not facts, that are drawn from past experiences and a sense of what the future is likely to hold. Decision making resides in unknown territory. As such, the self-governing subject's rationality is compromised during contract making. Second, consent focuses on individual intentions without taking structural vulnerabilities into real consideration. If you are a consent giver, you might be compelled to accept contractual terms, even if disadvantageous to you, to meet your basic needs. What would you do if you were a gig worker looking for a job to pay the rent who got an offer only for a highly undesirable job? What if you were a recent graduate looking for an opportunity to prove yourself who received nothing but an unpaid internship offer? It's unlikely that you would simply pass up the offer and walk away without securing a safety net or a backup plan.

Moreover, mutual agreement has little to do with freedom and equality in contractual relationships. Even if we think we know exactly what kind of business we're getting into, this does not guarantee equality between the two involved parties. The legal premise of a contract relies on an assumed meeting of minds. Two parties, who are supposedly equals, come to the table at the same time and shake hands; they are both fully capable, the logic goes, of negotiating their contractual terms, and they sign a contract to make their agreement official. Contract making in practice, however, is an asymmetrical assemblage of two parties. Consent givers, who are usually in vulnerable positions vis-à-vis consent seekers, are subject to the contract seeker's vested interest in the protection of their status, reputation, and property rights.[61] Thus, the fundamental issue with the legal premise of the contract is not individual indecisiveness but structural inequality.

The process that resulted in Kozai and other survey respondents' becoming AV actresses exemplifies this. Theoretically, all parties—the agency, the director, and the performer—should be able to bargain for what they wish. But this is not always the reality. Kozai's relationship with her agent, Aoki, does not sound even close to equality. Her vulnerable position, with no allies at the shooting studio, was a strategic advantage to the AV director (and the rest of the crew as well) throughout the process of filming. It is neither an autonomous process nor equal two-way traffic, particularly with contracts between a corporation and an individual.[62] However, the legal frame of the contract, as Hugh Collins argues, ignores how "the promise was made, how it fitted into a prior relation between the parties, how it affects other people, and how performance of the promise serves the interests and aspirations of the parties."[63] In this way, the legal frame of the contract not only flattens structural inequalities but also obscures involuntary consent, making consent givers structurally vulnerable under the Rule of Law.

## BOURGEOIS, MASCULINIST CONTRACTUALISM

Probing involuntary consent poses a stark challenge to liberal principles that put have-nots at risk of submission *by choice*. Meanwhile, in a liberal democratic society, the haves can take advantage of these principles, exploiting the have-nots with the full support of the law. Kozai's signed contract, as a legal document and material evidence, relegates everything not included within its terms to "he said, she said." There is no way for her to objectively measure the harms she experienced. As such, a trace of injustice is erased.

Moreover, politico-legal systems are inherently gendered, with the legal frame of the contract being essentially based on a gentleman's agreement. Feminist scholars have revealed how legal language and concepts are phallocentric and disadvantageous to women.[64] Linda Mulcahy contends that the legal premise that autonomous citizens freely give or refuse consent manifests "masculine ideals of the discrete arms-length transaction between strangers."[65] Contractual exchanges, in this view, are the "mere expression of economic relationships: a callous cash nexus divorced from intimacy."[66] Central to the contract, consent is founded on the "reasonable man" standard, or the masculinist logic of "separation, possessive individualism, certainty, security of transaction and standardization"—uprooting intimacy, interdependence, and everyday messiness as unreliable feminine traits.[67] In Japan, the concept of the consenting subject becomes possible only when the Japanese sense of the relational self, which often expects young women to resign themselves to harmonious social relationships, is dismissed. This means that women must act like "men" in principle while also remaining socially situated as women and expected to behave accordingly. The "reasonable man" standard, as Pateman has famously argued, not only protects men's freedom at the cost of women's subordination but also presents women's—more generally, feminized others'—submission as *by choice*.[68] In other words, bourgeois, masculinist freedom stands at the cost of the marginalized other at the intersection of gender, class, and age.

The issue of "forced performance" in Japanese adult videos provides a unique window into examining how structural violence is shored up through bourgeois masculinist systems. Unless juridically proven to be coerced victims, women in Japan are nominally autonomous legal subjects who are accountable for their own decisions—even if they suffer from unforeseen consequences. Their suffering is often understood as subjective, rarely associated with structural problems and hardly perceived as social suffering. Given liberal individualism and contractual premises, focal awareness is narrowly aimed at the consenting subject at the moment of signing the contract. Such a perception obscures what goes on behind the scenes: uneven distribution of social privilege, expert knowledge, and bargaining power between contracting parties and beyond. Putting the powerless at a disadvantage is one thing. Causing them much distress is another. The dismissal of structurally caused suffering itself functions as symbolic violence against those who suffer. Such structural violence, however, remains unrecognized in the narrow definition of violence—what sociologist Johan Galtung calls "personal violence." In commonsense understanding, violence, or "personal violence," involves a violent offender causing a victim injury directly, immediately, and physically. Structural violence, as Galtung points out, has "no concrete actors one can point to directly attacking others."[69] The contract itself is by no means harmful. Nor is it violent by nature. But the premises of autonomy and free choice on which the legal *fiction* of the contract is based generate a form of latent structural violence that, as I discuss further in the next chapter, leads to adverse consequences for the socially vulnerable while leaving few physical traces.

With laws being generally designed to protect the consent seeker's interests, the legal protection of rights is closely intertwined with social privilege.[70] Through labor contracts, for example, employers gain property rights over labor power and the things workers produce. Property is, as civil rights scholar Cheryl I. Harris succinctly argues, "a right, not a thing," and therefore, characterized as "metaphysical, not physical."[71] Put differently, property is not so much a specific object that a person owns but an intangible thing, such as legal rights one can exercise over what another person possesses—labor power, talent, and beauty. If the sexual labor required to produce adult videos is "property" women "contract out" to their employers in exchange for monetary compensation, that sexual labor and its pornographic products both become video makers' property. Out of this deal, women "sell" their sexual labor to receive wages, while the video makers "buy" this sexual labor to produce copyrighted videos and accumulate capital.[72] Furthermore, women's sexual labor is, to reiterate, not protected by any existing laws, whereas the video makers' sex commerce is well protected not only by intellectual property law but also Article 21, free expression, in the Japanese Constitution.

Giving consent to sexual performance on camera thus extends well beyond the narrow legal frame of the business contract. It exposes sex workers to the spell of bourgeois, masculinist, liberal contractualism—the politico-economic and juridical nexus that upholds the fictive and violent nature of autonomy, freedom, and even justice. How often do we provide "informed consent" in our everyday lives to receive medical treatments, join gyms, obtain credit cards, and download applications, to name a few such arenas? Don't we simply assume it's the *best choice* to accept what we are offered, without probing too deeply?[73] Consummating the legal premise of autonomy is therefore not a solution to contractual problems. Questioning liberal principles is the first step toward thinking critically and acting differently. Instead of asking what self-determination is and how to achieve it, the question should be: *what kinds of* autonomy and freedom are promoted, what do they *do*, and *for whom*? In the next chapter, I introduce AV actresses' narratives—their personal journeys while navigating bourgeois, masculinist liberalism—to illustrate how the "autonomous agent" and "coerced victim" binary collapses in their experience. I will discuss in detail why some women give consent to AV performance, what kinds of bargaining power they exercise, and how they cope with various forms of violence.

# 2

## THE ACTRESS

"What do I think of the 'issue of forced performance'?" Nakano Hiromi, a thirty-one-year-old retired AV actress and now AV talent agent, repeated my question listlessly and rolled her eyes, not even trying to hide her annoyance. I interviewed her at a Shinjuku cafe in 2018. I didn't expect her to speak openly. I was used to receiving a standard answer, "I'd rather not speak," when I recruited interviewees from the Japan Production Guild (JPG), a nonprofit organization of AV modeling agencies. Nakano, dressed professionally in a dark blue business suit, seemed reluctant to discuss the matter but also willing to give it a try.

"I don't think there is such a thing any longer," Nakano said, taking a sip from a cup of black coffee.

"Do you mean it once existed, but not anymore?" I pressed her.

"I don't know about the past. There might have been some awful agencies, but I don't think they could exist these days. I can't even imagine what kind of business such agencies could run if they did [force actresses to perform]," she said. "I am actually curious to learn how [they do it]," she added sarcastically.

Nakano's skepticism about "forced performance" is, as I later learned, fairly typical among people working in the AV industry.

From a mainstream perspective, by contrast, the human rights activists, reporters, and legislators I talked to all referred to the 2015 Tokyo district court case (discussed in the previous chapter) as a turning point in exposing wrongdoing in the industry. AV business insiders, however, have remained largely indifferent to the case. This is partly because most of the insiders I talked with did not pay much attention to things that would not directly affect their own business. Without much detailed information due to confidentiality, many were simply confused and overwhelmed by the multiple court cases and arrests happening at the time. Indeed, those I spoke with from the AV world tended to confuse the case with another—what they referred to as "the case of *you-know-who*," which sent a chill up the industry's spine. *You-know-who* is Fujiwara Hitomi, a *tantai* first-class actress who sued her talent agency around the same time the district court case was making headlines. Alleging forced performance, she sought to remove her videos from the marketplace. Representatives from her agency, known for its "conscientious and honest" conduct, were subsequently arrested, a move that business insiders believe was based on a "false accusation." They think Fujiwara lied, taking advantage of the politicization of forced AV performance to get herself out of trouble with her nagging fiancé, even though she reportedly enjoyed AV work throughout her acting career. Regardless of the circumstances, a long-lasting, "clean" agency was punished as a warning to others. Perhaps more as a reminder to themselves than anything, Nakano and others in the industry reiterated the same view: that actresses commonly "betray" the industry when they get into trouble, and law enforcement will punish talent agencies based on actress's false accusations. "The AV industry is the real victim," Nakano said. This perspective among industry insiders has kept the Tokyo district court case, which involved a little-known agency, under the radar for others working in AV.

"Nobody had any doubt how much *that actress* enjoyed her AV job," Nakano said. She had my attention. "She always looked so happy and enthusiastic while shooting. Who stays in the business over five years and appears in more than 400 videos if she has really been forced?" I was at a loss for words. In the cases reported by women's support groups and the mass media, several AV actresses reflected on their experiences of verbal and emotional abuse while working in AV, which they felt undermined their dignity and self-worth.

Nakano, however, vividly recalls the day Fujiwara joyfully announced her retirement for marriage. Lowering her voice, she said:

> Apparently, *that actress* had kept her AV job from her fiancé. One day, when [he found out about her past], she must have told him a lie, that her appearance in adult videos was against her wishes. Her fiancé [then] made her demand that all her videos be removed. Desperately needing to fix the problem before her wedding, she consulted a lawyer and learned that she could

make the request legally if she was forced [to perform in the videos]. That's when she made her allegation official.

Speaking all of this in one breath, Nakano then paused to take another sip. After catching her breath, she smiled at me. "Her case is known as *nanchatte*, mock-forced performance." *Nanchatte* is Japanese slang for a joke.

In the previous chapter, I argue that the mainstream view of AV performance, where sex workers were classified either as free agents or coerced victims, renders involuntary consent illegible. Business insiders, moreover, are inclined to protect their own interests, ignoring or dismissing involuntary consent as an issue. Either way, not enough is known about AV actresses' experiences, especially when they both give consent to perform in adult videos and suffer from the consequences of this choice. How do we know that Fujiwara's "happy and enthusiastic" demeanor on set is a manifestation of her free will? What if this look is a product of her emotional labor to fulfill her contractual terms (and make others happy)? Even if highly motivated to succeed in AV, most of the women I interviewed express still feeling trapped in moral dilemmas, and they constantly fear humiliation from romantic partners, family, friends, or the public. They are afraid of what they call *mibare* (having their identity revealed) and face a wide range of challenges: stigma; discrimination in marriage, employment, and social life; and psychological harassment via blackmail, cyberbullying, and sextortion. Consequently, their personal lives and work-related concerns are largely kept secret. Women performers' consent to sexual labor thus goes beyond the narrow legal frame of the business contract; rather, it is couched within infinitely expansive sociocultural and moral economies.

This chapter illuminates the experiences of actresses who have given consent to AV performance. For the most part, their jobs differ little from work in the service sector and gig economy. Uniquely, however, AV comes with a higher level of stigma attached to sex work as well as the greater risk of identity reveal. Nevertheless, most of the women I interviewed find meaning in their work once they decide to continue performing, even if they have to make difficult psychological calculations to endure what the job requires; for instance, they may diminish a traumatic event as a "bad day," describe it as a "hardship," or simply accept it as a part of their "work." In this way, they manage to persevere alongside everyday violence or even overcome it; some even express a great sense of achievement or a feeling of pride for their "victory" over suffering. Affective responses to violence are, as Veena Das reminds us, not limited to horror, fear, pain, suffering, and despair. Every conceivable kind of emotion or disposition could be felt, including feelings of courage, sacrifice, and heroism.[1] Drawing from this nuanced understanding of affect, I explore the inner workings of violence in the AV industry, illuminating how consenting actresses cope with often-invisible, everyday forms of harm.

Unlike other forms of physical, intellectual, and care labor, sex work in the AV industry requires physical proximity, emotional exchanges, and performance of sexual intimacy on camera. Japanese AV actresses also interact with their fans and the public increasingly through social media, while keeping their real identities confidential. As such, management of affect is part of their everyday lives, embedded in a sexist division of labor. These actresses perform strong-willed emotional labor to project a "playful and fun girl" image inside and outside their videos, rendering their suffering invisible to the public. Furthermore, they try to compartmentalize the violence they experience as a misfortune or misunderstanding. After all, actresses have given some degree of consent to AV work, juridically defined as "harmful work." Through the presumed consent given to acts that cause suffering, structural violence is normalized, perpetuated, and even glamorized—with the victims themselves, like other AV industry players, also contributing to the reentrenchment of such systemic norms.

## "FREE SPEECH" AT THE COST OF
## WOMEN'S *UNFREE SPEECH*

About a decade before our interview, Nakano, introduced above, had worked for two different agencies for over four years as both a *tantai* (first-tier) and *kikaku tantai* (second-tier) performer.[2] (Here, it is important to clarify the hierarchy among AV actresses. *Tantai joyū* (or simply *tantai*) are the highest paid, top-billing actresses who enjoy exclusive performance contracts with video makers. Below them are *kikaku tantai*, who are free to contract with various video makers but are paid less. The bottom tier actresses are the *kikaku*, low-paid performers who play supportive roles or appear in omnibus without credits.) After retiring from AV, Nakano now works as a manager at an AV talent agency. Her background, motivations, and emotional management strategies parallel the experiences of other women I have interviewed, in terms of both her initial interest in AV work and her moral struggles with her career path. Nakano's experience illuminates the complexity of AV employment, which is never black and white, and often misunderstood.

Born and raised in Kanagawa, Nakano moved to Tokyo after graduating high school to attend a two-year culinary school, where she studied pastry and baking arts. She landed a full-time job at a French restaurant in central Tokyo in 1997, when she was nineteen. As an apprentice, her day started at 9 a.m. to prepare for the lunch menu and finished after 11 p.m., with few breaks or space to relax. Despite her hard work, she earned only 150,000 yen (about US$1,500) in the first month. Meals were provided, but she could barely make a living. The following month, the restaurant's owner asked her to move closer to her workplace so that she could properly finish up at night without having to worry about missing the last train home. But with her low salary, she could not afford to move to the city. Finally, she decided to quit and go back to her hostessing job at a *kyaba kura* (a cabaret club where young hostesses flirt with male clients), where she had previously worked part-time, until she could find another job. As a full-time hostess, she made nearly 800,000 yen (about US$8,000) a month. While her earnings were substantially better than her restaurant job, she faced two issues. First, she had difficulty getting along with other hostesses in the club, who she said picked on and bullied her. Second, she was expected to engage in so-called pillow business: sexual relationships with loyal customers. This quasi-sex work, which involved seducing men into spending money on her and playing psychological games as their "girlfriends" or "mistresses," she found painful. Due to her mental stress, she began to think of *having sex as a job itself* rather than as a sales tool.

She contacted a street scout who had previously, and unsuccessfully, attempted to recruit her for AV. Although she had no idea whether he was trustworthy, she decided to visit a talent agency he recommended to see whether she would like it there. Before her actual visit, Nakano said she had a wild premonition: a staff person would request that she take off her clothes immediately. Her concern was misguided, however, as soon as she stepped into the agency's open and clean office. A soft-spoken staff member put her at ease. Based on an information sheet and questionnaire she was asked to fill out at the beginning of the meeting, he began to interview her politely, starting with general questions about her age, hometown, and current employment to break the ice. He then moved to questions the industry deems relevant to the work: her first sexual experience, number of boyfriends, favorite sexual positions, and "NG"—no good—out-of-bounds sex acts such as female-on-female, anal penetration, and BDSM.

The interview ended with marketing and publicity questions. The interviewer asked whether she preferred fame or money, or both, and told her that if she wanted fame, the agency would promote her via a variety of media, from mainstream television, newspapers, and magazines, to specialized satellite television and porn magazines. Afraid of revealing her identity, Nakano answered that she simply wanted the money. Although she was told that the more publicity, the higher the performance guarantee, she decided to keep a low profile. Looking back, Nakano says, "Honestly, I had no idea how much public exposure I would have or how much I could sell with minimal publicity at that point. I just wanted to avoid too much attention." She was especially concerned about her parents finding out, knowing that they would be deeply shocked. Sensing her anxiety, the scout, who sat right next to her, advised her to never admit to anyone that she performed in adult videos, even if someone confronted her. Nobody could actually prove it. At this stage, identity reveal was Nakano's main concern, so she asked no other questions before signing her management contract. As a manager at a talent agency today, Nakano told me that most women who seek AV work ask no questions at contract-signing time, even though agencies usually deploy soft-spoken staff for the "closing."

After she signed the contract, Nakano's agency footed the bill to have her damaged hair treated and worn-out fake eyelashes removed at a stylish hair salon nearby. With a "cleaner" look, she made a series of sales visits, along with her manager, to a handful of video production companies. At each location, she was asked to fill out a similar questionnaire soliciting personal information about sexual experiences and NG boundaries. Based on her questionnaire, a staff member or two at each video company would interview her for roughly half an hour. They typically videotaped a screen test to show to staff members and directors. Nakano knew the tacit rule in the industry: the less experienced sexually, the more valuable she would be as an AV actress. As such, she underreported her sexual experiences and presented herself as a "clean" woman. On the business side, there was no disclosure of her performance guarantees at any point. She would find out how many exclusive videos they would offer her depending on her openness to allowing wide publicity. A few days later, she got a congratulatory call from her manager. "You got an exclusive contract offer for four videos from Tiara, one of the most prestigious AV labels!" But when Nakano found out what her guarantee was per video, she was quite disappointed.

"I somehow expected more than a million yen (US$10,000) [per video], as that's what most ordinary Japanese would guess. So, my initial reaction was, that's way too little! The next moment, I found myself responding, 'Is that it? Are you kidding me?'" Nakano laughed.

"What made you take the offer?" I asked.

Nakano didn't hesitate: "Way more money than what I could possibly make in two days as a hostess, even though it was much less than what I expected."

Following the signing of her exclusive performance contract with Tiara, about a month passed before her first video shoot. At the time, she had no real sense of what performing in an adult video would entail. It all became real, however, when she finally received the video script a day before shooting.

"It all of sudden hit me that I have to do *konna koto* (this kind of [shameful] thing)," Nakano recalled. "I began to question myself, 'Is it really okay to engage in this kind of thing?'"

"What do you mean by 'this kind of thing'?" I asked.

"[It was] something that provoked an unsettling feeling of guilt, apology to my parents, and anxieties about what's about to happen," she explained, adding, "I became overwhelmed and couldn't sleep at all."

"What brought you to the shooting the next day?" I looked into her eyes.

"Well, I convinced myself, 'It's *a job* [I have committed to]!'" she said firmly. "I reminded myself of *how much fast cash* I could make."

Most of the first day of shooting was spent taking her cover photos. Then, after a late lunch break, soft porn scenes were shot until the end of the day. Nakano remembers the day being one of "unbearable stress." She was so exhausted that she barely remembered how she got home that night.

Alone in her apartment, Nakano said that she realized how physically and emotionally drained she was, and all kinds of negative thoughts filled her racing mind. She vividly remembered what it felt like:

> I just fell into lamenting what I had done and crossing a line I shouldn't have. Now that I had crossed that line, I knew I couldn't go back. I felt awful and became self-doubtful, questioning myself, "Have I really come all the way to Tokyo to perform in an adult video? What on earth did I need that much money for? I'm debt free! How can I explain to my parents if they find out about this? Have I just ruined everything they have done for me so far? What would they think of raising their daughter to become an AV actress?" I was too exhausted to find any answers, meanwhile I couldn't forget about the fact that I still had another full day of shooting ahead. I have to have sex on camera when the time comes. What should I do? I'm so lost. But I can't ask anyone for help. I don't want anyone to find out about this.

I was a bit surprised to hear about her detailed emotional turmoil since she had described herself as emotionally "dry" during my interview up to this point. Especially while sharing her views on *you-know-who*, she sounded calm and distanced. This sharp contrast further dramatized her narrative about the first night of shooting.

"I helplessly cried alone for hours and hours." Nakano paused.

"What made you go back to the set the next day despite *all* of this?" I was impressed by the fact that she did not give up.

"Suddenly it clicked when I noticed my face was puffed up, and it occurred to me that my eyes would be swollen the next day. At that moment, I realized that there was another self, deep inside [me], intending to go on," Nakano said, smiling gently.

With her new attitude, Nakano said she felt better the second day even though it was another long day and there were a couple of *honban* hardcore sex scenes. "Still, how did you feel *that* night?" I asked, wondering what it would be like for her to be alone in her apartment again. To my surprise, Nakano said she was "proud of herself," saying in her confident voice: "It was truly the hardest thing I'd ever tried in my life and the only thing I'd devoted myself to wholeheartedly. I was filled with a euphoric sense of great achievement and total satisfaction." Her enthusiastic narration made me think she had made a total transformation. To my surprise again, however, she stressed it was not such an easy and clear path. She once again went through the same emotional turmoil, though to a lesser extent, during her next video shoot about a month later. The process repeated itself for a few months, but she eventually gained more confidence that she was a trusted professional actress. "Once you go through a whole cycle of your work, you start to figure out what's next and mentally prepare for that. You get used to what you do, work-wise," Nakano explained. Nevertheless, she added, "mixed feelings about my job never completely went away throughout my AV performance career." Her remarks made me think of the complexity of the way she presented as a professional actress in front of people and what's behind the façade: changing temporal trajectories, reoccurring mental distresses, and shifting intentions.

Nakano's worries gradually eased over time. When she finally did experience identity reveal, she was not bothered as much about it as she imagined she would be. She first learned from her close friends that some acquaintances in her hometown, who found out about her videos, spoke badly about her; she let go of it, thinking they were not important people in her life. Her close friends respected her decision as something that she, a grown adult, had really thought about. Similarly, her sister understood her and simply advised her to make sure that their parents would not find out. (Luckily, her parents, according to her, have yet to find out about her past.) Relaxing her relational anxieties gradually, Nakano confessed to her boyfriend that she switched her career to adult video, but to her surprise he was not upset. Instead, he was more concerned about her financial difficulties, assuming that she was severely in need of money. "It was a bit disappointing," Nakano joked. She concluded that he was not serious enough to marry, although like other AV actresses, she had dreamed of getting married and quitting the job. "I was just a girlfriend he did not have to commit to or care much about, even though I was ready for marriage," she said. They broke up after all.

Fear of identity reveal, which potentially leads to severely negative consequences, is one of the most shared concerns among AV actresses in Japan. Although Nakano's identity reveal has not triggered severe discrimination or damaged her relationships, it could have, as it did in the case of *you-know-who*, introduced at the beginning of this chapter. Women like *you-know-who*, who sometimes reach out to support groups such as PAPS (People Against Pornography and Sexual Violence), have received blackmail and found screenshots of their embarrassing images widely circulated at work, at school, and in cyberspace.[3] Some have experienced severe sexual, psychological, and "moral" (or "power") harassment from their boyfriends, colleagues, and classmates, to the extent that they emerge broken. They are asked by administrators to leave their jobs and schools, are humiliated in front of people, and are discriminated against in marriage and employment.[4] A handful of women, according to case managers at PAPS, suffer from horrific hallucinations after receiving moral harassment. They imagine phantom others laughing and staring at them and as a result become socially dysfunctional. Others get into trouble with their family and neighbors, especially when they are from rural, conservative communities and their family is exposed to public humiliation.

Identity reveal—having the actresses' real identities revealed or personal information leaked—renders women especially vulnerable to cyberbullying. In her 2018 book *After Lives of AV Actresses*, Asami Yuma, an ex-*tantai* actress and now a television talent, revealed the psychological harassment she experienced online in 2013 when she made it public that she had her ovarian tumor surgically removed and went through chemotherapy. It was the most challenging time in her life, Asami said. Although the majority of her fans sent her supportive messages, some harshly criticized her, posting such anonymous attacks as: "You, AV actress, deserve ovarian cancer"; "Having too much sex is the cause of your sickness"; and "Your sin brought its punishment with it!"[5] Stressing that there is no scientifically proven causality between sex and ovarian cancer, Asami said she became keenly aware of the stigma attached to AV actresses.[6] Many AV actresses experience cyberbullying. AV actresses are always on the verge of public humiliation, even if they manage to keep their real identities hidden. Such symbolic violence, moral harassment, and anonymous bullying leads to emotional suffering and normalizes these everyday forms of violence as part of an AV performer's life forever after.

In addition to damage to their externally facing reputations, AV actresses face more private problems, such as relationships with potential marriage partners—even if they think their boyfriends understand their work. In *After Lives of AV Actresses*, a handful of former actresses agree that they have tended to feel inferior and guilty about their occupation and easily subordinate themselves to any man who will "accept" them. And if they do succeed in finding boyfriends who generally respect them as equal partners, they are not always on the same page about what AV work entails. Hasegawa Hitomi, a popular early 2000s AV actress, observed that her then-boyfriend got irritated as her shootings approached. One day, he exploded and yelled at her, "Do you allow other men to do things that you don't even allow me to do?" when he saw the words "anal ejaculation" in the title of her video script.[7] To her it is just a performance, not reflective of her desire or sexual interests—something that she does in exchange for money. Performing hardcore and challenging scenes, Hasegawa says, gave her a sense of achievement, but this was not something that she could expect her boyfriend to understand. Even though she was proud of her AV career, she had to keep this pride a secret in her private life.

Like Hasegawa's boyfriend, most men, according to these actresses, have difficulty dealing with jealousy, while actresses perceive having sex on camera as simply a job. "AV performance is a job, not like having sex at all," Asami said. "Even so, romantic partners might not be able to understand that. I sometimes think that AV actresses should not fall in love at all."[8] Asami's ex-boyfriend, who she was thinking of marrying, could not introduce her to his family as a serious girlfriend. He instead asked her to break up, not because he no longer cared about her but because he was afraid of making her quit her job and making her unhappy. Ai Kanade, another former AV actress, points out that AV actresses are not granted a seemingly ordinary life course—courtship, marriage, and children. Her boyfriend, with whom she was serious enough to think of having children, said to her, "I want you to be so successful in your AV career that our children would dispel prejudice and fight back against those who would badmouth their mother as a former AV actress." Ai understands that he said so to encourage her and support her work. Nevertheless, she confesses that she could not help facing the reality that men who marry AV actresses need to think through all sorts of challenges down the road.[9] Indeed, marriage in Japan is not only about a loving couple. It involves an entire family on both sides, as well as children. Performing in AV cannot be cut out neatly from the rest of the intimate relationships these actresses are nested within.[10]

Social webs are always already imbricated with moral economies. AV actresses constantly deal with sexual morality and manage their affect in specific contexts with particular individuals, including themselves, whether or not their identities are actually revealed to others. Nakano, for instance, faced a moral dilemma after her first video shoot. She felt that she had crossed a line. This is a peculiar feeling that derives from masculinist sexual morality, which ideologically imposes purity on female sexuality. The "line" is a metaphorical boundary that manifests upon transgressions such as losing virginity, having illicit sex, and engaging in commercial sex.[11] Nakano and other AV actresses demonstrate how they experience this symbolic violence, which causes their sense of guilt and moral dilemmas. Some women use the affective dimension of such violence as an interpretive cue to help themselves work through pain: in other words, to empower themselves, they internalize victorious survivor narratives about their lives. Others may become lost in their affective or psychological turmoil.

Regardless, with the threat of identity reveal ever present, many actresses refrain from talking about their job with anyone, contributing to their isolation. Their agencies, furthermore, keep them separated from each other so that they won't share information about how much they make and workplace abuses they may experience. As I discuss further in the next chapter, AV actresses, especially well-paid first-tier actresses, are kept in the dark by agency higher-ups.[12] Moreover, it is challenging for most AV actresses to go to the police and legal professionals for help—to go public, in other words—since they are afraid of possible identity leakage leading to social discrimination, compounding the violence they've already experienced. They have nobody but their agents to consult with. "AV work," as Asami Yuma summarizes, "is not a shameful job but a unique occupation that one cannot freely talk about to others without repercussions."[13]

Ultimately, AV largely silences women performers, leaving them alone to cope. Ironically, the *free speech* under which the production and circulation of adult videos is protected is made possible at the cost of the *unfree speech* of its actresses. If the *sexual entertainment* offered by the AV industry is officially protected from state censorship, insofar as it complies with obscenity laws, the *sexual labor* of the performer remains entirely unprotected. As the primary target of law enforcement, sexual labor is subordinated to the entertainment product for sale. Especially when compared to the AV directors, producers, and makers who can more easily make "free speech" claims on behalf of the products they contribute to creating, sexual performers are in a uniquely vulnerable position economically, legally, and socially.

## "I FELT AS IF I WERE RAPED"

What is the purpose of conceptualizing adult video as free speech? Whose free speech is protected by the law? AV advocates—lawyers, directors, and video makers—argue that erotic expression is an easy target of state censorship, and therefore AV functions as a fortress of free speech. In this argument, however, the primary purpose of AV remains unaddressed, even though the same people admit in casual conversations that AV is a mere masturbation tool for male audiences. Free-speech rhetoric yields to masculinist fantasies of female sexual purity—inexperience, shyness, and embarrassment—that constantly require new faces, devaluing experienced, "old" actresses. Indeed, these qualities of unthreatening femininity are at odds with the purpose of free speech for women, which implies a right to be assertive and opinionated. The paradoxical legal protection of masculinist *sex commerce* and *free speech*, at the cost of women's *sexual labor* or *unfree speech*, undergirds structural violence against AV actresses and normalizes the everyday harm these women experience.

Sato Jun's experience, among others', confirms the presence of such violence. Sato, a twenty-five-year-old *tantai* actress, made her debut video, "Sato Jun, 19-Year-Old Virgin," two years before meeting me in early spring 2018 for an interview. I met her at a Tokyo family restaurant, where her baby-faced small body in casual clothes—a beige hooded sweatshirt, brown shorts, and white sneakers—naturally blended into the crowd. I was mesmerized by the gap between her look and intelligence once she started to talk. She eloquently explained how she decided to become an AV actress and reflexively articulated her feelings of "being raped" while working in AV. Sato is by no means a "naïve" woman, even though she has undergone psychological terror. She is a deep thinker. Her story rather exemplifies the normalization of structural violence in the AV industry and beyond.

At our meeting, I learned that Sato was a virgin at the time of her debut, but she was twenty-three, not nineteen as advertised. As such, Japanese adult videos often mix *tantai* actresses' personal stories with fiction. Trying to get to know her better, I asked, "Did you intend to remain a virgin until then?" Drinking orange juice through a straw and giving it a stir, Sato slowly opened up about her past. A bad breakup caused her to seek something extraordinary in her life, she said. Meanwhile, her virginity had become burdensome. "Becoming an adult video actress was the perfect solution [for me] to kill three birds with one stone: getting rid of [my] virginity, recording the moment, and resetting [my] life." She smiled proudly, her face child-like. I asked her where she got the idea of becoming an AV actress. She told me that she saw AV actresses appear on television variety shows and was particularly intrigued by Sakura Mana, a popular AV star idol and public figure whose personality was, she felt, uniquely deviant from conventional femininity and also from ordinary AV actresses. Pointing out Sakura's intelligent and compelling writing in her blogs and novels, Sato said that she also wanted to use her writing ability and express herself in a creative way. "Of course, AV was not the only option I had, but [it was] a better one," she said.

Born in 1993 and raised in Chiba, she came to Tokyo to study computer graphics at college. After graduation, she worked at a restaurant and at a girls' bar when she needed extra cash. Sato claimed that she experienced sexual harassment at both workplaces before she became an AV actress. "I was so fed up with men's nasty looks and come-ons that I developed a great antipathy to men in general," Sato said. Noticing my puzzled face, she shyly smiled and continued, "I know it seems contradictory, but I can handle male actors who have sex as a job. I can also handle the male gaze on my body and their sexual desires as a job. It is just easier for me to deal with them, especially their raw emotions and lust, indirectly through the camera lens." Interestingly, I found that Nakano and Sato both struggled with men's sexual advances in other jobs and sought adult video as a better career choice than quasi-sex work, to avoid subtle sexual negotiations and psychological games altogether. Though inclined toward AV work like Nakano, Sato stayed as vigilant as possible to avoid trouble in the industry. When applying for the job, she carefully examined all available information online about talent agencies, as well as representative models and their private lives. She also assessed her commodity value before her job interview. "I believed I could make a *tantai* model even though I was not pretty or glamorous enough for that. I knew it because of my virginity, which is highly valuable." Her prediction was right. Promoting herself as a virgin, her agency secured an exclusive performance contract offer from one of the most prestigious AV makers in Japan.

Being cautious in the business, however, did not shield Sato from problems. She is still upset about the deceit she experienced in a couple of her videos. Widening her tiny nose and round eyes, Sato started angrily, "I could have filed a legal case against my agency regarding this incident if it actually happened as it was intended." Implying sexual violence, she described what happened and how. She was initially shocked when she saw the words "internal ejaculation" in the script title she received on shooting day. "I felt as if I had received a death sentence," Sato said. Internal ejaculation, especially the genuine act, is widely known as a last resort for declining actresses. At this point, Sato had released only two videos, both of which had sold well. Sato noted that it was far too early to degrade herself by doing that act. Nonetheless, she couldn't say no to the director's face, even though it was unacceptable. "I couldn't stop thinking that I was, after all, a disposable commodity to them. It hurt me since I felt nobody cared about me as a human being although it turned out to be a fake [ejaculation]." Similar to sex workers who draw a line and eschew kissing as an essential part of sexual intimacy, actresses in the AV industry differentiate "fake internal ejaculation" from the "genuine one,"[14] and list genuine ejaculation as an NG act to perform. At the time, Sato did not quite register the technical distinction. Nobody, including her agent, explained it to her in detail. As a result, she simply felt that the words "internal ejaculation" signified a massive reduction in her value: that she'd become a throwaway sexual product.

Some might not quite think this counts as violence since the actress had signed up for sexual performance and no physical harm was done to her. Beyond such a positivist view of violence, however, what Sato experienced resonates with various definitions of violence, including sexual and symbolic violence. Having someone engage in unwanted sex is sexual violence. Perpetrating a less physical form of violence—micro-aggressions, verbal abuse, and/ or ostracism that assault others' dignity and sense of self-worth—is symbolic violence.[15] In Sato's case, her dignity and self-worth were symbolically violated by the cultural meaning of internal ejaculation in the AV industry and, arguably, by her agency's negligence. Like other AV actresses, she wished to avoid this particular sexual act as long as possible but was pressured to accept it at this particular time—too soon to accept such a degrading hardcore act, but too late, under the pressures of shooting, to fight back against it. Furthermore, she was not properly informed about the technical difference between fake and genuine internal ejaculations, and as a result she felt deeply offended. Even if none of Sato's narrated examples had clearly passed the threshold of commonsensically understood violence, they all illustrate a series of near-misses. Thus, violence is, as medical anthropologist Nancy Scheper-Hughes puts it, "a slippery concept."[16] While physical violence may create a spectacle or leave bodily evidence of its presence, forms of symbolic violence, which may be more chronic and less visible, often remain unrecognized in everyday life.

At the end of the day, Sato did receive fake ejaculate in her body, not genuine semen. Recovering from this near-miss at being violated, she calmed her nerves. However, she recently learned from her current agent that she *was* scripted to receive genuine internal ejaculation during the above scene; her current agent had her former agent intervene on her behalf to have the script changed at the last minute. A video producer allegedly tried to persuade Sato's former agent that hardcore porn, performed by a burgeoning star like Sato, would shock audiences and increase DVD sales. Her current agent, who worked for the same office, happened to overhear the plot, and proposed fake ejaculation, which he claimed would create equally sensational effects in the eyes of viewers. This is partly because, like Sato, the audience usually do not know the nuanced technical differences. "I was horrified to imagine what would have happened if my current agency wasn't there on that day," Sato said, her voice trembling with anger.

> I couldn't believe [that] such important decisions were being made behind the scenes without notifying me at all. If it were a genuine internal ejaculation, I needed to prepare for that accordingly. Otherwise, I would have become pregnant! I still can't believe that such a crucial decision that directly impacts a woman's body and mental health was made inconsiderately by [male] staff.

This is the part she was greatly bothered by, to the degree that she would have sued her agency if it actually happened. It was "sexual violence," she insisted.

In hindsight, Sato explained how a "miscommunication" possibly led to such risky business. She reminded me that she was not only sexually inexperienced but also unfamiliar with technical AV jargon when filling out questionnaires during her job interviews asking about "good" and "NG" sexual acts. Internal ejaculation was one such act. She asked her ex-agent what it meant and learned that "good" meant she was fine with real semen inside her on a cum shot. Although she did not feel that he was pressuring her to mark "good," she remembers that he was trying to convince her that she should be fine with it if they use fake semen and edit the scene as if a man came inside her. Unable to decide on the spot, she followed his advice to leave the question unanswered. She assumed that they would ask her about it again later. "There was a blind spot there," Sato said irritably, inferring that her ex-agent took advantage of her lack of an affirmative no and bought into the producer's sales pitch.

Such ambiguity derives from a blurry line between fiction and reality. Exemplified by Sato's debut video, which contained a touch of documentary realism in its focus on her virginity, the production of pornographic fantasy in Japan is designed to fool the audience into believing that what they are seeing is real. Most internal ejaculation videos on the market are fiction, though they are promoted as if real. Meanwhile, the minority of videos that document "genuine internal ejaculation" are sold as *"genuinely* genuine." These subtle demarcations in the production and marketing of pornographic illusion are not always evident to outsiders, especially newcomers to the industry. In this context, what Sato has claimed—miscommunication—is no simple misunderstanding between two equally informed parties; it can be intentionally created and abused, due to the uneven knowledge and power dynamics between talent and the AV industry. As I continue to problematize throughout the rest of this book, AV actresses are often left in the dark as a means of ensuring that their decisions will align with the industry's economic interests.

Women's structural vulnerability in the AV industry is the root cause of their suffering from sexual and symbolic violence. Nonetheless, this suffering is often trivialized. Sato shared an episode that she found herself troubled by, involving a scene that featured a nurse assaulted by a stalker patient. As she recalls it, the script simply stated that there was a sexual assault scene during which she would have sex with the stalker in the general waiting area of a hospital, in broad daylight. No details about the scene nor any indication of penetrative sex were written. In her experience doing this kind of story-based performance, directors typically shot numerous scenes in which the actors performed fake sex[17]—so that, once edited, they appeared to be having sex all over the place. Despite what she thought, however, it turned out to be real penetrative sex for this scene. The perceptional gap between what she expected and what she was about to experience put her in a difficult position; quickly, she had to mentally prepare for it. Meanwhile, she struggled to get into her regular acting mode inside a rented outpatient clinic. Entering a studio space, she said, would help her swiftly transition into acting mode. But being on set in such a public space, during the day, she could not entirely leave her everyday self behind. She also had a hard time dealing with the male actor who performed the stalker role. He was perfectly cast—someone who was careless about his appearance and had bad breath.

Sato's "misunderstanding" about the script continued. To her surprise, dozens of extras were brought in to stare at her private parts while she was already being "assaulted" sexually by the stalker on camera. Reflecting on this particular scene, her face clouded, and she said angrily:

> I felt as if I were raped. I understand that exposing my private parts to male actors and directors is part of my job. But how on earth do you think I feel, to be surrounded by all kinds of strangers and subjected to perverted looks at almost arm's length? I cannot have sex in those circumstances!

Even so, she did not stop the camera. She stressed that she felt obliged to be professional, once the camera was going, no matter what. While her body was assaulted on camera, she said, she was thinking her misery would feed into what the director wanted: a realistic reaction by an assaulted nurse through unfiltered expressions of disgust, agony, and humiliation. Being caught by surprise, she made the split-second choice to complete the scene instead of stopping the camera and going through it all again later for a retake.

Although Sato spoke no further about her rape-like experience, it occurred to me that it must be tricky for AV actresses to walk such a thin line with dignity. In the above hospital scene with unexpected onlookers, Sato was in the complex position of juggling multiple factors—her bodily discomfort, mental distress, disgust about her sexual partner, and sense of humiliation, while also calculating the cost-benefit of stopping the camera. She decided to complete the scene because she had already committed to it and found no better options in the given situation. Since much of what happened was not what she originally intended to consent to, the stalker-rape scene could certainly be considered sexual violence. However, Sato narrated her experience as almost, but *not quite,* rape: in her own words, "I felt *as if* I were raped." Drawing from Sato's nuanced language, a *rape-like* experience is indicative, I argue, of the multilayered ambiguity embedded in the AV performance contract: its unenforceability, despite the fact that a contract is, by definition, a written or spoken agreement that is intended to be enforceable by law; AV actresses' commitment to going through with challenging scenes, even if they have given consent only reluctantly; and AV's fictionality, despite its marketing as "real." Filming actors' "genuine" reactions might be a director's dream, even in mainstream television and film. This is particularly so in Japanese adult videos, wherein pornographic illusion is produced and marketed in a way where video users' sexual fantasies are satisfied largely through the belief that they are seeing something "real" (in chapters 4 and 5, I discuss more about how AV is produced and consumed).

But this kind of illusion keeps the abuse actresses experience in the realm of fiction—including legal, as well as narrative, fiction. As with most people who give consent to sexual partners, AV actresses "decide" whether to consent to sexual acts in advance. The ritual of consent giving, however, guarantees neither consensual nor violence-free sex. Consensual sex is, as Joseph Fischel points out in his book *Screw Consent,* presumed to be "good" in the equation of consent-plus-desire-equals-pleasure, whereas a lack of voiced consent implies that "bad," unwanted sex (i.e., rape) is happening. This formula determines what counts as good and bad sex, even when the sex consented to turns out to be terrible and the sex not overtly consented to surprisingly good.[18] As such, it is not the actual sexual experience but communicated willingness that determines whether sexual violence is present. Such communication is further complicated when a business contract is involved. It is assumed that the performer will deliver what she has agreed to once consent is given. Thus, signing an AV performance contract might appear no different on paper from other business transactions. But actresses are not always ready to perform sexually.[19] This is where sexual consent in private life and a *sexual contract in business* differ from one another. While the former is not enforceable by law, the latter becomes less clear-cut in practice, even though the Tokyo district court ruling clearly states that sex during AV filming cannot be forced against one's will. Moreover, the ruling is not commonly known among AV actresses. Like Nakano and Sato in this chapter, as well as Kozai and others in the previous chapter, many women do appear to feel obliged to finish a job they have committed to rather than quit and walk away.

No matter how much AV actresses may feel pressured to complete a sexual performance, the transaction appears to be smoothly completed once they get paid for the work. It may look like just another business agreement. As a result, any abuse or exploitation that they may experience—unwanted sex, agony, and humiliation—is swept under the rug. In the process of actualizing AV performance contracts, extralegal factors such as body conditions, sexual compatibility, and other special notes fall into a zone that entails—at least theoretically—individual negotiations among involved parties. Practically, this means it is oftentimes easier for AV actresses to bear the agony for a moment rather than stand up for themselves and renegotiate. Like Sato, another actress I interviewed told me that she did not ask to stop the camera even though her vagina ached badly during a scene involving penetrative sex. She needed a rest but was concerned about taxing her partner to get hard again later and about making the editor's job difficult when piecing together different cuts. Rescheduling the shoot was out of the question since she was not paid hourly; in addition, she was afraid of being labeled as an actress who frequently stops the camera. These women feared losing their jobs or damaging their reputations. Their choice to endure pain rather than stop filming is not the only one they have; it is, however, the best choice they can see in a situation containing a host of structural constraints.

## EVERYDAY VIOLENCE UNDER THE RADAR

Violence becomes accepted and normalized under such circumstances, where individuals give involuntary consent by "choice." Meanwhile, social suffering is cast as a personal issue, with AV actresses put in a position to privately deal with issues they face in and beyond the industry. Their only real choices are to leave their AV jobs or adapt to them. Either way, the process exposes them to various forms of violence: sexual violence, when a scene is not fully explained in advance or something goes wrong on set; symbolic violence, when nonphysical forms of abuse such as micro-aggressions, verbal harassment, and social discrimination assault one's dignity and sense of self-worth;[20] and structural violence, where systemic injustices cause tangible harm to individuals' health and wealth as a result of uneven distribution of resources, legal protections, and mental health care.[21] These forms of violence overlap and intersect with each other, discursively. As such, suffering cuts across physical, psychic, and affective dimensions.

To my surprise, AV actresses who have decided to stay in the business attempt to cope with their suffering and accept violence. Having experienced deception and humiliation, Sato Jun, for example, still defends her agency and the AV industry at large from accusations of systemic wrongdoing. "Things are not so black-and-white," Sato says. "I do not think the entire industry is evil. There are only a handful of dishonest people in this industry, just as in any other fields." She believes that the majority of industry professionals work hard to produce better-quality adult videos that cater to users, not to hurt women. She self-identifies as one of those, saying, "I honestly like this job and the laid-back culture of this industry." For this reason, Sato avoids saying anything that harms the entire industry. She rather tries to find ways to fix problems by herself, such as switching her agents and accumulating wisdom to better protect herself. Sato says she is proud of these and other changes she has made to improve her working conditions. Thus, though actresses like Sato have suffered harm while working in AV, they are put in a position where the choice to remain in AV necessitates adjusting to industry conventions rather than challenging them. On a micro level, Sato has hardly been a passive player in this adjustment process, however; part of the pride she takes in her job is based in her ability to succeed within the system while continuing to advocate for herself. Nonetheless, on a macro level, Sato and other actresses' adjustments render them integral players in the maintenance of a system that perpetuates violence against women.

A system that causes adverse outcomes is, in turn, naturalized. Indeed, when asked pointed questions about forced AV performance, many AV actresses and other business insiders alike become defensive about their practices. As Nakano contended at the beginning of this chapter, actual forced performance is rare in the eyes of business insiders; the mainstream definition of an *uninformed* or *misinformed* woman being forced into performing in adult videos does not apply to how AV actually operates, they believe. By Nakano's accounting, coerced women would most likely never return to set if they were truly experiencing violence, even if they managed to persevere the first time. On the other hand, "false allegations of forced performance" are, she argued, made by actresses who want to have their cake and eat it too: maintain a well-paying job in the industry and garner paternalistic sympathy from mainstream society for working in AV. For someone like Nakano, who confronted her difficulties and overcame them "righteously," others like *you-know-who* are, in her words, "irresponsible nuisances."

I understood Nakano's view as a talent agent today, but I wondered whether she had sympathy for struggling actresses as a former actress who went through her own hardships. Her words seemed to feed into a victim-blaming narrative. "What do you mean by 'irresponsible nuisances'?" I asked. Nakano was straightforward. "They are the people who tell haphazard lies to protect themselves, selfishly and irresponsibly, without taking into consideration other people." I was speechless—but Nakano insightfully unpacked her opinion for me. Forced performance, she explained, essentially involves false accusations against the AV industry; but the public simply takes actresses' "comments" on their AV performance experiences at face value. Looking into my eyes firmly, she said:

> The whole thing is a joke. It has nothing to do with forced performance per se. It's merely a personal issue that derives from the perceptional gap between their anticipation and [unfavorable] outcomes. Instead of blaming themselves, they try to accuse the AV industry—an easy scapegoat—for their unwished-for consequences by taking advantage of public pressure against the industry.

She subtly sneered. As she saw it, these women were troublemakers.

I couldn't fully comprehend what she was trying to say here since, as I will detail shortly, some women I had spoken with were clearly traumatized, turning to victim's support groups for help. I didn't feel those women were simply "irresponsible nuisances." I was frank with my questions. "Isn't the perceptional gap—what you consent to in advance and what you actually experience later—symptomatic of some sort of wrongdoing? I wonder what you would think of it especially as someone who went through excessive distress before your first video shooting, for example." She replied, without hesitation:

> I don't deny that AV actresses face a series of hardships. It's not an easy job. But whether one takes the hardship unfavorably or favorably, it is, after all, no more than her personal opinion. In my case, I never predicted [that I would experience] emotional turmoil. But *nobody forced me* to perform in AV. I made my decision and nobody else did it [for me]. I put myself in the position, and I felt it was harder than I anticipated. As such, this was *my opinion*.

Her remark that "nobody forced me" reminds me of a commonsense understanding of violence that is based in a positivist view of causality: only identifiable individuals, whose direct acts cause harm to immediate others, can be offenders, and observable scars on the victim are the evidence of physical violence; everything else is relegated to the realm of subjective impressions and opinions. From this positivist perspective, violence must be physical, direct, and immediate.[22] Nakano raised a rhetorical question about AV exceptionalism:

> Are there any other business fields wherein contractors are allowed to leave projects without delivering what they have agreed to and instead blame the industry for their failures based on their opinions that the job was harder than anticipated? No way! Why do people pressure only this industry to apply a business double standard, allowing actresses to come and go as they wish?

She rolled her eyes. I was sympathetic with her frustrations when I put myself in her shoes as a talent agent. At the same time, I was concerned about the rhetorical effect of such questions on AV actresses who have far less power than their agencies and video makers.

To start with, a contract for sexual entertainment is and isn't a business contract, simultaneously. It is not clear-cut in its enforceability. If the Tokyo district court ruling were strictly applied, actresses could come and go as they wish, as no sexual acts can be enforced against one's will. But AV contracts are written in an ambiguous way in order for the industry to conduct its business under the protection of free speech, even though sex work is prohibited by law. AV business insiders, not actresses, benefit from this situation. I eventually came to see that, as discussed in the introduction, actresses' consent—a must-have condition in AV—falls into a legal loophole created by three different legal systems: free speech, anti-rape, and labor laws. These systems protect *sexual entertainment*, *sexual victims*, and *wage workers*, but not *sexual labor*, *consensual sex*, and *sex workers*. Under such conditions, AV actresses are left vulnerable to moral harassment, sexual violence, and economic exploitation. They are caught in this quagmire not because of their poor choices or false consciousness but because of the nature of sexual labor in Japan, which is deeply embedded in the paradoxical existence of sexual entertainment. Lacking other legal protections, some performers may see "forced performance in AV" as the only card available for them to play to get out of their mess. From this perspective, the choices of seemingly "irresponsible nuisances" are, in fact, byproducts of a system that offers them few other viable ways out.

Of course, structural violence against workers is pervasive in capitalistic profit-seeking businesses, not just in sexual commerce (in chapter 5, I discuss this aspect of precarious labor conditions among Japanese men working in other fields). But in the Japanese AV industry, actresses tend to be an easy target of symbolic violence within and outside the business. Some pro-AV actresses, including Nakano, symbolically assault fellow anti-AV actresses as "liars" and "irresponsible nuisances" who have "betrayed" and revolted against the industry. When the politicized discourse of forced performance was at its apex, influential *tantai* actresses such as Sato Jun, Sakura Mana, and Amatsuka Moe used their social media accounts to criticize those who (in their view) took advantage of mainstream prejudice against the AV industry, emphasizing that sex workers were not all brainwashed victims. For example, Amatsuka commented in her Twitter post, "Most [street] scouts are quick to walk away once you simply say, 'no thank you.' I cannot imagine there are such forceful scouts."[23] In the popular weekly tabloid magazine *SPA!*, Sakura asserted, "This [forced performance] issue sounds like falsely accusing someone of groping on a crowded train. This is particularly so, since the negative image of the AV industry assumes some wrongdoing."[24] In this way, a handful of outspoken actresses "canceled" the victims of what they refer to as *nanchatte*, or mock-forced performance. Yet these actresses also soon became targets of symbolic violence themselves. Called out as privileged AV idols—lucky minorities—who were not entitled to speak for other actresses, they were quickly silenced.

Women's subjection to unfree speech by "choice" is thus the result of the symbolic bashing they face once they try to raise their voices. As exemplified by the defendant in the Tokyo district court case, victims of forced AV performance rarely speak up. Instead, their lawyers and case workers speak for them. By the same token, most actresses who support the AV industry largely remain silent as well, while privately pointing to their opponents as the symbolic offender. Sato Jun blames abolitionist lawyers, case workers, and social justice activists for their failure to protect sex workers who wish to continue their work. She said privately:

> Outsiders, including policy makers, human rights activists, and women's support groups, have a preconceived notion that sex workers are all victims. The default is no voluntary consent to sex work. This view not only deprives women of their autonomy but also leaves no room for self-determination. Even if someone like me claims that she has made informed decisions and achieved self-empowerment, she is still a poor victim, who is brainwashed to believe so, to these people. So, it doesn't matter to them if an allegation of

forced performance is true or false. What they intend is to dismantle the AV industry, not to understand women's experiences and improve their work conditions. Any policy and sanction based on such a biased view is not helpful but detrimental to women working in this industry.

Sato eloquently articulates the multilayered hypocrisies in anti-porn abolitionist claims. Even so, her sound criticism can be easily canceled and her voice lost once sex work is cast as fundamentally illegitimate within a dominant legal and moral framework.

It is a form of symbolic violence when women silence other women. It is, however, symptomatic of a deeper form of structural violence to stage the problem as primarily a fight between women over their ideological differences, which deflects public attention from the fundamental problem—sexism. The pro- versus anti-sex work battle demonstrates this. Pro-sex work AV actresses accuse those opposing pornography and sexual violence, many of whom are women, of depriving women of their agency. The anti-sex work camp fights back against such claims as false consciousness, or AV industry indoctrination. Both regimes narrowly focus on sex work, overlooking other systemic problems endemic to Japan's precarious labor market. Women are marginalized to "choose" low-paying secretarial work, care work, or gig economy jobs such as freelance or contract work, with low incomes and job insecurity being their default. Working "regular" service sector jobs, as Nakano and Sato's experiences exemplify, women earn much less than their male counterparts, and their experiences of sexual harassment can be just as bad, if not worse, than what they experience in AV.[25] Sexism and paternalism are found everywhere, from mainstream workplaces to grassroots activist and policymaking spaces. Nonetheless, an easy target like sex work is singled out for reform. In this way, seemingly opposing pro- and anti-sex work regimes become two sides of the same coin, upholding a masculinist script of fragile femininity imposed on women. Pro-sex work AV actresses perform submissive femininity to capitalize on men's sexual fantasies. Their anti-sex work counterparts victimize sex workers by indulging their paternalistic "savior" fantasies. Structurally vulnerable women are thus constantly put on the frontlines to fight a proxy war over a masturbation tool for men, while male bystanders largely dismiss the issues at hand as "women's problems." Thus, both masculinist sexual commerce and the juridical system perpetuate the sexist status quo.

## PORNOGRAPHIC ILLUSION AS SYMBOLIC VIOLENCE

As Nakano and Sato's cases illustrate, actresses who have decided to work in the AV industry constantly manage their emotions inside and outside the workplace. Being "loyal" to the industry means that they also interact with AV fans and users accordingly, adding another layer to the management of their emotions. The women I interviewed stress "support from their fans" as a major reason they keep performing and nurture a sense of *ibasho* (belonging). By the same token, pleasure and danger are often closely intertwined in how they engage with their fans and general AV audience, and how they balance their privacy with publicity. Men expect emotional exchanges with AV actresses (as I detail later), entailing what feminist sociologist Arlie Hochschild calls emotional labor: work that produces emotional satisfaction on the receiver's end.[26] For those who provide such labor, however, the work does not necessarily coincide with their personal beliefs or feelings. Such emotional work, which is rarely compensated for in wages and yet is imposed on women as part of the gendered division of labor, is another realm of structural and affective violence enabled by male AV users' sexual fantasies. As a result, many actresses suffer from emotional burnout, psychological turmoil, moral qualms, and other symptoms of alienation from their own feelings.

It is interesting to note here the difference between the Japanese and US AV market. In the US, mainstream adult entertainment video is precisely that: entertainment. The implicit understanding among viewers is that the sexual performance depicted is essentially fiction, something akin to pro wrestling. By contrast, in Japan, adult video is produced and marketed like reality television—not quite real but not quite fiction either. The industry believes that male viewers' vicarious pleasure is provoked through their invested, affective involvement with the story. Mentioned above, Sato Jun's debut video, "Sato Jun, 19-Year-Old Virgin," is a good example of such "realistic" fiction.[27] "I guess men can't jerk off if they know women are faking," Sato said. "Sexual pleasure is a physiological phenomenon and AV has to deal with that. If AV users want what's on the screen—women's gasping, facial expression, and sexual scripts—to be real, I feed into that fantasy." Successful actresses, for their part, are then able to market their videos as authentic and manipulate male psychology.

This job requirement, however, can at times create a moral dilemma for AV actresses. For example, Sato's internal ejaculation video (discussed above) was promoted as a "documentary" in which her secret curiosity about this sexual act was satisfied. She admitted to me that, when fans at marketing events would express concern about her participation in such a hardcore video so "soon" in her career, she pretended that she had genuinely embraced the experience. Of course, this was not true. Sato felt the same way and had an emotionally draining experience. But she hid this from her fans. Other fans expressed serious concerns about her mental health due to her hardcore performances, including rape scenes. This reaction deeply hurt her feelings too. In those moments, Sato would still smile at her fans and thank them for their kindness and try to insist that she enjoys her AV job and there is no need to worry. However, she confessed to me, "I am neither grateful for their kind thoughts nor scornful of their pornographic illiteracy. I am simply hurt. My heart is broken by the fact that I am perceived as 'that kind of woman' who is fine with her body used as a sex object." Japanese AV actresses are subjected to sexual fantasies peculiar to their audiences, who expect both pornographic illusion and their interactions with AV actresses to represent reality. Teetering on the edge between the pornographic illusions they create and men's projected fantasies, AV actresses thus juggle the management of their own feelings with their emotional work for others.

In a sense, Sato is caught in a catch-22 between unfree speech and sexual integrity: if she reveals her true feelings to her fans, she will break the tacit rule of the industry to uphold pornographic illusion, betraying male sexual fantasy. But if she suppresses her feelings, her core identity is consumed by the industry's pornographic representation of her as a sex object. Sato underscored this dilemma by noting the no-win situation she faced dealing with her internal ejaculation video. Even though she cared greatly about the difference between real and fake internal ejaculation to maintain her integrity, such nuance is lost among her male audience. "Facing this reality, I get hurt and depressed. To be honest, I'd rather not have someone I don't love ejaculate inside me." Sato sighed. Her experience illuminates how the nuanced moral boundary that women performers cling to can be symbolically violated—dismissed and even shattered—when they uphold pornographic illusions that degrade them. Sato, who infers from her fans' reactions that she is perceived to be helpless, says, "It would be wise to appeal to their 'poor little thing' fantasy and capitalize on their sympathy." This is her best choice, given that fan support is a must for many AV actresses to simply survive another day in the industry. Though such calculated emotional labor is not part of the performance contract they sign, it is widely provided by AV actresses, as if by choice.

Nevertheless, women like Sato are hardly helpless victims of men's sexual fantasies. She and other opinionated AV actresses pointed out that many of their fans expect them to be the "poor little thing" so they can imagine themselves as heroic, paternalistic saviors. Imai Haruka, a twenty-eight-year-old *kikaku tantai* (second-tier) performer who describes herself as a physically and mentally tough person, claimed:

> Many men simply want to fantasize about AV actresses as tragic heroines who are troubled with huge debts, suffer from mental problems, and whose flawless beauty is spoiled by a dirty job. In their fantasy, they indulge in themselves as nice guys who are sorry about these poor little girls. They believe that they provide necessary support—DVD sales, loyal fan base, gift giving, and moral support—and rescue poor actresses from their tragedy.

As these observations suggest, pornographic illusion serves men's sexual desires, inflated egos, and moral redemption arcs—all of which are masturbatory. It is, of course, the sexual and emotional labor performed by women that enables this illusion. Knowing the sales value of pornographic illusion, however, both Sato and Imai demonstrated a maternal-like understanding of male psychology. This knowledge is acquired as part of their AV job, which requires them to monetize catering to such fantasies.

AV actresses, however, do not simply conform to what's expected of them; they look for ways to carve out space for their agency, even within an industry that allows them little room to do so. Sato, for instance, regularly shares extended thoughts on her blog, which she describes as a way to display her "brain" to the public. Initially, a video producer advised her to stop posting because men could not masturbate to smart women. But she soon discovered that another director was a big fan of her writing. He told her that her writing moved him to tears several times and begged her to keep writing for men like him. Since then, Sato's writing has gradually gained support from her fans and general audience alike, to the extent that some truly understand her life philosophy, and many others simply want to support her no matter what. This unique experience gave her new insight about expressing her philosophical side more openly. Sato told me:

> I hated being accused of being too smart during my upbringing. My parents, who can't process more than three sentences at once, kept complaining that my utterances are too complex and difficult to understand. Most of my friends stayed away from my philosophical discussions. I only communi-

cated [in this way] with a much older man who I could openly talk to about anything but could not date for reasons I cannot disclose here. I feel I can finally express something difficult and intelligent now, because a woman who has sex on camera is perceived as intellectually nonthreatening.

Her remarks suggest that women's intelligence is symbolically violated at home, school, and elsewhere in society. It is, then, the prejudice against sex workers as "stupid" that paradoxically allows Sato to express her smarts safely. Still, "it is extremely difficult for someone like me, who has a brain to make my own decisions and act responsibly, to pretend as if I were a brainless bimbo who easily gets in trouble and helplessly waits for [male] rescue," Sato said. Her relatively free speech thus always hinges on masculinist assessments of women's intelligence, whether it is to be berated, celebrated, or canceled.

Like Sato, Imai, the "physically and mentally tough" woman, has found her own ways of coping with symbolic violence, particularly cyberbullying against AV actresses. Originally from Fukuoka on the southern island of Kyushu, Imai used to practice karate. She has long been curious about the human body and increasingly became interested in sexuality. For her, an AV job was a means to both satisfy her sexual curiosity and escape from a series of what she described as "monotonous low-wage jobs" in her hometown: care worker at a nursing home; shop clerk at a retail cell-phone store; and line worker at a medical equipment factory. None of these jobs satisfied her and none paid more than 160,000 yen (US$1,600) a month. Needing the money, she decided to give AV work a try five years ago. She immediately fell in love with her new job. "It's the only work I have found myself truly enjoying while making a living," Imai proudly said.

Despite her affinity for the work, she suffered from offensive comments and cyberbullying via social media. Sporting a casual T-shirt, pants, and sandals during our interview in an agency meeting room located below her provided apartment, Imai frankly shared with me numerous derogatory comments made about her physical traits, AV performance, and morals. To name just a few: "flat chest," "dirty ass," "stupid face at orgasm," "How on earth do you cling to this dead-end job?," and "Don't you have any sense of guilt about shaming your parents with what you do?" Echoing Asami Yuma's experience with cyberbullying when she was going through her ovarian tumor removal (discussed above), Imai says that she initially felt hurt, upset, and depressed by how total strangers, who exposed nothing about themselves, gave her such harsh one-way criticism. She was most offended and traumatized by one scornful comment left on her Twitter account: "Ignorance is bliss. You, brainless woman, are lucky enough to enjoy spreading your legs without thinking twice. No wonder your little brain is located in between your legs!" The nasty remark was published when she was still struggling with her own prejudices about her new job. "It reminded me of the injustice that AV actresses are subject to, since such hate speech is unforgivable in the outside world but largely tolerated when it's directed toward us," she sighed.

The cyberbullying hurt her, but Imai told me that it also enabled her to uncover strengths necessary to overcome it over time. Persevering in the business and interacting with her fans and general audience, she has gradually learned how to deal with such public humiliation, mainly, she says, through understanding bullies' psychology and reorienting their comments toward her triumphs. She shared this journey with me, breaking it into three phases. She began by using the logic of pornography to reinterpret negative comments. Pornography, as she sees it, requires eroticism and perversion to provoke and monetize viewers' sexual arousal. From this perspective, she reinterpreted the derogatory comment she received, "little brain is located in between [her] legs," as the highest praise an AV performer can earn. "It means that not only her private parts, but her entire body, her heart and soul, emits an erotic aura," she explained to me. As such, Imai welcomed any and all comments as a sign of her victory over the commentators who, after all, watched her videos and contributed to her sales records. The next step was to figure out the real intention behind the inconsiderate comments. She noticed that some men did not intend to hurt women but rather wanted personal attention; they obviously did not know how to communicate with women. Based on this observation, Imai spoke to their real intentions by ignoring troublesome individuals. For those who were looking for personal attention, she thought the worst reaction from their target was receiving no attention. As her coping methods advanced, she warned persistent individuals that she would block them if they did not stop "misbehaving." To her surprise, she received replies from her harassers such as, "I welcome any criticism from you to deepen our conversation" and "Please forgive me. I just wanted to play a game." Taking it one step further, Imai criticized the person who wanted to "play a game" for his selfish behavior that possibly hurt many women and caused mental breakdowns. He sincerely apologized to her, thanking her for her frank speech and promising to stop acting like a jerk.

Sato and Imai, who self-identify as a "smart woman" and "tough person" respectively, used their affective responses to violence—getting hurt, upset, and depressed—to make sense of their suffering and empower themselves. But not all actresses share their smartness or toughness to handle their situations in the same way. According to Imai, if a woman shows vulnerability, she will be attacked further and caught in a vicious cycle: the more bullying, the more suffering:

> If a woman responds with, "Why do you say such an awful thing to me?," her harasser could come back with remarks like, "Because you deserve it" and "You are hurt because it's true, right?" In this way, she would allow the harasser to gain the upper hand and drag her further down.

Only after Imai figured out her own three-step method has she become able to greatly reduce unwelcome comments. Otherwise, she thinks she may have been dragged down herself. Indeed, some women might face more severe forms of violence such as moral harassment at daytime work, blackmail, and sextortion, and feel completely victimized by the abuse. Imai told me that she might have just quit if she hadn't reached her own epiphany.

AV users are largely responsible for bullying AV actresses. However, it is also AV fans who help actresses feel a sense of satisfaction in what they do. AV fans, as I further detail in chapter 5, are central to AV actresses' careers. "I can get going because of support from my fans," Imai said. Her first encounter with fans occurred at a photo shoot before her AV debut. At the event, a dozen AV actresses and nude models posed for photos. To her surprise, a handful of regular men approached her to talk while shooting photos. Imai said:

> At that moment, I had a weird sensation, as if I were all of sudden transform-ing from a nobody into someone like a celebrity. I didn't quite register having fans. But I was so happy to have someone who wished me luck since I was still torn between the AV job and my own prejudice against it.

After doing more events, Imai realized that there was nothing she could do about those who spoke ill of AV actresses; but she could work for those who supported her for what she did. Even though she had originally planned to make quick cash and quit AV after a few months, Imai wound up working in the industry much longer because of this support. Maintaining fans' support is not always an easy job for even skillful actresses, though. Imai explained the intense scrutiny she feels at fan events, where she is the center of attention, constantly gazed at from all angles. If she loses concentration or lets go of her smile, her fans will pounce on her. Some fans have been vocal: "You look unpleasant today," they say, suggesting they regret coming to the event. Some other followers read into every detail of her appearance, speech, and body language, feeling entitled to scrutinize her.

Among other actresses, Amatsuka Moe (discussed in the introduction), known for her remarkable handling of her fans, told me that she totally dedicates herself to public events and typically ends up staying in bed on her off days due to excessive physical fatigue and emotional exhaustion. "Patrons are extremely sensitive," Amatsuka said. "Once disappointed for any possible reason, they get turned off." She added, "Fans go where their fancy takes them, from one actress to another. It is sad to let go of mine. But that is the nature of AV fans." Even if a fan's loyalty is fickle, commercially successful AV actresses still manage to find profound significance in their followers' support and spare no effort to provide intensive emotional labor. Such a tender yet tense relationship with fans can put actresses on an emotional roller coaster: winning celebrity-like support in some moments, while losing dignity and respect in others.

## IN SECRECY

All the actresses in this chapter have given consent to AV performance. But none of them seem to fully understand the extent of this consent, beyond performing sexual scenes in exchange for money. It is especially difficult to predict what kinds of unwritten risks, harms, and abuse lie ahead once consent is given. By signing contracts, AV actresses open a Pandora's box, whereby they are left alone to figure out how to best cope with it behind a shroud of secrecy.

In Japan's AV industry, what I call a "secrecy loop" consists of five interrelated layers. First and foremost, AV actresses must hide their real identities to avoid the prejudice, stigma, and discrimination that come with participating in adult video. Hiding real identities is always concomitant with the risk of identity reveal. Another layer of secrecy involves concealing their true feelings in the process of AV production. Actresses often prioritize the completion of shooting over their own wellness when they face unbearable physical and mental challenges, since they are paid per performance, not by the hour. The third secret requires aligning pornographic illusion with viewers' sexual fantasies, to sell the realistic fiction of AV actresses as a commodity. For this, actresses, especially *tantai* actresses, constantly perform ideal femininity on and off camera, even though they are oftentimes offended or outraged by their representation in videos. The fourth layer of secrecy involves masking the management of affect. Actresses I interviewed have struggled to uphold their integrity while providing emotional work, exchanging civilities with fans and the public, people in the business, and their significant others. The last and deepest layer of secrecy revolves around their self-respect. Actresses often suppress their real feelings out of a sense of guilt and shame in relation to their intimate others, while doing the same out of a sense of duty in relation to their enthusiasts. Either way, their own emotional needs remain unfulfilled.

In this multilayered secrecy loop, AV actresses seemed to me to have lost their strong sense of the self and self-esteem. I was surprised by how unduly humble AV actresses seem to be even in victorious moments. My own reaction made me think of their self-esteem issues. In my interviews, I often heard actresses refer to themselves as *konna watashi* (this kind of [unworthy] person). In her short speech at the event I attended, for instance, Amatsuka Moe showed appreciation for her fans by stating, "I thank you all for cherishing someone like me who has *no particular merits*." Another actress described her sense of euphoria at gaining new fans: "I was nicely surprised by the fact that some got aroused by *an ordinary woman* like me." These lines of self-expression align with how Imai described her sense of elevation from a "nobody" to "someone like a celebrity" upon gaining her fans. Elaborating further, she said:

> I genuinely thank those who support someone like me. I'm humbled to know that I have been doing something meaningful to gain their acceptance and support even though I am *no good* as an AV actress.

Although the expression "this kind of [unworthy] person like me" is a humble way of framing the speaking subject in a Japanese linguistic context, AV actresses' excessive use of the form strikes me as part and parcel with their low self-esteem. Even if not exactly the case, the repetitive utterance of such phrases has the potential to performatively constitute their subjectivity as "unworthy" and "no good," whereby they symbolically violate themselves.

In a slightly different context, Nakano referred to her AV performances as *konna koto*—"this kind of [shameful] thing"—describing it as a job that makes her feel guilty and ashamed, and lamented her line-crossing. If "this kind of thing" suggests the other side of the shore from a morally sound choice, "this kind of person" connotes the opposite of a morally sound human deserving of dignity and respect. Synthesizing their speech patterns in context, AV actresses risk internalizing a sense of themselves as "not worthy" due to perceived dishonorable acts for which they've already been stigmatized by Japanese society. As one ex-actress pointed out in *After Lives of AV Actresses*, AV performers carry emotional baggage filled with a sense of guilt, humiliation, and inferiority that impacts their self-worth and intimate relationships with others. As such, AV actresses are symbolically violated not just for what they do to make a living but also for who they are.

When the secrecy loop fuels injustices that cannot be freely spoken of, systemic issues remain intact. AV actresses refrain from expressing their true feelings, which cuts them off from necessary avenues for support and care. Even if they are subject to multilayered sexual, symbolic, and structural violence, they keep their heads down and remain silent. If they do try to reach out to friends, the police, or legal professionals for help, they risk identity reveal and "second-hand" harassment. Many believe that illegitimate sex work is, after all, the kind of job where one can only blame oneself for work-related problems. A *kikaku* third-tier actress who worked in various sex-related entertainment venues said, "Sex workers cannot complain about their work to others openly. If they try, even close friends silence them by simply responding, 'You choose the work because you like it, don't you?'" In this way, consent to sexual labor is taken as an agreement to bear all kinds of abuse and exploitation within and beyond the AV industry. The implication is that an actress should quit the job if she doesn't like it; otherwise, she must enjoy herself. There is no in-between. So often, the secrecy loop hides violence and suffering deep within its layers.

Meanwhile, AV idols like Amatsuka Moe shine radiantly on the stage with their cheerful and playful façades. The AV industry continues to welcome young, inexperienced women with open arms as untainted, valuable commodities, without fully disclosing what it really means to sign a contract. As I write, there is a strong likelihood that another woman is giving consent to AV performance, voluntary or otherwise.

# 3

## THE MANAGEMENT OF GIRLS

"The court case was sheer madness! It is unthinkable for a talent agency to file a lawsuit against an *onna no ko* (girl)," an exasperated Sakai Yoichi told me as he exhaled a thick cloud of smoke from his cigarette. A talent agency owner in his early fifties, Sakai works from a tiny studio apartment office in Shinjuku, Tokyo, where I first interviewed him in 2018. My intent was to get an agency's point of view regarding the 2015 Tokyo district court case involving a talent agency that took their AV actress to court for contractual nonperformance. Casually dressed—unbuttoned cotton shirt and worn blue jeans—and eloquent, Sakai expounded on how the New Gates talent agency, the plaintiff in the case, broke unwritten AV industry rules. "There are some good customs in this industry," Sakai said, taking another drag on his cigarette. "We all know that there is no way for us to win any sort of legal dispute, especially against *onna no ko*. (Like many others in the male-dominated AV industry, he often refers to AV performers as *onna no ko*, literally a female child, suggesting belittlement of adult women.) It is common sense that we should keep our heads down and do our business quietly in the corner." Sakai claims that New Gates, which he described as an "outlaw agency," made a big mistake and damaged the industry. "They are nuts," he said, blowing smoke through his nose.

I wondered why Sakai was speaking so frankly when nobody else in the business seemed comfortable talking with outsiders about "forced performance in AV." I had a particularly hard time finding any talent agency that would speak to me. Yamada Masaru, an independent AV director in his seventies who I met by way of an AV actress I interviewed, arranged my interview with Sakai. Yamada, for whom Sakai supplies his talent, insisted that he wants to reform the industry so that directors like him can continue to produce their creative works. Both Yamada and Sakai want to see changes in the industry. "Yamada and I are the rare minorities," Sakai told me. "So, I don't think our opinions are representative, but I feel I need to speak up to root out the evils in this field. The mass media, along with women's support groups and human rights activists, severely attack us without really knowing our business." Along the same lines, Sakai told me that law enforcement had so far arrested only talent agents and scouts, not video makers or directors; the police constantly dodge giving clear answers as to what rules talent agencies should follow. In this way, he thinks the police could arrest them anytime, if they wish, for violating the "harmful job" clause under the Worker Dispatch Act and Employment Security Act. The bottom line is that supplying sexual labor violates labor law, whereas using sexual labor to produce pornography complies with Article 21 of Japan's constitution: freedom of speech, press, and all other forms of expression.

"Our existence itself is unlawful and therefore, we are an easy scapegoat," Sakai scoffed. His remarks suggest that sexual labor suppliers (talent agencies) and buyers (AV makers) are put into different legal categories and divided by their (il)legality. To complicate the situation further, the adult video industry, which is mostly self-regulated, established the AV Human Rights Ethics Committee in 2017 to combat forced performance. The committee grew out of the Intellectual Property Protection Association (IPPA), established in 2010 by AV makers to protect their intellectual property rights; its mission was later extended to create the "legitimate AV" label and protect AV actresses' human rights.[1] "The committee ultimately seeks to protect AV makers' free speech, not performers' human rights, as it consists of legal professionals and scholars of free speech, not human rights," Sakai pointed out. "They simply create rules and impose them on us without knowing what's really going on. Such top-down regulation doesn't work." Meanwhile, legal firms, Sakai claimed, prey on AV actresses who need help by charging outrageous consultation fees. "Look, it's chaotic. But it's not a big deal for the majority of mainstream Japanese," Sakai said with frustration. Extinguishing his cigarette in the ashtray, he looked at me firmly. "This whole situation doesn't solve any problems concerned. I wish to bring the truth to light."

Sakai is, however, reluctant to speak up in public. He is afraid of having

his identity revealed due to not only the stigma attached to sex-related business but also the criminality associated with AV talent agencies. As a result,
he thinks talent agents are silenced and made scapegoats of forced AV performance. He told me that he decided to speak to me, someone he thought of as
"neutral," in the hope that his voice would be anonymously delivered to the
world. His fears and frustrations, as I found out later, are largely shared with
other talent agents and scouts. They are keenly aware that their legally gray activity renders them vulnerable to being blamed for AV-related problems, while
AV makers, who rely on the labor talent agencies supply, are unfairly shielded
from accusations. Nonetheless, AV agencies cannot confront AV makers, the
buyers of their labor supply. Despite the complex, twisted power dynamics at
the intersection of legality, employability, and mutual reliance, both parties
walk hand-in-hand in terms of their primary business interest: making profit
out of AV production.

In the previous chapter, I discuss how actresses who have consented to performing in AV engage in a host of invisible labor behind the scenes, juggling
a wide range of issues including fear of identity reveal; relationship problems;
and discrimination in marriage, employment, and social life. Contract making
thus goes beyond the narrow legal framework of discrete commercial exchanges of sexual labor for payment. AV performers are systematically vulnerable to moral harassment, social discrimination, and mental distress, while their
suffering is normalized as part of the job. In this chapter, I delve into structural aspects of the adult video industry from the standpoint of talent agencies
(and scouts), revealing what's hidden from AV actresses. Contract provisions
are presented in intentionally confusing ways to keep actresses in the dark, for
example. Failing to disclose the full amount that video makers have agreed to
pay women performers, agencies extract more than 50 percent as a commission
fee—sometimes 70 to 80 percent—and pay their actresses the rest.

AV infrastructures are built and (ab)used for what scouts and talent agencies refer to as the "smooth closing" and "management of girls." Based on their
narratives, I show how recruiters pilot women through Tokyo's cityscape into
AV contract making and performance. An "invisible hand" incites women to
give consent to exploitative work while guiding them to function within the
highly controlled ecosystem of Japan's AV industry. Agencies engage in what
I call the wholesale management of their talent, a job that extends beyond
simple booking and sales to include managing performers' earnings, mental
care, and *irekomi*—bringing actresses to studios for shoots, through coercive

means if necessary. For such services, Japanese talent agencies charge exorbitant commission fees, justifying this for their talents' peace of mind. Revealing the organizing principles that maximize the industry's business interests at the cost of AV actresses' autonomy, I illuminate how structural violence against women is deeply embedded in AV infrastructure and perpetually rendered illegible under the guise of paternalistic protection.

## "I'M JUST A DECENT PERSON WHO ENGAGES IN . . . ILLICIT THINGS"

"Simply put, there are so many agents who do not really understand their girls," Sakai said, pointing out a fundamental issue with talent agencies. Most talent agencies, he says, proceed according to the assumption that nobody will 100 percent voluntarily take off their clothes and have sex on camera. They therefore manage AV actresses through various coercive means, including flattery, attentive care, empty threats, penalty fees, and contractual bondage. Sakai insists that he sincerely wishes the industry consisted only of women who give enthusiastic consent to performing in adult videos. This is one reason Sakai did not adopt contract making as a business practice until recently, following the AV Human Rights Ethics Committee's 2018 mandate that all agencies and video makers use standardized forms of contract. "Who the heck would trust sleazy talent agents to make a contract? I wouldn't. If I were an AV actress, I would rather rely on a trust-based relationship than a paper-based binding to obligations." Criticizing the process of contract making, Sakai explained that nevertheless agencies have long used contracts to prevent their actresses from freely moving from one agency to another. Against this practice of binding a woman to an agency, Sakai reminded me of his business metaphorically. "It's really like a matter of what you would do if your girlfriend wants to move on to another man. Would you force her to stay with you? I wouldn't. I'd let her go and wait for the moment to have her back and hear her say, 'I love you more than anybody else.'" This is what Sakai said he means by a trust-based relationship. "The key is," he asserts, "I don't press on anybody what I don't want for myself." Sakai believes that his talent knows where they feel most at home and likely won't leave him even if they are baited a trap with better offers elsewhere.

Born in the mid-1960s, Sakai is originally from a Tokyo suburb. He moved to central Tokyo to work for a men's apparel company after his high school graduation in the early 1980s. After a few years, he thought about launching his own clothing store and sought out a childhood friend who was successfully running an AV model agency in Shibuya. In need of money for his start-up, Sakai decided to work for the agency. He told me that he had sensed how lucrative the AV industry was at that time, as an "AV boom" was emerging. Nonetheless, he was still pleasantly surprised by the pay scale. The starting salary at his friend's agency was 300,000 yen (US$3,000) a month, 100,000 yen more than his previous job, plus the sum of commission fees—10 percent of performance guarantees for actresses he booked. Quickly saving up money, six months later Sakai launched a men's apparel wholesale company and retail store in Shibuya, the mecca of Japanese youth fashion in the early 1990s. A severe sales slump in the mid-2000s, however, forced him to close his businesses. Sakai went back to work for his friend once again, who convinced him to switch his business to AV talent management. Sakai already had some work experience in the field and an office setup that even came with former employees. His company was well equipped to make a smooth transition. It turned out to be good timing since the AV industry was still highly profitable—just before the internet age hit culture industries hard.

Sakai's company has grown into one of the largest AV talent agencies in Japan over the last fifteen years. At his office, 80 to 100 actresses are constantly on standby, and a dozen of them are regularly booked. Despite his business career and success in the AV industry, Sakai maintains job confidentiality with not only his acquaintances but also his wife and daughter. To my surprise, he insists that nobody has asked him in detail about what he does. His friends and family alike apparently assume that he still works in the fashion industry. "I simply haven't had a chance to tell anybody that I switched my business to a talent agency," Sakai said, innocently smiling at me and lighting another cigarette. Maintaining his routine—dressing in the same way, leaving home at the same time, bringing in the same amount of salary every month, and maintaining the same office and even the same business homepage as backup, Sakai pointed out that nobody suddenly asks him what he does out of the blue. "I don't want to have my identity revealed and get into trouble," he playfully stated. "I understand how AV actresses feel and I don't press on them against their wishes." Exhaling his cigarette deeply, Sakai mused, "There are things in the world [for which] ignorance is bliss." As he sees it, he remains silent out of consideration for his family, given how pervasive and entrenched occupation-based discrimination is in Japanese society.

While Sakai, a former owner of an apparel company, differentiates his management style from that of others in the AV industry, I have found that all agencies essentially face the same issues and struggles over their business's legality. Sharing business challenges and personal concerns in common, they develop similar identity management tactics. To avoid hassles, as Sakai does, many agents strategically register their business as something other than an AV talent agency. Official classification as an entertainment service, a modeling agency, or something similarly vague allows their business to function as a "dummy" company to the public. They also hide their occupations when renting office spaces and opening bank accounts, to avoid the likelihood that their applications would be rejected if they honestly reported their sex-related businesses. Thanks to the high level of anonymity in a big city like Tokyo, they can maintain a low profile about their occupation and dodge their nosy neighbors. Just like AV actresses who are concerned about identity reveal, the talent agents I met are especially concerned about social discrimination against their families and particularly their children.[2]

Reemphasizing his unique background as owner of an "ordinary" (or legitimate) apparel company, Sakai maintains that he conducts his business according to a commonsense understanding of women's needs. To exemplify this, Sakai shared an anecdote with me. One of his former actresses, who assumed that talent agents were all evil, said to him upon her retirement:

> Working with you, Sakai, reminds me of The North Wind and The Sun [in one of Aesop's Fables]. I have long waited for the moment that you shed your mask and show your evil self. But you have never changed. I now think that you are like the Sun. A genuinely nice person!

The way Sakai narrated this story was so pleasant and entertaining that I didn't think twice about it being a truthful account. He simply made me smile. But in the next moment, Sakai lowered his voice, sharing his ambivalence about the actress's judgment:

> People often say to me, "Sakai, you are such a nice person." But I'm not. I am really not such a nice person. If I am, I wouldn't be involved in this kind of business at all. I am just a decent person who engages in what's considered to be illicit things since any sex-related business is labeled as *yūgai gyōmu,* a harmful transaction, and can be busted anytime in Japan.

It occurred to me how profoundly layered this anecdote becomes when analyzed in the context of Japan's AV industry. From the North-Wind-and-Sun metaphor, I inferred that talent agencies may employ seemingly opposing—coercive and inducive—approaches. Like the North Wind, an agent who tries to force an actress to take off her clothes on camera will likely face her strong resistance; whereas like the Sun, an agent who knowingly provides what she may need to feel comfortable will more likely succeed in convincing her to go naked. Despite these seemingly opposing methods and results, it is therefore shrewd preparation on the part of the agent that underlies, if not determines, how she will react. In other words, when an agent manipulates the situation in a way that coaxes an actress toward a decision he wants her to make—however "sunny" his approach may be—that decision is not truly hers alone. Even if his actresses all appeared to be enthusiastic consent givers, this would be, to some extent, the result of him functioning as the inducive Sun. From this perspective, I better understood what Sakai said about himself, that he is perhaps "not such a nice person" after all. His ambivalence became even more pronounced when Sakai expressed that he would not want his daughter to perform in adult videos. I began to see decency as a matter of degree, rather than kind, in Japan's AV industry.

Sakai's decency is manifest in the fact that his office houses only a few top-tier actresses with full publicity despite boasting a good-sized talent pool. This is, according to him, the embodiment of his best practice—understanding women's needs and concerns. As he sees it, there are only a handful of women who are both pretty and willing to perform in adult videos openly because high publicity increases the risk of identity reveal, which is typically AV actresses' main concern. So Sakai is suspicious of talent agencies that line up a good number of highly publicized *tantai* actresses. He believes those agencies conduct what he describes as *hamidashi eigyō* (shady business).

When a woman comes to the agency for an interview, whether she is brought by a scout or has applied by herself, staff assess how to best promote their model to AV makers. If she exhibits the hallmarks of conventional physical beauty—a pretty face, nicely proportioned body with large breasts and shapely hips, and smooth skin—and requires fewer restrictions on her publicity and sexual performance, they can better capitalize on her in their negotiations with video makers who might be interested in her. For example, first-tier *tantai* models, who secure exclusive performance contracts with particular video makers, settle on a pay range of 800,000 to 2,000,000 yen (US$8,000–20,000) per video, whereas second-tier *kikaku tantai* and the rest, *kikaku*, can expect 250,000 to 600,000 yen and 100,000 to 150,000 yen, respectively. A very pretty woman whose appearance qualifies for *tantai* might be classified only as a *kikaku tantai* or even *kikaku* and paid accordingly if she wants to minimize public exposure, limiting her sales potential. "High risk, high return," Sakai reminds me of the nature of economic investment that intertwines with AV actresses' dignity. The balance among her physical appearance, the range of sexual activities she is willing to perform on camera, and her comfort level with publicity becomes a very delicate issue. As I describe in the previous chapter, women who are not familiar with the AV business largely rely on their agents' expertise. Sakai thinks this is the moment when greedy and manipulative agencies will downplay potential risks and persuade women to aim at the *tantai* class for its prestige and lucrative pay.

My later interview with Kanda Reiji, a former talent agency employee and handsome AV actor in his late twenties, reinforced Sakai's assessment. Like Sakai, Kanda claims that agents strive to gain the upper hand over women in business negotiations throughout. I met Kanda by way of Yamada, the independent AV director who regularly hired Kanda to perform in his adult videos and who also introduced Sakai to me. "One way to gain the upper hand," Kanda said, "is to obtain necessary information from the target first, so that you become better equipped to judge her moves and respond to her questions and concerns strategically." The point, he told me, is to let the target reveal herself, allowing him to understand her needs. This process starts with the very first meeting, where the goal is to make a service contract. Like a used car dealer, Kanda's talk is unanchored, smooth, and witty to the extent that he openly admits that others often find him *usan kusai* (fishy). He graduated from a top high school in Gifu, central Japan, in the early 2000s, and came to Tokyo for college, where he developed an unorthodox sexual fetish: an interest in feces. He self-analyzed that he has learned to create a verbal smokescreen to mask his secret obsession, which he keeps deeply hidden. As a young, handsome, and smart man with a hidden sexual agenda, he struggles to develop any trustworthy relationships with his love interests.[3] But his smokescreen scheme, cultivated to pursue a secret passion, has apparently been useful for him when trying to do business with the AV talent he manages.

To illustrate how this "smokescreen scheme" works, Kanda showed me a few sets of interview sheets and a questionnaire that talent agencies and video makers ask women to fill out, soliciting personal information and details about their sexual backgrounds. To my surprise, Kanda shared documents with me that were filled out and signed by actual interviewees; he grabbed a few originals out of hundreds of confidential records that were scattered around the office, he explained, when he quit and left his agency two years ago. Casually grabbing from his backpack, he put the forms on our table at a busy family restaurant in Ikebukuro. He did not seem to care about others' proximity to us while we discussed these documents.

Like a thorough medical questionnaire for first-time patients, the interview sheets contained a wide range of personal information, including full names, home addresses, birthdays, birthplaces, marital or relationship status, dependents, emergency contacts, family members' occupations, height, weight, body size (bust, waist, and hip sizes), daytime work, and banking information. One sheet, called "questionnaire," consisted of eighty-one more questions about family, work experience (including sex work), hobbies, health conditions, menstruation, sexual history, fantasies, and "NG" (no-good) performance acts. It inquired about the applicant's first sexual experience; number of sexual partners; erogenous zones; frequency of masturbation; and whether one can, cannot, or can "maybe" do each among dozens of sexual acts (acceptance of cum shots on the face, swallowing semen, anal sex, female-to-female play, SM, urination, etc.). The last thirty questions focused on one's feelings about drug use, work ethic, sexual morality, money worship, hopes and dreams, and self-esteem.

Kanda took a bite of his pizza. "With the given information," he said, "you can better understand women's background, personality, motivations, and weaknesses, so that you can appeal to their needs and vulnerability more effectively." He smiled at me proudly. I was mesmerized by his nonchalant, unapologetic attitude while sharing confidential information with a stranger like me. I could only imagine how these women would have felt if they knew how their personal information was being handled. No wonder the women who provide talent agents with such questionnaires tend to comply with what they are told to do out of fear of information leakage, even though they are technically free of legal obligations. In addition to the tacit coercion contained in these information-gathering practices, talent agencies also offer the irresistible pull of imagination. "If a woman is materially obsessed," Kanda explained, taking another bite of his pizza, "you can use material wealth as a talking point to convince her that she can easily afford multiple designer bags, an expensive sports car, and a luxurious condominium with the money she earns from performing in adult videos." If a woman dreams of fame, he would advise her to start out with an AV job to cultivate her popularity and fan base, suggesting that this would lead to eventual opportunities in mainstream show business.[4] To a woman who has been working a regular office job, he would highlight AV's lucrative pay and flexible scheduling; she could reallocate her money and time, he'd suggest, toward cultivating her beauty, hobbies, and self-growth. "These are the [rhetorical strategies] that talent agencies frequently use to persuade women to sign their contracts," Kanda summarized.

While listening to Kanda's detailed explanations, I noticed an intake sheet on which a thirty-six-year-old woman described her parents as "absent." I asked him what this information meant to him. Kanda explained that her parents could be dead or her ties cut with her family. "In any case," he stressed, "a woman with a special circumstance has a tendency to have fewer strings attached and fewer hurdles to become an AV actress openly." To avoid problems, he explained that agencies were cautious about hiring women whose family members, particularly parents, are politicians, lawmakers, law enforcement officers, or reporters; they also avoided foreigners, as well as Chinese and Korean residents in Japan. Pointing to "Tokyo" as her birthplace, her "absent" parents, and "earning a living" as the reason behind her pursuit of an AV job, Kanda asserted that this woman would be a "safe" bet. With further information provided about her sexual experiences with more than ten people and her work experiences as a hostess and so-called delivery health provider,[5] he predicted that she would make a smooth transition to having sex on camera. He also estimated the minimal impact of identity reveal on her, if it happened, based on her family background, single-room occupancy residence, and no work experience at large corporations.

Kanda helped me to understand how each piece of seemingly trivial information becomes gold for a talent agency as it proceeds with contract negotiations. Even if it does not obtain enthusiastic consent, it can effectively persuade women into agreeing on AV performance by removing their concerns and fears one by one, to the point that they no longer have a good reason to say no. This is evident in the Cabinet Office's 2017 survey on sexual violence against women, which detailed the reasons that young women did not or could not refuse to sign AV contracts. Of those who made talent management contracts, 41.6 percent reported that they had "no good reason to refuse"; 15.2 percent thought that "nothing would go wrong"; 12.2 percent confessed that they wanted money; and 11.2 percent answered that they were told they could choose their job, did not have to do anything unwillingly, or that the job did not require nudity.[6] The remainder reported that they did not think they could refuse; talent agents pressured them to sign; they were afraid of their provided personal information being abused; or that they did not think they could go home unless they made contracts.[7] The survey revealed that the majority of these women did not say no firmly—they felt they could not—and as a result gave their consent involuntarily. The survey results reinforce what Kanda explained to me: AV talent agencies craft their tactics of persuasion based on manually collected and accumulated personal data.

Contract making in the industry suggests that consent giving is not solely based on the consent givers' wishes and desires. It is rather the result of rigorous negotiations, which reflect personal and business interests unevenly on both ends: on the one hand, women's interest in modeling, economic and material needs, life experiences (including sexual and work history), family background, social network, and ethical concerns; and on the other hand, agencies' interest in women's market value, work ethic, and willingness to perform a wide range of sexual acts on camera. Furthermore, contract making in Japan customarily requires a "good reason to refuse." This allows a senior negotiator (or a superior) to save face when a junior (or an inferior) declines an offer. At this negotiating table, set up with social expectations in a hierarchical manner, the haves—in this case, talent agencies—gain the upper hand over the have-nots—young, inexperienced women.

## AN INFORMATION GAP BY DESIGN

Contract making in Japan goes beyond the temporospatially bounded moment at a negotiating table. In Japan's AV industry, seemingly unrelated factors—publicity campaigns for AV idols, online classified ads, and street scouting—are all potential influences on would-be actresses. Despite the Tokyo Anti-Nuisance Ordinance (revised in 2013), which banned street scouting, street scouts have played an especially important role in recruiting beautiful *tantai*-class models for talent agencies.[8] Though this part of the AV production process often remains invisible due to its criminality under the current ordinance, scouting is invaluable to the industry; business insiders refer to it as a "lifeline" and "corporate secret."

After having a hard time locating any scouts who would speak to me, I finally found Takai Ryo, a self-identified twenty-six-year-old former middle school teacher, through Twitter direct message exchanges. He actively recruits young women to the sex industry from the streets and through social media. Unlike other shady scouts, however, his Twitter account caught my eye. With a clean-cut, handsome profile photo and the title of certified teacher, he uniquely promotes a wide range of life coach–like consultation services, from job searches and work-related troubleshooting to housing arrangements, financial advice, and health and beauty consultations. His consulting services include finding clients an apartment that requires no upfront payment, arranging an alibi company to conceal sex work, and matchmaking clients with sugar daddies in exchange for commission fees. "I think my street scout work is a kind of social work," Takai stated in his message to me, "since girls need more support [than young men] to make a living when they finish their schooling." One afternoon in October 2017, I met him for an interview at a coffee shop in Roppongi. I then realized that I had naïvely accepted his Twitter profile at face value. His appearance was much different from his profile photo, but he insisted that everything else posted on his blog and Twitter was true. Even though his trustworthiness was questionable, I had no other contact at that time. Most scouts I approached were too afraid of being arrested to talk.

Differentiating his line of work from illegal street scouting, Takai introduced himself to me as a "life supporter," describing his motivations:

> I do care about girls genuinely whether as a teacher or as a life supporter. As a teacher, I helped them go through compulsory education, but I felt my role was limited. As a life supporter, I now extend my support to many girls and help them live independently in a big city like Tokyo, by securing job opportunities in *fūzoku* (the sex industry) and providing necessary assistance.

Takai has a keen eye for finding young women who might need his help. He says he learned how to identify a "target" based on his own inferiority complex in the big city as well as through observation of general behavioral patterns. Originally from Ibaraki, Tokyo's neighboring prefecture, he was often ridiculed during his early days in Tokyo for his fashion sense, accent, and unfamiliarity with the urban landscape. He looks out for the same traits when trying to identify outsiders. "Those who carry suitcases and aimlessly wander tend to be runaway youth or new arrivals from rural Japan. They are often in need of a place to stay and eager to find a job as soon as possible." According to him, newcomers usually stop and listen to strangers, as they are not used to the speed of the city and the customary practice of ignoring others on the street; they also have few acquaintances or friends in Tokyo to rely on. Women who hang out on the streets during the daytime on a weekday are also targets because they tend to be either unemployed or nonregular workers. College students are another group who, he thinks, are generally interested in opportunities to polish their fashion sense through creative work like modeling. Despite his street wisdom, he speaks to hundreds of women daily. In his experience, only a handful of women will stop and talk to him, and even fewer show interest in his services.

Takai, however, does not give up easily. He sees all young women as potential clients since most are, he believes, struggling economically. His tireless attempts occasionally yield fruitful results. Once a woman shows interest in his services, he "helps" her determine whether hostessing, AV performance, or *fūzoku* (all other sex work, from hand jobs to costume play, BDSM, and prostitution) is a good fit depending on her appearance, social skills, and preference among these three major types of sex-related work. If she is attractive and sociable, he would help her find a hostess job that does not require physical contact. If a girl falls short of these qualities, he recommends sex work for which physical beauty and communication skills are less important. Takai told me that discovering a *tantai*-class AV actress is the most challenging task since beautiful women who are willing to perform in adult videos are scarce. Due to this scarcity, a scout typically receives a lucrative commission fee for recruiting a *tantai* actress, roughly 25 percent of what AV makers pay the actress per video—800,000 yen to 2,000,000 yen—as long as she continues to perform in adult videos. In other words, a scout's earnings increase in proportion to what his AV recruit earns.

Scouts like Takai therefore stand to gain financially by helping women find high-paying jobs in the sex industry. This payment scheme made me rethink Takai's stated motivations. Though he claimed to genuinely care about young women, I wondered to what extent he did the work for *himself*; not only did the job come with economic benefits but also symbolic recognition as a "resourceful and reliable man" from the women he "helped." My suspicion was reinforced when he explained how he found meaning in his scouting work. "I have found that young women are easily ripped off when they try to find a sex-related job without knowing the nature of the work and how much they should get paid," he said. In his mind, his job is to protect these women from such risks and maximize their earnings under more reasonable work conditions. "Sex workers are," he added, "discriminated against in society too. So, these girls need well-rounded protection." Although his justifications sounded sincere, I couldn't stop thinking that his work—harvesting sex workers *and* protecting them in and outside the sex industry—is in fact a conflict of inter-est. It makes sense only according to his distinctive interpretation that what he does is "just," and everything else is unjust. For him, mainstream Japanese society, wherein young women are left alone with their economic struggles, is useless. The sex industry, through which business insiders rip off sex workers, is detrimental to struggling women as well. This logic turns him into a heroic figure who rescues women from social injustice and economic exploitation. To "protect" these girls, however, he paradoxically transforms them into sex workers and gets them involved in the very industry that mainstream society would likely say they need to be "protected" from. At the same time, if the sex industry didn't prey on young women's vulnerability, perhaps he wouldn't need to provide such paternalistic "protection" in the first place. His contra-dictory logic itself sounds to me like his work, after all, needs justification for *himself*, not for these women *per se*.

After "catching" his target on the streets, Takai brings her to a nearby talent agency for what scouts and talent agencies call *kurōjingu* (closing)—a process culminating in the moment when a woman makes the decision to sign a contract, like a fisherman bringing a freshly caught fish from a stream to the kitchen for cooking. "It is important," Takai stresses, "to have a seamless flow from recruitment on the street to signing a talent management agreement at a nearby office. Any extra time or disturbance of the flow creates a moment for a woman to think twice." Like Sakai's office, most talent agencies are con-veniently located by train stations in Shibuya, Harajuku, and Shinjuku. They use apartments as office spaces. With no signage or nameplate on the building, they conduct business literally behind the scenes.

At the office, according to Takai, an agency staff member greets the woman he brings in, explaining to her their wide range of services, from commercial modeling to body parts modeling to acting in adult videos; the staff member then asks her to fill out the paperwork discussed above. Prepared to begin the process of persuading the woman to work in AV, the scout and agency staff expect her to ask about the risk of identity reveal, as this is the foremost worry among AV actresses. To ease her nerves, they typically use the metaphor of a traffic accident:

> You never know that you are completely safe when you drive a car. But think of the probability that you would be killed in a collision. It is extremely rare, isn't it? You might experience a near miss or a scratch. The same thing with

identity reveal. It is an accident. But there are thousands of videos released per month. Their shelf life is very short, too. What do you think the probability is that someone finds you in the millions of copies circulated in the market? Hardly, right?

If the woman is still concerned, they would say something like:

You'll look totally different, given a makeover by a professional makeup artist. Your video package will also be heavily photoshopped to digitally enhance your aesthetics. So, it is not easy for anyone to identify if the actress is you.

Depending on the woman's reaction, the staff might go even further, explaining how to deal with the situation if someone asks her whether she has performed in adult videos.

With professional makeup and a photoshopped package, believe me, you do not look like yourself at all. So even if someone asks if it was you in an adult video, insist that it's not. There is no way for anyone to prove the likeness is yours unless you admit it. Most identity reveal happens when performers make a slip of the tongue.

Nakano, the former *tantai* actress introduced in the previous chapter, has received this advice. Like Nakano, most women, who are already interested in AV performance to some extent, are simply anxious about what's ahead, according to agents like Sakai and Kanda. "By asking the question [about identity reveal], what they really wish is not to hear the truth, but rather confirmation that they will be fine," Kanda confidently asserted during my earlier interview with him. With the truth unknown, however, their rhetoric helps women to eliminate their concerns to the extent that they exhaust "good reasons" not to sign a contract. At this point, a staff member will encourage the woman to register her name and profile photos so she can see what jobs are available, and then pick and choose. As discussed above, she most likely does what she is asked. Registration is simple and easy: providing a photocopy of her ID for age verification and signing a contract.

While Takai works independently, a scout who works for a recruitment agency may be part of a more elaborate team effort to persuade an indecisive woman like Kozai Saki, the top-selling *tantai* actress who came out as a victim of forced AV performance in 2016. As I discuss in chapter 1, Kozai went through months of what she called "brainwashing" before she appeared in her first adult video; the owner of her talent agency, his employees, and other social actors such as a famous fortune teller all engaged in the process; and she wound up appearing in a sexy image video without realizing it was actually an adult video. After my interview with Kozai, I met Ueda Kenta, a scout in his mid-twenties who works for one of the largest recruitment agencies in Shinjuku, by way of a Japanese sociologist who studied street scouts. Although most other scouts and talent agencies I met avoided discussing the topic, Ueda defined the term *closing* as a process of "forcing an unwilling person to change one's mind."[9] He described it not exactly as deception but as something like a conversion of values or exaggeration in advertisement, so to speak. "It is," he said, "the most crucial aspect of the business since it determines whether or not [we will] transform women into commodities."

Upon my eager request for an anecdote, Ueda agreed to share what he witnessed one night when the CEO of a leading talent agency garnered enthusiastic consent from a targeted woman Ueda had scouted from the streets. The persuasion process impressed him. According to Ueda, the CEO invited him and the woman to a high-end, members-only *ryōtei* (a traditional Japanese-style restaurant) in an upscale Roppongi neighborhood, where celebrities and showbiz moguls hang out after hours. Without any visible signage, the restaurant's entrance was not clear to first-time visitors, but once they managed to enter, a woman-manager in a kimono elegantly guided them to a private room. Chic Japanese-style architecture with refined background music and art created an extraordinary atmosphere. Ueda remembers that the recruit kept repeating, eyes sparkling, "How gorgeous this is! I can't believe [this]. I can't." It was obvious to him how pleasantly surprised she was to be in such an exclusive space as a young woman with little money and social status. It was the same for him. Ueda, a high school dropout with a juvenile record, had never experienced something like that. Originally from Akita, a mountainous area in northern Japan, he was unfamiliar with Tokyo's luxurious spots. "Honestly," Ueda said to me, "I never knew such a place existed!"

Over a preordered dinner of eight courses, the CEO was in a good mood, telling amusing stories about the success of his talent in music, acting, and modeling, and dropping names of celebrities and influential people he knew in show business. His stories, which kept grabbing the recruit's attention, climaxed with his persuasive closing. According to Ueda, the CEO looked into the recruit's face and confidently said:

You know? You are a person who can make it in *kocchi no sekai* (this side of the world). Would you rather stay at the place where you are now? It's a waste of your talent and potential. You'll never grow younger. Don't you wanna come over to this world when you are still young and beautiful?

Ueda vividly remembers how the young woman's face lit up at this invitation. Although he did not elaborate further on the episode, I felt that the CEO's rhetoric, particularly "this world," evoked an imaginary land—the glorious field of show business—wherein great opportunities await a young, beautiful woman. She could embark on an unknown yet exciting journey and rely on the CEO's expertise to guide her. I shared my thoughts with Ueda. "Indeed," he nodded. "The whole setting nicely paved the path for a smooth closing."

The information gap between a woman and the industry is obvious throughout contract making. Although closing is "the most crucial aspect of the business" to recruiters and talent agencies, none of the AV actresses I met were familiar with the terminology. The whole process, which goes way beyond the negotiating table, is calculated and staged, even if it appears to be an accidental development from the standpoint of passersby, including the target herself. The everyday cityscape and the fast, smooth flow of Tokyo pedestrians makes outsiders highly visible, and vulnerable women are especially identifiable on particular days, at particular times. The agencies' conveniently located offices condense the multiple steps—from street interaction to contract making—into a kind of one-stop shopping.

Street scenes and cityscapes are thus not simply out there. The infrastructure—roads, buildings, and railways—that undergirds everyday life in a modern society enables those who know the architecture to (ab)use it. Infrastructures, as anthropologist Brian Larkin claims, shape "the nature of a network, the speed and direction of its movement, its temporalities, and its vulnerability to break down."[10] Certain individuals can take advantage of a structurally created flow and subtly manipulate those who are unfamiliar with its design. Uninformed others cannot see or predict the infrastructure of contract making. Once made, contracts are kept confidential. Until Kanda unexpectedly provided me with signed contracts, there was basically no way for me to access them. The AV actresses I met neither received a copy of their contract nor asked for one. For the most part, they do not wish to possess any evidence that they have performed in adult videos. As such, power dynamics, played out in a nuanced way, disappear into seemingly apolitical infrastructures without a clear trace.

## "A MANAGEMENT CONTRACT HAS NO ENFORCEABILITY"

It is a political illusion that, as I argued earlier, a contract is made in the mise-en-scène of a gentlemanly handshake between two parties coming together to assert "I hereby agree." This illusion erases not only the temporospatial trajectory of how contract making itself embeds in pre- and extra-contractual contexts but also the customary practice of how a contract unfolds in everyday life. Closing is the emblematic endpoint of contract making within a legal framework. It is also the official entry point into an uneven contractual relationship between new AV actresses and their agencies throughout AV production, which requires what talent agents refer to as *irekomi* (bringing performers to shooting sites), *gyara kanri* (managing performance guarantees), and *kokoro no keā* (taking care of women's psychology).

To explore what a contract means to talent agencies and how they use it, I interviewed a dozen AV talent agency owners, managers, and staff members. I recruited them through the Japan Production Guild (JPG), a professional association of AV talent agencies, newly organized in 2017 as part of the effort to prevent forced AV performance under the AV Human Rights Ethics Committee. Despite my initial struggle finding agents to interview, Sakai, who has many friends in the field, and Sugimoto, the owner of AV idol Amatsuka Moe's agency and the founder of JPG, helped me find agents who wanted their voices to be heard.

Kimura Naoki, a talent agency owner in his mid-forties who is known as a "clean" and "considerate" agent among JPG members, responded to my interview request in early 2018, inviting me to his office near Harajuku station. Thanks to the success of a number of his *tantai* actresses, Kimura's recently renovated office, freshly painted in white, was much more spacious and open than Sakai's studio office. Despite the spatial differences, I found that Sakai and Kimura shared some similarities; both were chain smokers and eloquent speakers. Seating himself at a table, Kimura lit his first cigarette and began to talk frankly about one of his top actresses who recently "disappeared" without completing her performance contract. He was clearly frustrated. "I'm in trouble to pay back the AV maker for the damage her no-show caused," Kimura said as he exhaled smoke, telling me that he had another "disappearance" just a couple of months before. "It is not always AV actresses who are the victim," he said, inhaling deeply. "Talent agencies are also often victimized by their women." I sensed that he suffered from the financial burden that these incidents caused. At the same time, I didn't quite get it. Why so often? Was it sheer bad luck or due to some fundamental flaw in his management? I pondered these questions but refrained from vocalizing them. I asked instead what he thought was the most important element in talent management. Based on his business experience since the mid-1990s, he insisted that providing emotional support for women performers' mental health was a crucial component of his management.

During his early twenties, Kimura began working part-time for a modeling agency that a high school friend ran in Shinjuku. The agency, which specialized in booking models for sexy photography, expanded its business to include AV performance and sex work in general a few years later. Kimura, who liked the "looseness" of the sex industry, decided to stay in the business after graduating from college in Tokyo. He eventually started his own agency in the mid-2010s. Soon after, along with a few other talent agency owners, he was arrested for violation of the Labor Dispatch Act when the police discovered that his talent performed with Fujiwara Hitomi, the actress who, as introduced in the previous chapter, filed a case of forced AV performance against her agency after reportedly appearing in more than 400 videos.

I wanted to understand talent agents' motivation that would explain their professed concern about AV actresses' mental health, among other things.

"What kinds of women perform in adult videos?" I asked Kimura.

"They are just *futsū no ko* (ordinary girls)." He rested his cigarette in an ashtray.

"Do you mean ordinary girls, but in need of mental care?" I pressed, thinking about his earlier comments regarding the emotional support he provides.

"Well, they are not ordinary in the sense that OLs [office ladies] are." He slowly exhaled smoke from his cigarette, as if looking for the right words. "Honestly, they have a few screws loose. In a word, they snap!" he said with a laugh. This sounded sexist to me—pathologizing women as if they just snap out of nowhere.

"Do you mean they become that way? Or does the AV industry attract such women?"

"I have encountered quite a number of women who used to work as typical OLs and became unhinged working in this field," Kimura said.

"Is that because the work environment in this industry is 'looser' than the Japanese corporate world, and they adapt to it?"

"Um. . . ." Kimura was being careful. "It's a job to strip naked and sell sex.

So, a woman constantly deals with moments when she doesn't want to have her body exposed on camera; she would think twice about taking off her panties if she found an ugly pimple on her butt or started menstruating, for example. If she were working as an OL, a pimple or menstruation wouldn't bother her." He looked at the cigarette butts piled in his ashtray. "Of course, we understand such women's needs."

The more I listened to him, the clearer it became to me that the main task for the talent agent is *irekomi*: delivering AV actresses to the production site, where the director and crew then take over handling them. "As long as we deliver a woman to a studio," Kimura said, "we make money." However, most actresses understand their commodity value and do not easily oblige their agencies' orders. When they feel confronted or pushed to the edge, they snap and say things out loud like, "It's your job to take care of the mess we create since you guys are the ones making the most money off of us!" Kimura said he gets upset about such attitudes but tries to let go of his anger and focus on the deliverable. Otherwise, his agency would go out of business.

Kimura shared some difficult moments he has had with his talent. It is typical, he said, to have a model who suddenly becomes reluctant to perform and wants to cancel a shoot at the last minute. In such a case, Kimura said he first acknowledges her feelings, saying "I got you. I understand how you feel today," and yet reminds her that everybody is ready for the shoot. He patiently persuades her to go no matter what it takes, whether it is a taxi fare, a gentle hug, or a promise to take her out for a meal. (This is what he means by the industry's "leniency.") In another case, Kimura vividly recalled one *tantai* actress he struggled with. According to him, she tended to be late for filming because she frequently drank all night long with her male companions at host clubs. To avoid any further trouble with a video maker over her tardiness, Kimura told her, "I will pick you up you tomorrow at 9 a.m. in front of your apartment and drive you to the studio." Arriving at her place the next morning and calling her from his car, he received no response; after several attempts, he finally reached her. Half asleep, she answered, "Hello. What's up?" He replied, "Didn't I tell you yesterday that I would come to pick you up at this time today?" She indifferently responded, "Oh, you meant today by 'tomorrow'? It's too bad. I am now at my parents' home in Niigata." Niigata is about 150 miles north of Tokyo. Kimura was furious and screamed "Stop it!" in his mind, but he managed to control his anger and instead begged her to take a super express train right away to come back to Tokyo. His persuasion brought her all the way from her Niigata home to a Tokyo studio, although it caused a five-hour delay. It was costly on his end, but he avoided a huge no-show cancellation fee. Such a bill could be anywhere from 750,000 yen (US$7,500) to 2,000,000 yen (US$20,000).

I asked Kimura how he was able to manage his emotions with his talent.

> If it is worth scolding and accusing, I'd love to. Believe me. But it doesn't work. It only makes the situation worse. Girls get scared and quit. I'd rather suck it up and let it go than lose them.

Kimura's accommodating attitude toward his talent feeds into the industry's leniency. The agents I interviewed unanimously stressed the importance of their emotional labor, particularly patience, neither getting upset with their actresses nor confronting their irresponsible behaviors. They understand their main role is to supply their talent to AV makers and fulfill performance contracts. For this mission, agents cultivate their own tactics. Sakai told me that his trick is to infantilize his talents' "nonsense," sending them to the set like a parent bringing his unreasonable three-year-old to kindergarten. Kanda, a former talent agency employee who works as a male AV performer, commented that he was trained to understand women as finicky creatures, taking their complaints with a grain of salt so that he can focus on what he needs to do. His strategy is a common business practice that many agents follow: "Give a girl 90,000 yen [US$900] for her performance gig if you pay her 100,000 yen," Kanda said. "Use the other 10,000 yen to take her out for a meal so that you seed a sense of indebtedness."

Despite their patience and lenience, however, these talent agents remained silent about the use of management contracts for *irekomi*, which literally translates as stuffing things into a container. In the industry it refers to bringing women to the set for filming, but the connotation is that it is done in a forcible manner. The language not only undermines women performers' legal status as independent contractors but also reinforces the view that they undertake what they are reluctant to do. As mentioned earlier, the ambivalence about women's consent to sexual labor made *irekomi* a sensitive topic. The closest I got to an honest assessment of the issue was Kanda's comment about how money overpowers unwillingness. "The default is that AV performers are in a bad mood since they are being asked to do things that they don't really want to do. Without being paid money, nobody would have explicit sex on camera." As he sees it, the industry uses money to "silence actresses and get them to work."[11] No one else in the industry was willing to discuss the topic further.

Something unexpected happened, however, during my interview with Miyata Miki, a rare female talent agency owner in her early forties and a former AV actress. We met at a Shibuya cafe in early 2018. We were having a regular conversation about the AV industry, but when I brought up the Tokyo district court case, Miyata raised her voice. "Some influential public figures think women are bound to contracts and forced into performing in adult videos," Miyata said. "This is such nonsense! What they claim is unthinkable. If anyone is troubled, it is an agency that subjects itself to women's unpredictable behavior." Sipping a soda to calm herself down, she added:

> A management contract has no enforceability. It is a mere *ikaku* (empty threat). It functions as a threat against girls not literally, but more symbolically. We simply use it as a preventive measure to avoid performers' irresponsible behaviors such as no-shows, last-minute cancellations, and tardiness. Its legality is out of the question. We all know that there is no way for us to win any legal battles since our business is so gray.

I was taken aback by Miyata's frank disclosure about the function of a contract—another strategy to bind performers to AV filming. Amano Koichi, a former talent agent in his late thirties who I had interviewed a week before, kept telling me that nobody would share any controversial information—about closing strategies and details of the management contract, for instance—related to the issue of forced AV performance. He arranged my interview with Miyata, even sitting in with us, with her permission.

"The contract is simply an 'empty threat'?" I queried.

Nodding, she elaborated that "the contract is, for us, no more than one's word to follow rules. It's made only for the purpose of restraining free movement."

I was astonished by her claim that contracts are actually null, as I believed that contract making was a ritual to render the terms of the work officially enforceable, or that at least the agency intended this. Otherwise, what's the point of a contract? Miyata's remarks opened my eyes to how the meaning, use, and function of a contract is determined by the ways in which those who participate in the contractual relationship perceive, interpret, and practice it. More than anything, it is used to block women performers from freely moving from one agency to another or keep them from causing problems on the job. I also began to wonder what it means for contractors to sign a document that is, in reality, null and void. How do they reconcile it, or even try to reconcile it, when both parties have different understandings of what a contract means and does?

"Do you mean," I asked Miyata, "that some women naïvely believe in the legality of the contract and bind themselves to AV performance, although agencies perceive the contract as nothing more than an empty threat?"

"Well, some girls might take it literally. That's too bad." She sounded dismissive or even irritated. "What they should have really done is to reach out to the police for help. That's it!"

"So, do you mean that a contract is a mere token to implement the rules and that it's an AV actresses' responsibility to figure out the real nature of the contract?" I looked at Miyata and Amano to confirm whether I understood correctly.

"I think so," Miyata answered swiftly. "If any problems occur, it's not about the issue of the contract itself but more about the problematic business management of an agency."

Amano agreed. "There is hardly any case in which girls have actually gone to the public for help, as far as I know. [This] is exactly what talent agencies are so vigilant to avoid. Decent agencies would notice girls' distress and address it before it becomes something serious; they could even provide some money to silence them if necessary. We do everything to prevent a girl from running to the police. We all know that our business can only exist at the margins, under the police's mercy."

Miyata and Amano's remarks highlighted that talent agencies set and implement rules for which a contract is made, practiced, and justified accordingly—despite the lack of its enforceability.

If it is true that agencies define contractual terms and decide how to use them, this Japanese AV business model is quite different from the one used in the US. In the US porn industry, performers hire booking agencies and generally pay a 10–15 percent commission fee per booked performance. As such, contractual terms are straightforward. An agency's service is clearly defined. Taking actresses out for meals, bringing them to the studio, and performing emotional labor on their behalf won't be part of it. If a car-less actress needs to hire her agency to give her rides to sets, she has to make a special arrangement for the service and pay extra fees. Both male and female actors in the US are expected to manage themselves, except during contract booking, whereas the same is expected in Japan only for male AV actors. Women performers in Japan's AV industry are made to depend on their agencies, like small children dependent on their guardians. In other words, an actress does not hire her agency; they hire her.

This power dynamic is largely behind actresses' erratic behavior. The

AV industry relies on women's sexual labor, and everyone knows that. The sex work they perform feeds their agencies (and scouts), while it caters to AV consumers' desires and enables video makers' capital accumulation. Despite the central role that women's sexual labor plays in this profit-making cycle, their actual earnings are systematically minimized. The industry makes up for the imbalance between the value of performers' sexual labor and their lack of proper monetary compensation by treating actresses, especially top-selling ones, as VIPs, at least symbolically. This is why the Japanese AV industry tolerates actresses' "nonsense" behaviors. The information gap between the industry and women performers is thus translated into an uneven relationship through which the former infantilizes adult performers, binding them by an "empty threat" called the contract. And yet, this situation remains camouflaged by the status of the performer as an independent contractor, nominally.

## "[GIRLS] ESSENTIALLY PAY FOR 'PEACE OF MIND' "

The use of an empty contract and the wholesale management of money-making actresses are at the heart of a talent agency's profit-seeking strategy. For the full-course service, agencies charge exorbitant management fees, usually in the range between 50 and 80 percent of performance guarantees. I asked how such a high rate was set and by whom. My interlocutors had no clear answer, simply saying, "I don't know. That's how things have been done." They knew very little *why* they do what they do and kept their actresses uninformed too. None of the customary practices around commission rates, wholesale management, and the nature of contracts are fully disclosed to women. Nor are these customs spelled out in the service contract. Very few resources are available for performers, either. This is partly because agencies typically ban exchanging personal contacts and sharing business information. This is also the result of the high turnover of actresses, producing very few with accumulated knowledge. In this way, agencies keep actresses in the dark, disempowering them to challenge the status quo. Thus, the performer is not inherently naïve but rather in a disadvantaged position, playing an away game by someone else's rules.

When challenged in my interview, the talent agents largely justified what they do and pointed the finger elsewhere. An easy target was video makers, who set the budget for performers' pay and make all decisions regarding video content and marketing strategies. Sakai, the former apparel business owner, remarked, "We just serve as a go-between for video makers and performers.

Our job is supplying girls to the makers . . . we never wish our girls to perform ever-intensifying hardcore scenes that only shorten their lives as AV actresses. It's video makers who demand more and more for less money." Sakai expressed that today's AV industry is far more competitive than during the early 1990s and that video makers have gained much more power over agencies. Talent agencies in the 1990s satisfied video makers by simply providing pretty girls who would go naked on camera. "We now struggle with finding and supplying better looking girls with not only nice personalities, but also the capability for self-promotion on and off line," Sakai said.

Other talent agencies similarly pointed to video makers' excessive demands—women with higher "specs," willing to perform in harder-core sexual performances at more hours per day—for less money. Sakai told me that women's performance guarantee is now one-third of what it was during the 1990s AV boom. There was a big shift in the mid-2000s when, as I discuss in the introduction, increasing numbers of young women were recruited to the AV industry, resulting in a buyer's market. Changing information technologies have also intensified demands on the sexual labor AV actresses provide. In contrast with VHS, DVDs enabled much longer recording time and higher picture quality. That technological change translated into the demand for longer filming (and work) hours and flawless beauty in performers. Meanwhile, DVD prices dropped by half from VHS prices, and video makers shrunk production budgets accordingly.

"Women performers are 'disposables' today," said Sugimoto, the manager of AV idol Amatsuka Moe and a JPG founder. He explained current practices. "Video makers can afford the high turnover of fresh actresses since there are plenty of pretty girls they can pick and choose from." According to Sugimoto, video makers used to offer a *tantai* actress a year-long exclusive performance contract, meaning a total of twelve videos with once-a-month releases. In this way, talent agencies could afford to nurture their actresses, slowing down their declining commodity value. Such an offer is extremely rare today. As I discuss further in the next chapter, major video makers now commit to only a debut video before deciding whether to renew an actress's exclusive performance contract. Describing the negative impact of this practice on actresses, Sugimoto said:

> For the [contract] renewal, video makers usually request more explicit sexual acts, wider publicity, and the like. That means a girl has to release perfor-

mances, rapidly, that include acts she would have specified as "NG" ("no good" acts on camera) in her contract. This degrades her market value drastically and lowers her salary, destroying her.

In this business context, Sakai and Sugimoto, among other agents, maintain that they are there to "protect their girls." One way to ease the sharp decline in AV performers' earnings is through an agency's management of monetary flow in general. Management companies keep financial details confidential from their performers, justifying this as part of their job.[12] Some agencies explained that this was out of necessity, to absorb the shock of sharply declining guarantees. Others defended the high commission rate to cover fees and expenditures necessary to holistically care for performers. And yet others felt performers should be excused from the graphic negotiation scene wherein video makers put prices on them. Despite their different justifications, they believe that this practice contributes positively to an actress's mental health. According to Amano, the former agent, it is discouraging and even depressing for performers to see their market value decline rapidly, no matter how much effort they make or how much their acting skills improve. So, in his view, it is important to avoid disclosing a sharp fall in their earnings:

> To make it a "soft landing," decent agencies try to even out a performer's earnings as much as possible. It would be pretty much standard in this business to give highly paid *tantai* performers roughly 30 percent of what they earn from their performances. For example, an agency would pay her 1,000,000 yen (US$10,000) and save 500,000 yen out of her full performance guarantee of 3,000,000 yen (US$30,000). In this way, the agency can afford to keep paying her 1,000,000 yen even when her guarantee would drop down by half.

I asked what he thought about the fact that 70 percent of an actress's hard-earned money goes into someone else's hands, even when some of it is being saved for her future. He was quick to justify:

> It is no good to give too much money to young girls in their early twenties. They would end up blowing the money on things that are fun but not necessary. It is also extremely difficult for anyone to lower their standards once they live in a luxurious condominium and take taxis all over the place. So, it's better to have a stable income and live within it.

This is the reason, Amano stressed, that a talent agency manages performers' finances: out of goodwill. The performer, however, never asks for such a service nor agrees to it in the management contract.

Monetary flow and management manifest who is in power. Extracting as much money as possible from high-earning performers, Amano explained, allows agencies to avoid financial challenges and focus on what they prioritize. "People in this industry," he said, "tend to prioritize making money and moving forward rather than being caught up in trivial things. They also let go of money here and there as a necessary expense to manage girls. So, they are willing to use money to solve problems instead of fighting legal disputes." Obviously, they are doing so with money extracted from their top-earning performers. Amano pointed out that agencies attempt to extract money from a video maker, too, or solicit better business deals when their actresses are injured or abused at work.

"What happens in cases involving injury and compensation?" I asked. "How do you split the money with the performer?"

"Honestly"—Amano paused and restarted slowly—"We only reimburse medical expenses when she submits receipts."

"There is a flow of much larger sums of money you receive than that, right?"

"It might sound cruel [to the injured actress], but it's more important for us to think of our business first and pool the money for miscellaneous business costs," Amano responded defensively. "It's a great business chance for us to negotiate with video makers for better deals when they are indebted to us. Otherwise, we lose an important negotiation card."

To me, Amano seemed concerned only with the business perspective, with little concern for performers' safety or needs. I felt compelled to pry open the inner workings of this arena, wherein actresses experience everyday violence and accept it as something that they cannot fight against.

"So the injured actress might not herself benefit from future business deals?" I asked. "Another lucky actress might get the chance made from someone else's loss?"

Amano nodded. "To tell the truth," he said reluctantly, "there's nothing you can do about it. Indeed, it's not fair. Such is life."

"Do you think she would understand if you fully disclosed what's going on behind the scenes?" I might have sounded accusatory. I sensed Amano was slouching in his chair.

"Well . . . ," his voice sounded zoned out. "She cannot help but accept it. That's how things work in 'the adult world.' " He looked away.

As Amano justified it, talent agencies have to invest in newly recruited performers even before they make any money. Such an investment is made possible, he explained, out of other performers' earnings. "In that sense, it's like insurance whereby everyone helps one another." Interestingly, his insurance metaphor, which stressed mutual assistance among performers, omitted how the system itself is completely controlled by the agency. These examples further demonstrate that, above all, agencies hold the upper hand throughout contract making, the distribution of compensation, and troubleshooting.

Some might wonder why women performers don't become freelancers, managing their own bookings and finances. I asked Sakai about that.

"There is no way," Sakai responded definitively, "for young, inexperienced women to navigate through the crowd of outlaws and perverts in this industry. Please think about that, Ms. Takeyama!"

I didn't know what to say.

"Without know-how," Sakai continued, "it's impossible to do business in this field. Girls can perform safely only because their talent agencies protect them." Like others in the industry, he patronized adult women by referring to them as *onna no ko*—which, as pointed out above, literally means a female child in Japanese.

Sakai was convincing, but I still sensed the injustice of the service, for which an agency charges such a high commission fee. "Isn't it too much for an agency to extract more than a half of what a video maker pays an actress for her performance?" I pressed.

"Commission rates might sound too high. But we pay all sorts of fees and fares, including transportation, STD testing, and lodging for women who come to video shootings from rural Japan," Sakai commented.

My skepticism about the agencies' self-defense faded away when I came to realize that the Japanese AV industry wouldn't allow independent actresses to benefit much from freelancing. To avoid "trouble," video makers won't hire *tantai* actresses unless they have agencies, though they do occasionally use non-*tantai* freelance performers. Makers offer freelancers only half the performance guarantee they would offer to agency-based actresses. In other words, video makers, not performers, save an amount equivalent to commission fees. Furthermore, unlike an agency's actresses, who can ask their office to intervene when they have issues with video makers on site, freelancers must represent themselves if they are put in a tough spot. They gain virtually no benefit. What would be the point of AV actresses becoming independent? This unfavorable situation for performers is thus systemically nested in the business customs of the AV industry.

For most talent agencies, video makers are, after all, employers of their talent. In their view, agencies and their models are in the same boat in their relationship with their employers who represent the industry and set rules. From this perspective, agencies are simply taking advantage of the existing scheme. Furthermore, the industry knows that no matter how little AV actresses are paid, their income is still high compared to what they would make in other service sectors. Sakai asserted:

> There are few girls who would think that their earnings were too little and their pay to agencies was too much. They essentially pay for "peace of mind."

As Sakai's remarks suggest, what Japanese AV talent agencies provide is wholesale management, with performers essentially receiving holistic care services.

Still, some agents I met were more skeptical about the management system than those trying to do their best within the given structure. Matsuda Akira, thirty-seven, reflexively looked back at his experience working for an AV talent management office a few years ago. When I asked him what he ultimately learned from the experience, he paused for quite a long time. The moment was accentuated by his smooth talk once he began speaking. "I guess, I learned my own weakness more than anything," Matsuda said. "I came to realize that I was such a weak person who had no guts to make changes for the better." Originally from the southern island of Kyushu, where he performed in a rock band after graduating from college, Matsuda moved to Tokyo in 2007 at age twenty-six, seeking new opportunities. He wanted to become a comedian but struggled financially. So he made a living working for an AV talent agency. "Although I technically had no problem persuading unwilling girls into performing in adult videos, it caused a moral dilemma and psychological burden," he said, biting his lip.

Matsuda slowly began to talk about his journey of self-transformation over time. Despite his belief early on that he was "rescuing" girls into the AV industry, his feelings began to change. One day he asked the owner of his agency, over drinks, whether it was the right thing to coerce women into AV performance. As he remembers it, the owner replied, "Those girls, who have special circumstances, are fated to drift to *kocchi no sekai* (this world) sooner or later. So, it's important to help them to make money and obtain happiness. Otherwise, they are doomed to misery." Despite some initial doubts, Matsuda told me that he tried to believe this, to do his best. "I didn't want to do a halfway job for the owner and for his agency," he said. But something about what the owner said afterward stuck in his mind: "Girls would eventually betray [me], so my employees and family are more important to me than those would-be betrayers." The more Matsuda got to know the actresses, the more he felt he was dishonest with himself:

> Indeed, there are many unhappy girls out there, as the owner pointed out. But they don't have to become AV actresses to find their happiness. The job would potentially ruin their happiness instead. I started to feel responsibility for them as someone who guided them to *kocchi no sekai* (this world). My skepticism grew into the conclusion that it was wrong to highlight only positive aspects, while ignoring the risks and harms they face. I came to realize that I was lying not only to them but also to myself. The fact hit me hard. At that point, I decided to quit the job.

Matsuda now thinks that what the owner maintained was simply whitewashing, and it is better to reveal all possible risks up front to performers. I asked him whether it is typical for talent agents to struggle with moral dilemmas as he did. He responded:

> Even though we are going through similar struggles, most agents, including myself, would likely reconcile it with monetary gain. That's the weakness of human beings. It was for money that I put everything aside and convinced myself to do my job. Some could go quite far for the sake of money, but I couldn't.

His remarks suggested that something important was hidden from performers, glossed over with shrewd reasoning and persuasion. Compared to other showbusiness fields, like comedy, Matsuda pointed out the difficulties AV performers encounter. He thinks both comedians and AV actresses provide something intangible—funny jokes and sexy images. Both are commodities in themselves since they have nothing but their own talent to sell. However, unlike comedians, who can arm themselves with jokes and comedic gestures, AV performers are literally naked, vulnerable to all the social stigma and discrimination attached to sex work.

Kanda, the former agent and AV actor, metaphorically explained what it would be like to be an AV performer, based on his own performer experience and dialogue with actresses. Illuminating the peculiar nature of AV work, he said:

AV performance as a career is useless. It's like candle wax that simply runs down. It never grows back. With AV performance, your commodity value diminishes quickly; you never really advance your acting career or anything. You might enjoy momentary fun. But that's all. It's literally "candlelight just before it goes out."

Kanda insisted that a job in AV catalyzes an ever-growing sense of emptiness under the countdown to the end of one's short-lived career. Indeed, I do not know of any other occupation in which one's salary decreases as one's career advances and one's dignity is questioned forever after.

With the dead end ahead, Kanda has observed that actresses seek their exit by finding men, ideally future spouses, who can financially support them; but they often wind up hooking up with good-for-nothing men, as the majority of sensible men will stay away from them once they discover their past; women performers, in turn, go for men who accept them, even when the men are abusive or financially dependent. "It's the lack of self-esteem," Kanda asserted. "They end up selling themselves short." Most women leave AV jobs quickly unless they are lucky enough to become a breakout star. There are a handful of women such as Sato Jun and Imai Haruka, introduced in the previous chapter, who gain some success and self-confidence. Most actresses, however, constantly struggle with their self-worth—commodity value *and* human dignity, as the two are inseparably intertwined in the pornographic illusions that adult videos produce. Even if, as agencies claim, women would be willing to pay extraordinarily expensive fees for "peace of mind," the coverage area seems to be limited to what agencies care about most—having actresses show up at shootings and complete their performance contracts—even though these women's lives continue beyond the realm of the AV world. Their vulnerability to stigma, discrimination, and relationship problems remains uncovered.

## VICTIM-BLAMING OR SELF-ACCOUNTABILITY?

I wondered where agencies think accountability lies when women suffer from identity reveal, social stigma, and sextortion. To my surprise, Kanda, who is especially empathetic with AV actresses based on his performer experience, said it would be the woman's responsibility to deal with such consequences since she "bought the AV industry propaganda." Sakai, the self-claimed "decent person who engages . . . in illicit things," also stressed the fact that the actress was "not threatened to perform under force of arms," and therefore, it would ultimately be her problem.

Once I got to know Sakai better, I revisited his earlier comments and asked him rhetorically, "Isn't this victim-blaming?"

He laughed my question off as groundless. Reminding me of how women are recruited on the streets, not kidnapped, he alluded to women's carelessness to be blamed, if anything. "Would you, Ms. Takeyama, stop when a stranger speaks to you on a busy street and tries to sell you something?" He looked into my eyes confidently.

I thought about it and shook my head. "Well, maybe not."

"See!" He gave me a victorious smile. "That's the way reasonable people behave. I have a teenage daughter, but I don't think she would. Those who stop have an issue with their risk management."

Sakai saw my skeptical face and continued:

> When a stranger says to you, "You have the potential to become a celebrity," 5 percent [of you] may feel flattered and pleased. But 95 percent [of you] would be aware that something is not quite right. Look, there are so many points at which you can notice signs of risk before you sign a contract and perform in AV. What business would you think allows contract workers, who gave consent, to freely walk away by them simply saying, "Whoops, I didn't mean to participate in the project"? Can you think of any?

I couldn't think of any off the top of my head. It was also difficult for me to cut in throughout his animated, self-assured speech. Sakai always spoke in such an engaging, smooth manner—asking rhetorical questions, noticing my reactions, and throwing another ball into the conversation, one after another, rhythmically. Much later, Nakano, a talent agent and former actress who appeared in the previous chapter, asked essentially the same question regarding AV exceptionalism that I couldn't answer either. I now know, however, that sex work *is* exceptional, not because of its indecency but because of its illegitimacy in Japan; AV performers technically can say no to sexual acts anytime and make AV performance contracts null and void.

Sakai's speech continued and concluded with him pathologizing street scouts, talent agencies, and AV actresses alike in a gendered way. In his opinion, the AV industry consists of "psychopathic men" and "women with developmental disabilities."[13] He elaborated on what he meant by this:

Scouts and agencies do anything for money without a sense of guilt. . . . Profit making is their sole purpose in life. They wouldn't notice it unless a girl says to their faces that she was hurt. On the other hand, girls lack the ability to see ahead and manage risks. They can foresee only one or two steps ahead. They understand the very basic thing, such as doing this makes this much money. That's pretty much it. They cannot think further than that. As a result, when they face trouble that could have been predicted, they blame someone else for deception. Those girls never think things through carefully. They just go with the flow.

His description of male recruiters and agencies echoes what Matsuda described as his own "weakness," that is, reconciling his moral dilemma with monetary gain. Sakai's view on women performers' unreasonable behaviors also aligns with how other agents such as Matsuda's boss and Nakano characterized AV actresses—women as "would-be betrayers" and "irresponsible nuisances." This kind of construction of recruiters, agents, and actresses allows narrators to differentiate themselves from troubled others with personality disorders. It also reduces structural violence against women to an issue of individual flaws or pathologies. There is no black-and-white causality to locating accountability when structural violence causes individual suffering. This is particularly the case when, unlike coerced victims, those suffering have given consent to the acts causing the suffering. As a result, consent givers are blamed and made accountable for their decisions. Equating victims with those who are "threatened to perform under force of arms," Sakai and Kanda imply that all others are essentially stupid people who "bought AV industry propaganda" and failed to "manage risks." In this view, all consent is, unless overtly forced, voluntary no matter how reluctantly it may have been given. It is not the industry, sexism, and infrastructures but the consent giver who is being put on trial for accountability. Sakai's solution reinforces this point:

> It's important to teach them to think twice before they commit to something that sounds too good to be true. It's also important, I think, to let them make mistakes and learn from the experiences. Otherwise, they would never grow up to be responsible citizens.

His paternalistic claim infantilizes adult women in the industry and expects them to become self-responsible citizens. In this view, which aligns with the Japanese government's political goals I discuss in the introduction and chapter 1—the "self-governing subject" under the Rule of Law— very rarely are they perceived as victims of structural violence or objects of systemic harm.

———

The deck is heavily stacked against those who are socially vulnerable and enticed into unknown territory. In Japan's AV industry, the "wholesale management of girls" starts with recruiting and moves on to closing in contract making; ensuring that performers arrive on time for their shoots; providing emotional labor for actresses with mental health issues; and controlling performers' finances. Such management is deeply embedded in infrastructures of contract, through which the business side customarily holds the upper hand within a male-centered industry culture. They create and enforce the rules. Physical, symbolic, and cultural infrastructures that are obvious to them are not so clear to performers. Furthermore, such customary practices and structures are not easy to reveal and prove, with material evidence, as the cause of violence and exploitation against women. This point leads to another. Women's vulnerability, which is discursively shaped through the information gap, perpetuates their disadvantage in the AV industry. This vulnerability carries over to mainstream Japanese society, which would label them undeserving of the status of victim. AV actresses are caught in the catch-22 situation of being involved in a risky business while simultaneously being blamed for their "risk management" failures if they encounter trouble.

As such, the focal emphasis on individual responsibility renders structural violence invisible. AV performers who understand their financial value might have a "so-what" attitude toward their agencies and exercise symbolic power in everyday forms of resistance. Their overall lack of familiarity with AV business operations, however, usually keeps them from challenging the status quo. Furthermore, talent agencies are not at the top of the AV food chain, either. The industry's hierarchical structure originates in the difference between scouts and talent agencies, a distinction often lost on AV outsiders. To Sakai and many others who work in talent management, scouts are a "different species." They point to the fact that street scouts were banned in 2013 under Tokyo's sweeping Anti-Nuisance Ordinance and try to separate themselves from these "criminals."[14] By the same token, agencies cannot completely cut scouts off because, after all, they depend on them for recruitment of women with high "specs," or *tantai* actresses. The same paradoxical system, as I discuss further in the next chapter, is deployed against talent agencies by AV directors and makers. Meanwhile, women performers, situated at the bottom of this business hierarchy, are structurally kept in darkness.

# 4

## THE INDUSTRY

On a clear and crisp winter afternoon in February 2018, I entered Ueshima Coffee in Tokyo's upscale Aoyama shopping district. I had come to interview fifty-six-year-old Akasaka Mitsuo, a porn director known as "Mr. Nice." Akasaka lives in the area, the wealthiest in Tokyo. In contrast to the cold and wintry gray outside, the coffee shop was warm and welcoming, with a fresh coffee aroma. A radiantly smiling man sitting alone amid the shop's stylish interior caught my eye. It was Mr. Nice. Wearing a pastel blue ironed shirt and khaki pants, he waved his hand and politely greeted me. After introducing ourselves, we ordered handmade pour-over coffee and got settled in for the interview. Akasaka is one of the most successful and well-known AV directors in Japan. A graduate of a top-ranked private university in Tokyo, Akasaka wanted to produce feature films but found it difficult to do so in Japan's hierarchical and competitive film industry. Meanwhile, he found that he could direct his own adult videos almost immediately. After six months of acquiring necessary skills under a famous AV and mainstream film director, Akasaka shot his first adult video in 1993 at age twenty-nine. With his film background, he produced drama-infused videos in a newly developed genre, *bishōjo* (beautiful girls), which became highly popular and influential in the 1980s. In the new millennium, he launched a wholly new genre called *jukujo* (mature women) and made it a big success, when few in the industry believed women over thirty could star in adult videos. Akasaka is married to a former actress who made her AV debut in one of his videos.

Akasaka and his wife have been outspoken in their belief that forced AV performance is nonexistent in the Japanese AV industry. Although some people inside and outside the industry doubt the claim, Akasaka seemed unfazed. I was intrigued by the difference between the sweeping generalizations he subscribes to and his sincere demeanor. He did not appear to be lying or covering something up. And, based on his friendly manner, sincere tone of voice, and polite attitude, I began to understand why he is known as Mr. Nice. His frank, witty talk about his upbringing, career, and family was entertaining. To my surprise, he told me that he used to be very shy around women—to the point where he would sometimes shake uncontrollably—because he felt he was unlikeable. Nearly thirty years of directing adult videos has helped him figure out how to become likeable, he said. "It's the [director's] likeability," he insisted, "that determines whether actresses have a pleasant experience on set."[1] I asked for his thoughts about forced AV performance, as someone who has been in the business for such a long time. "I don't know why, but I have never met anyone who was forced [into AV performance] in my entire career in this industry. I have interviewed over 2,000 potential actresses and actually worked with more than 1,000 actresses. Everyone I have worked with has said to me, 'It was so much fun.'" Akasaka added, "I don't think they would have lied to me."

While actresses appear to have "so much fun" while shooting on set, as chapter 2 illuminates, they also experience mental distress inside and outside AV production. Put another way, having "so much fun" while filming is one thing, but facing occupational discrimination is another. The latter may not be obvious to other people, including those the actresses work with. Akasaka's perspective helped me understand how ones' life philosophy and positive attitude determine what to see and what not to see. I gradually came to the conclusion that those who are in privileged positions may be attuned to overlook (consciously or unconsciously) the structural violence against less-privileged others.

In our interview, Akasaka stressed the importance of considering others, especially AV actresses, as a director strives to create a pleasant space on set. "I am always thinking of how I can please the person in front of me. I want [her] to like me and enjoy working with me," he said. He was beginning to cast his spell on me too. I sensed his will to be likable and could easily imagine his likability being contagious on and off set. His considerable efforts, he explained, start before shooting takes place. At auditions, he sets a disarming, genial tone and shows his genuine interest in a performer. He carefully listens as she discusses her background, what she enjoys doing, and her future goals. These are all important pieces of information for him to win an actress's heart on set. He has his assistant director prepare her favorite snacks so that she starts the day feeling catered to. If he discovers that she is performing mainly for money, his shooting prioritizes efficiency by cutting back on breaks and moving from one scene to the next as quickly as possible, so that the actress feels her hourly earnings are maximized. If she wants to build an acting career, he spends time discussing the particulars of her performance and reshooting scenes until she is satisfied. Observing his personality and consideration for others to meet their ends, I was persuaded by the positivity Mr. Nice exuded.

Even though Akasaka insisted that he had never met anyone who was forced [into AV] in [his] entire career, I pressed him further to get his take on how women are recruited. "I am a person on set, working all day long to produce videos," Akasaka said defensively. "I have no idea how women are brought to this industry. Honestly, I don't even want to know. I only deal with actresses who have already made up their minds." His "I-don't-even-want-to-know" answer puzzled me; such uncaring words seemed to contrast with his pleasant personality. But other AV directors, I soon learned, shared his view. They unanimously said the same thing during interviews, as if prepared for this particular question: "Our job starts when women arrive on set. They've already made up their minds."[2] Their remarks demarcate the compartmentalized process of AV production, in which talent agencies undertake packaging talent to directors like meat in a supermarket: the less the customer knows about how it got there, the better. The trace of the supply chain can be easily erased and forgotten. Unseeing by choice is, after all, entangled with the privilege of selective seeing. Structural violence often remains invisible to the socially privileged due to its nondirect, nonimmediate, and nonphysical nature. As I discuss in the previous chapter, those who are in a position of power and familiar with the infrastructures of the AV industry can use and even abuse them to take advantage of others who are not familiar with the industry's design. Like Akasaka and other directors, the "haves" might not necessarily grasp the scheme entirely—but this is because, I argue, they are privileged enough to get to decide whether they want to know something or not. Put differently, those in power can hurt and exploit disadvantaged others indirectly without knowing it. This kind of nuanced power dynamics, enabled by structural inequalities, cancels out such superficial binaries as intentional and unintentional acts, truth and falsehood, and honesty and dishonesty. To reinforce this view, Sakai, the talent agent I introduce in chapter 3, commented, "What Akasaka sees as reality is true to him. Nobody can see everything and therefore, people tend to assume what they see is reality." A director who used to work with Akasaka elaborated further: "He is, after all, in an elite position. He never has to get his own hands dirty. Someone else does the dirty work for him. Because of that, Mr. Nice can remain a genuinely nice guy."

Because compartmentalization and the division of labor remain so integral to how AV is produced, few in the industry understand—or even try to understand—the effects of what they do beyond their immediate purview. In the previous chapter, I demonstrate the ways that talent agencies and scouts (ab)use AV infrastructures of contract for what they refer to as smooth "closing," the delivery of actresses to film sets, and wholesale management of their talent. I argue contract provisions are intentionally kept in the dark for AV actresses. This chapter explores how AV directors fit into this infrastructure of AV production—and how male production staff and even male actors align with the directors' prerogatives. By the same token, AV directors subordinate to their employers, that is, AV makers. The AV industry is stovepiped, I contend, from talent management to filming to marketing and distribution. Talent agents supply actresses to video makers; directors rely on this stream of actresses to produce master tapes, to be sent to video makers; and male performers and the production crew follow directors' orders on set. Within this loosely organized arrangement, video makers are the capitalist class: they own the means of production and commodities—adult videos and their copyrights.

If talent agencies are the dealers who help women find AV jobs and provide AV makers with sexual labor, video directors, production teams, and male performers are the craftsmen behind the commodity called adult video. Actresses are the raw input in the production of the good. Nevertheless, their positionality in the AV production process is rather ambivalent. Actresses' consent to performing in adult videos puts them at the bottom of this hierarchically compartmentalized infrastructure (per my last chapter). In other words, their consent to AV performance is automatically translated into not only business contracts with AV makers but also social contracts with the male-centered AV industry at large.

It is essentially the social contract that AV actresses involuntarily consent to, even if they give enthusiastic consent to their business contracts. The social and business contracts are inseparable in AV production, and yet, the former is not spelled out in the contracts they sign. Through contract making, they wind up accepting subjection, as if by choice, whether they are cognizant of it or not. This custom complicates the contract-making process, which is based on the legal assumption that all parties fully understand the contractual terms and have provided informed consent to them. Thus, a host of unequal relationships in the labor process and involuntarily consented to social contract premises fall within the cracks of the hierarchy—which, by design, functions by keeping structural violence against women intact and invisible in and outside the industry.

## "AFTER ALL, IT'S VIDEO MAKERS WHO PAY US, NOT ACTRESSES"

"When I started to direct videos for the rental market in the early 1990s," Akasaka said, "I never felt pressured about sales numbers. I only focused on how to please women and make good videos." Early on, Akasaka mostly produced *bishōjo* (beautiful girl) videos, which were enjoying a boom when he began his career in 1993. However, young, pretty models never appealed to his personal tastes, as he preferred sexy, mature women. Akasaka brought his idea of filming mature women to mainstream video makers, who at that time produced adult videos for rental only. Nobody took him seriously at first; they assumed the younger, the better when it came to appealing to the dominant rental market. Akasaka's experiences mirror the rapid changes in Japan's AV industry,[3] which transitioned from offering rental videos to consumer-direct sales videos in the 1990s, and then to streaming videos in the 2010s. As these delivery formats changed, however, video makers' profit margins became smaller and smaller. When producing *bishōjo* videos during the home-video rental explosion, Akasaka did not have to think of end users or profits; he simply devoted himself to his craft.

By the late 1990s, Akasaka had firmly established himself as an AV director, winning a best director industry award in 1998. But at the peak of his career, he lost motivation to continue making *bishōjo* videos. Around this time, he was approached by Iwasaki Gen, a former mainstream television producer who founded a consumer-direct sales video company that has grown into one of the largest Japanese AV makers today. Back then, Iwasaki was struggling to find directors and actresses willing to work for him; enjoying industry hegemony, rental video companies often prohibited their directors and performers from contracting with sales video makers. Akasaka, however, shared Iwasaki's vision for the creation of a consumer-oriented sales video market. Moreover, when Akasaka revealed his wish to film sensuous, mature women, Iwasaki shook his hand and said, "Let's produce our customers together and cultivate a new market." He offered Akasaka four million yen (US$40,000), twice as much as his average rental video budget. The fusion of sales video pioneer and award-winning director spawned a new AV genre, *jukujo* (mature women), among other lucrative endeavors.

Due to their marginalized status in the predominantly rental-based AV industry, sales video makers and directors were free from the self-regulation of conventional video making. At the same time, they were under pressure to cultivate new markets. "Iwasaki thought there was an untapped reservoir in the adult video market and therefore novel videos would create new consumer needs," Akasaka said. In the early 1980s, when rental videos were the primary format, the retail price of videos was fixed at 15,000 yen (US$150). Once a master tape was produced, it was recorded in VHS and sold to rental video shops, of which there were more than 6,000 throughout Japan. As such, sales of at least 6,000 copies per title were guaranteed, a remarkable number by today's standards.[4] Though the rental video price was eventually reduced to 9,000 yen (US$90), rentals remained profitable through the early 1990s.[5] But by the mid-1990s, a sales video maker, Soft On Demand, began selling its videos directly to consumers for 2,980 yen (US$29.80), a third of the rental video price. Iwasaki's sales company also began producing cheap, uniquely marketable videos. While excited about the new opportunity, Akasaka faced a new challenge: sales videos are meant to sell. "Unlike rental video makers whose sales were predetermined, sales video makers had to make a profit," he said.

To sell videos, Akasaka decided to become a good "*himo*" (pimp) for the first time in his AV directing career. I asked what he meant by that. To him, a "good pimp" meant a man who makes money off women but produces neither victims nor unhappy individuals. "Ideally," Akasaka added, "I wish AV actresses would continue being happy even after they leave this industry." His remarks suggested that these women could face challenges when they reintegrate into mainstream Japanese society, after the euphoria of the AV industry fades. Akasaka further explained, "There would be no victims if there were no stigma or social discrimination against women who have performed in AV. But reality is not that way. So, AV performers must hide their past and live with fear of victimization." Understanding that actresses carry psychological baggage, Akasaka further explained, "Though I can't do anything about that fact,

I can work on the area [in which] I am in charge. So, I make sure that actresses enjoy working with me. Without actresses who are willing to go on camera, our job is impossible."

Specifically, Akasaka strives to provide emotional labor while directing videos. "I film actresses very closely for an entire day or two, and therefore a bad relationship makes everyone's jobs difficult," he said. Of course, it is not always easy; sometimes, even Mr. Nice encounters a woman he would like to stay away from. "In that case, I force myself to like her no matter what. Once I decide, I usually start to see positive aspects of the person." He squinted his eyes and smiled. Akasaka's remarks imply that in any business relationship, no one is completely free from the need to compromise. He calls his self-imposed commitment "binding oneself to liking [the other]."[6]

In contrast with AV actresses' bondage to sexual labor, "binding oneself to liking" made it sound like Akasaka was involuntarily consenting to his own will. To characterize the situation that way, however, necessitates flattening structural inequalities—creating a surface equivalency, perhaps, between Akasaka's challenges as director and those of the young women he films— while the hierarchical infrastructure of the AV industry remains firmly in place. Obviously, an elite's subjection to his own will is not the same as a socially marginalized person's subjection to someone else's will. The former is more *voluntary* self-imposition than *involuntary* consent. There are certainly parallels between the emotional labor Akasaka prides himself on providing and that performed by the actresses he directs—but they have different goals, while both essentially serving AV makers' profit-making motives. For example, Akasaka must produce a marketable, quality picture that will satisfy the AV makers he works for, while AV actresses care about satisfying multiple male actors in and outside the AV industry: AV directors, whose command and control they are subject to; AV makers, who decide whether to rehire them; AV actors, who take the lead in sex scenes; and AV fans, who purchase their DVDs and determine their career longevity. Directors ultimately create self-contained products within their niches, while actresses provide other-oriented servitude that extends beyond the realm of video production to include lengthy social contracts with the AV industry at large.

The self-contained AV production process allows directors to focus on what they do well. As a result, they can remain unfamiliar, by choice, with the dark side of AV. "It's beyond my scope and I don't know how women are brought to me for audition interviews," Akasaka said. I was empathetic to his difficult position but, at the same time, disappointed by the seemingly willful narrowness of his thinking. If he wished to, I thought, he could expand his scope and probe into the structural limitations, just as he succeeded in creating and establishing an entirely new AV genre. It was his choice not to inquire more deeply into the life trajectories of the actresses he professed to care so much about. His own words reinforce this view: "I listen to what a woman has to say, if she ever mentions it, about why she decided to perform in AV. Otherwise, it's none of my business."

Akasaka's reluctance to know the truth is shared among other directors I've interviewed. Thirty-year-old Honda Makoto, who recently quit directing adult videos, shared his thoughts:

> There is nothing good about knowing the truth. We can do only so much even if we find out there is some wrongdoing. Why bother if the truth depresses everyone and disables your ability to do your main job?

Honda's intentional oversight, as well as Akasaka's willfully limited scope, suggests that a tacit don't-ask-don't-tell policy exists in the AV industry. Honda stressed that AV directors are not in the position of asking how a woman has been recruited into the AV industry. "It is taboo. Our job is to make a video, not make enemies of talent agencies, given the fact that our job relies on their supply of actresses," Honda added.

Honda quit his AV job when his in-laws pressured him to change his occupation for his daughter. Despite my expectation that he could more openly share what he knew about women performers than those who still worked in the AV industry, he was still hesitant. "I only have a vague idea about AV actresses. I'm afraid of categorizing them out of pity." I pressed him on what about them made him feel pity. "There are certainly a lot of girls who have self-inflicted scars on their wrists," Honda said. "I feel sorry for them." He paused, searching for the right words. "I would definitely try to stop it if I found any of my female friends wanting to become an AV actress." The sacrifice, he reasoned, was far greater than anything they could gain out of such a short-lived career.

I asked, "How did you reconcile your personal feelings and occupational obligations?" "Um . . . ," he answered, "they were separate issues in my mind." He focused specifically on drawing beauty from actresses rather than letting his personal feelings intervene.

"Once filming was scheduled, I devoted myself to working with the actress collaboratively to produce a good video," he said.

"Did your passion to depict women beautifully clear your mind of any responsibility for their experiences?" I asked again.

"A subtle unease never vanished completely." He continued, "I think every director has that moment where they question whether it's right or not to turn a nice girl into an AV actress."

"When did this occur to you?" I asked.

"A sense of guilt hit me, especially, when I became empathetic toward a nice girl with a future."

His face clouded up. "But I realized a guilty conscience compromised my work and resulted in producing an unsatisfactory video and making the actress unhappy. Why bother continuing your work if you make everybody unhappy?"

For this reason, Honda did his best to shed his personal feelings and focus on creating the best possible picture. However, his guilty conscience deepened as his daughter grew up and he eventually quit AV. Thanks to skills he cultivated through AV direction and production, he now freelances producing music videos, television commercials, and promotional films.

While most AV directors remain guardians of their own territory, a few have traversed other fields in AV production, starting out as AV actors themselves. These men had a different take on the issue of forced AV performance. Suzuki Seiji, a fifty-four-year-old director, former AV actor, and talent agent, highlighted how his lack of knowledge about adult videos confused him early on. Born in 1966 in a Tokyo suburb, Suzuki started filming and starring in his own 8mm *pink eiga* (pink films), a Japanese-style soft-core film genre, when he was a high school student. One of his films won a prize at a 1984 film festival. Following his award, he was invited to observe how studio pink films are produced and was occasionally asked to act in a film. Pink films required covering up genitals and pretending to have sex on camera. This worked on screen because private parts were fuzzed out with a mosaic anyway under the movie industry's self-regulated obscenity rules. One day Suzuki was invited to an AV production, where he was asked to briefly appear in the video. Assuming it was the same thing as a pink film, he did not think twice about it. Suddenly, an actress began performing fellatio on his penis, and he realized that he had consented to something he did not expect. Confused yet feeling aroused, he ended up having sex with the actress on camera. "Knowing very little about the technical details," he said, "I had no idea what I had consented to." He learned afterward that some directors allowed sexual intercourse in AV, while most directors at the time adopted the obscenity rule that applied to pink films.

It became clear to him that those without industry knowledge were in danger of involuntarily consenting to things they didn't understand or expect. Suzuki also pointed out the gendered aspects of this danger. Male actors, he said, usually enter the AV industry after watching adult videos extensively, but female performers do not have the same level of familiarity. In the internet age, he acknowledged that more women have easier access to AV. "This doesn't mean, though, that they know what they would be made to do even if they willingly sign performance contracts," Suzuki said.

As discussed in the previous chapter, talent agents take advantage of women's naïvete about AV performance and its social consequences when they solicit their consent. AV directors' willful ignorance of this situation, as well as the tacit don't-ask-don't-tell policy in the industry, eclipses gray areas. In this context, what Kozai referred to as brainwashing in chapter 1 and Sato called miscommunication in chapter 2 exemplify structural violence embedded in the gendered knowledge gap and the have-nots' vulnerability. Kozai's claim that she agreed only to model in a sexy image video, not AV, resembles Suzuki's experience consenting only to appearing in a pink film. Sato's complaints about the violation of her personal boundaries (e.g., ejaculation in her body and an unexpected rape scene) also resemble Suzuki's unease about the unexpected fellatio. None of them, however, revealed their stories until years later. As such, this kind of structural violence, induced by involuntary consent, is normalized to the extent that it is taken for granted as "miscommunication" or "confusion"—an accident of everyday life. Thus, simply asking for a woman performer's consent won't solve the fundamental problem of ambiguity in the process of contracting for AV work. It only reinforces the political fiction of the consenting subject, a façade the AV industry is intent on maintaining.

Aware of the fundamental problem of consent, Suzuki is caught up in his own dilemma as an AV director: righteous indignation about issues he knows well, and his contractual obligation to direct videos for AV makers. It is not solely his decision to stop a camera when he senses something is wrong with an actress. He could technically cease shooting, but he then has to face consequences. If he fails to deliver a master tape by the deadline agreed to on in his contract, he would be paid neither for the work already completed nor the cost related to canceling the shoot. He is, after all, a freelancer who works for video makers. If he gained notoriety for canceling and causing "trouble," he could be blacklisted. Significantly, AV production entails both women's sexual labor and video makers' capital. It is the directors' job to use these resources and create videos. It is, however, not that easy on set. Suzuki shared his frustrations as a director; he has worked with a few actresses who seemingly enjoyed themselves on previous shoots but suddenly became reluctant to perform. "I think everyone has a moment to think twice. I understand that. But I also understand how it frustrates directors who work under time pressure, and that irritates them. They would wonder why she can't do things she's had no problem with in the past." Suzuki pointed out that this was a situation where a director would likely pressure her to complete her work. According to him, it is expected that the director will give her the necessary push. Otherwise, directors won't survive in today's profit-seeking AV industry.

Without clear guidelines from video makers, Suzuki claimed that most directors would be too afraid of repercussions to do anything besides silencing actresses and completing the assigned filming. He recently brought this issue to a producer at a major video maker in hopes of a top-down reform, asking him to clarify a hired director's responsibilities on set. A few weeks later, the producer reported back that the company decided to remain "low key." Suzuki's request for clearer guidelines was declined. He told me that he was just a director for hire who was caught between video makers' business interests and actresses' bodily needs. "What I can do is limited. It's, after all, video makers who pay us, not actresses," Suzuki said.

To secure sexual labor, AV makers must obtain women's consent and have them agree to a performance contract. The irony is that, as discussed in the previous chapter, the contract itself is not enforceable by law because sexual labor is a type of work that cannot be coerced against one's will. In other words, performance contracts do not bind performers to AV work. This is why talent agents are in charge of reliably delivering women to film sets—or handing them over to directors, one could say. If talent agents provide excessive emotional labor and wholesale management service, video directors employ their own methods to please women and create a "nice" work environment. All efforts in the industry are directed toward the completion of AV production. AV makers' hesitation to set clear industry guidelines for such a case that AV actresses become reluctant to deliver what they agreed to could be indicative of maintaining such a situation unimaginable and keeping a walk-away option unthinkable. The bottom line is that AV production stands on the built-in fragility that actresses could freely walk away from their signed contracts anytime if they knew the facts and exercised their rights.

The AV directors I met all contribute to further obscuring actresses' access to this scheme when they knowingly focus only on what they like doing—*monodukuri* (producing things). Pleasing actresses on set may put them temporarily at ease and help directors get better results on camera. But it does not address the systemic harm actresses face within the compartmentalized infrastructure of the AV industry. Out of their domain of accountability, directors overlook structural violence and remain loyal only to their employers—video makers—whose priority lies in profit making, not fair labor practices.

## "WE, AV ACTORS, ARE CLOSER TO THE PRODUCTION SIDE"

Male actors, who work under AV directors, are indispensable players in AV production—even though their role is often supportive in bed and their positionality is ambiguous in the production setting. They are not at the center of attention, though they are generally afforded a dominant role over actresses in sexual scenes. They are expected to function primarily as a conduit to bring directors' intentions into being. How do they understand their roles and positions? To what extent are they aware of AV actresses' concerns about involuntary consent to AV performance and the social stigma attached to it?

Most AV actors, called *AV danyū*, engage in AV production or consumption before they become performers. Some become AV actors by being casually asked to perform minor film roles while engaging in AV production as assistant directors or other assistant jobs on sets. But most apply for the sex work themselves. They have typically enjoyed watching AV and became interested in getting involved in productions. Finding job information in magazines or on the internet, they directly contact video directors or makers, not talent agencies, about job openings. Unlike AV actresses, they work as independent freelancers who are hired and paid by video directors directly; neither talent agencies nor commission fees are involved. AV actors' guarantee is fixed per scene and based on their classification categories: top stars make from 50,000 to 70,000 yen (US$500–700) per scene; midrange actors, 15,000 to 30,000 yen; *shinjin* (new faces), 10,000 to 15,000 yen; and the so-called *shiru danyū*, faceless "semen actors" whose sole role is to ejaculate on actresses, make 5,000 to 7,000 yen plus sometimes an extra 1,000 yen for public transportation. Actors typically start at the very bottom. It takes an "ejaculator" a few successful gigs to prove his potency in front of a group of people under the bright lights before he is promoted as a "new face." Growing into an *ichininmae* (fully qualified) actor entails more than 1,000 scenes performed over a one- to three-year span, on average. According to my interlocutors, there are only about sixty to seventy male actors who make a living in the industry. Once qualified, male actors usually do not face the rapid drop in market value and short-lived occupation like their female counterparts.

Motohashi Tamotsu, in his mid-thirties, is a top male AV star, performing in at least one porno scene every single day and making 20,000,000 yen (US$200,000) annually. Top-tier actors are well known for their ability to break the ice and bring scenes to life, skills Motohashi described as a "combination of pleasing women like male hosts (paid companions) and providing sex like male escorts." In addition to people skills, skilled actors are equipped with a wide range of knowledge about camera work, visual effects of certain body movements, and how to create action on screen without hurting actresses. This is one of the biggest differences between male and female performers who perform active and passive sexual roles on camera. With directors' nonverbal cues, male actors calculate bodily positions carefully, lead women smoothly, and control the best timing for climactic ejaculation. Their role is akin to male ballroom dancers, who lead female partners to create dazzling moves on the dance floor. Thus, they are an important asset for video directors to shoot erotic spectacles. "Even though [we] appear on the screen with AV actresses, we [AV actors] are closer to the production side," Motohashi said.

Performing in AV used to be, and is still, a dream job for Motohashi, who has long fantasized about the AV industry as a "fun and pleasant place." Born in 1979 in a Tokyo neighboring prefecture, he graduated from one of the most prestigious high schools in Japan, which is famous for their placement of students at the University of Tokyo. Despite his good academic record, he did not share the same ambition as his classmates of going to the University of Tokyo and getting a high-paying job in government, banking, or academia. He began feeling isolated at school and escaped by watching adult videos. Upon graduation from high school, he applied for an AV job he found in a classified ad in the back pages of a dirty magazine. Dialing the number, he recalled nervously shivering, as if he were about to do something fatal, as much as he got excited about the possibility that the telephone line would connect him to his dream job. He hung up the phone to think twice about what he was doing. But his sexual appetite—"I was desperate for sex"—pushed him to book a job interview. He clearly remembers feeling as if he were on a "one-way journey to a world from which [he] could never come back again" while on the train to his interview.

Motohashi's metaphor of a "one-way journey" sounded much like female actresses' expression of "crossing a line." Once they cross the line, they know that they cannot go back. In this respect, both male and female performers may go on a similar guilt trip to the other side of the shore, though, as I will elaborate shortly, they face gendered consequences. Even though Motohashi enjoyed his work, he could not shake off a sense of guilt for a long time. Looking back, he thinks he had internalized social stigma, thinking of sex work as shameful. Worse, his parents found out what he was doing soon after he became a fully qualified actor. His father confronted him, saying, "Shame on you! I didn't raise you to do this kind of thing." His father's hostility made him realize that he was living in *hikage no sekai* (a world in the shade, or underground world) from a normative perspective. But his family's sense of shame in his occupation also reinforced his belief that *hinata no sekai* (the world in the sun), meaning mainstream society, was superficial and vain—all about keeping face. For him, living in the underground was more truthful to his heart. Motohashi explained:

> In the world in the sun, titles and social status are everything. People live as corporate employees, academic scholars, and husbands and wives, for example. They remain in these roles when having sex, too, as if taking no clothes off in bed. In the underground world, naked humans encounter other naked humans. We have nothing to hide. We have sex once without knowing occupations and even real names.

Motohashi thinks those living in the underground world can be honest about what they like and dislike on a visceral level. "People in mainstream society," he said, "tend to be intimidated by revealing their 'faces behind masks' or private selves, but I think it is an effect of false pretenses." Once he began thinking this way, his sense of shame lessened as simply a cultural construct in the "sunny" world. He no longer cares about how other people judge him, though he used to be easily bothered by hypocrites who enjoy watching AV but look down on people who perform in it.

Motohashi's swift transformation is, I argue, gendered. Although male performers are not completely free from social stigma, they seem to experience it much less intensely than women. This is because the social perception of the gendered division of sexual labor creates a buffer against the stigma attached to men's sex work. In the dominant script of heterosexuality, men play an active role as initiator and doer since sex is understood as something done to women by men.[7] As a result, men remain in the position of self-control and get credit for their potency. In contrast, women performers are subject to a masculinist sexual script that degrades and eroticizes them. Conjuring the mixed feelings that AV evokes, AV makers and users alike describe how women are depicted with expressions like, "What a pity that such a pretty girl is made to endure *konna koto* (such [horrible or embarrassing] things)," or transform into an object of shameful sex. They emphasize women's passivity, humiliation, and devaluation. A similar sentiment might be expressed toward inexperienced men who appear in gay porn videos, but not usually toward male actors in mainstream heterosexual adult videos. Within this gendered sexual script, the inner conflicts of heterosexual male actors become more manageable than those felt by AV actresses, whose human dignity is forever compromised by the sex acts they perform. Reinforcing this view, Motohashi commented on his process of shedding the dishonor he once felt: "I have probably given up what's considered to be socially respectful. Respect based on superficial factors like social status, fame, and credentials certainly does not make me happy."

Motohashi understands his marginalized status in mainstream society, but he can manage it with his own brand of masculinist logic. He is "choosing" an alternate life path and thus remains in control of his destiny, at a psychic level. By the same token, he does not have to strive to retrieve his dignity as women performers do. For heterosexual men, sex is not associated with a loss of dignity.

One's "social status" is thus only a superficial thing unless the loss of it causes unbearable harm—a gendered privilege that most women in AV can't take for granted. Motohashi feels lucky to be a male actor who is paid for what he enjoys most. "You have to pay young women to have sex. But I'm paid to screw pretty girls one after another!" This masculinist logic is his mantra. Whenever he questions what he does for a living, he always goes back to his original motive. "You must be desperate for sex . . . after all, it comes down to your sexual appetite. You have to be sexually aroused. You can't fake it. Worshiping money doesn't get you hard." For this reason, he maintains his hunger for women and lives his life accordingly. He is abstinent from sex in his private life, neither having a girlfriend nor utilizing commercial sex. He believes that he would lose his sexual appetite if he had easy access to women. "I'm sure that other actors have their own methods. Mine is to worship female genitals wholeheartedly on set," Motohashi said. With this method, he has been performing sex day after day, without any break, for the past fifteen years.

This is one area wherein male and female performers experience different kinds of social pressure based on their sex roles within what Adrienne Rich calls "compulsory heterosexuality."[8] Men's role requires self-motivation to get aroused, initiate sex, and control scenes. Potency is a must-have condition. "Women can pretend to enjoy sex on camera, but men can't. We have to physically showcase sex drive with an erection and ejaculation," Motohashi emphasized. For this reason, male actors are most afraid of what is called *tachi machi* (literally waiting time for erection) on set. When this happens, they make others wait and cause a production delay. And the longer they struggle with erectile difficulties, the more pressure, anxiety, and embarrassment builds, further increasing the burden of achieving an erection. Male performers' fears revolve around their sexual performance, while as chapter 2 demonstrates, AV actresses' anxieties are based mainly in identity reveal and social stigma.

Reflecting their less-stigmatized status, men's pay is far less than what actresses make. Male actors are also paid fixed rates for their sexual labor, whereas female actresses' market value fluctuates widely. Motohashi, a top-ranking actor, is paid 50,000 yen (US$500) per scene, equivalent to what the lowest-ranked *kikaku* actress receives. He books thirty to forty scenes a month, each of which can be as short as a few hours to an entire day. Although the annual income is high, he is concerned about his future. "This is a short-lived occupation. The work ends if you ruin your health or develop erectile difficulties. So, you want to earn as much as possible when you can," he said. While top-ranked AV actresses are paid ten to fifteen times more than Motohashi, their shelf life is far shorter. Most *tantai* actresses secure this highest-ranked status only for their debut videos and lose luster immediately after, descending to *kikaku tantai* or *kikaku* ranks. Two-thirds of actresses are replaced with new faces annually.[9] Despite this gendered labor precarity, male actors, including top-ranked veterans, often refer to their employment as "day labor," conveying no job security or benefits.

Interestingly, none of the AV actresses I encountered described their far more precarious job situation in the same way. This perceptional gap made me think of the intersection of gender, class, and labor. "Day labor" connotes lower-class physical labor for men, in contrast to full-time middle-class employment; whereas for women, there is no reference point equivalent to day labor. Women's labor precarity and lower-class status have long been taken for granted. Stigma attached to women's sexual labor is also normalized by sexual double standards. Male actors may not register their privileges.

Unlike AV actresses I interviewed, they often refer to their sexual labor as just another job.

Yamaguchi Yoshihisa, a fifty-one-year-old veteran performer, said, "Performing in AV isn't much different from working at a construction site, though the content of the job is completely different." Originally from Kyushu, a southern island of Japan, Yamaguchi came to Tokyo in the late 1980s for college. To earn extra money, he soon started part-time work in construction, making about 9,000 yen (US$90) a day and working twice a week. One day a construction worker friend invited him to join him on a nude modeling job, where he would only have to pretend to have sex for a magazine shoot. Yamaguchi at first said no; he was too shy to do anything in front of people. But at his friend's insistence, he decided to give it a try and see what it was like to pretend to have sex for a couple of hours. The pay was 15,000 yen (US$150), five times better than his construction job—though as Yamaguchi learned, the work turned out to be far more psychologically demanding than he realized. "It requires a hundred times more mental energy," Yamaguchi laughed. Unlike the construction site, where he often would carelessly drop things, in AV he had to learn how to treat women gently, create a nice flow, and bring life to the picture. He must make himself presentable to his performance partner; avoiding eating smelly food, for instance, is a must before shooting. He thoroughly cleans his body, brushing his teeth, scrubbing under his armpits, and even soaping in between his toes. He also shaves closely and has his fingernails and toenails clipped short and filed meticulously. His goal is to present his body with "no taste, no smell," and cause no harm. "This job entails careful attention since what you are dealing with is human beings who have feelings and emotions and react to what you do," Yamaguchi explained.

Despite his professional attitude and veteran status in AV, Yamaguchi still equates AV work with day labor due to the "loose" nature of the work. He is one of a few AV actors who have played minor roles in mainstream movies. "Performing in AV is completely different from acting in feature films in terms of seriousness, intensity, and depth," he said. Feature film actors are expected to fully prepare for shoots by understanding the plot and developing characters. For such gigs, Yamaguchi carefully reads a script days before shooting and memorizes his lines so that he can focus on his on-set acting. By contrast, for AV, he usually receives a video script on the spot, often just saying what's written out loud on camera. "Nobody cares about the quality of acting as long as sexual intercourse is filmed. So, nobody prepares for anything," he sighed.

For most male actors, performing in AV does not advance their acting career beyond the "AV village." Even top stars never exceed 50,000 yen (US$500) per scene, nor do their roles and names occupy a major place in the credits. No matter how many videos they may appear in, male performers remain shadow figures in adult video.[10]

For both men and women, a career in AV is short-lived and precarious. AV actresses, at the center of pornographic entertainment, enjoy relatively better pay and greater admiration than male actors. But their sex role, which revolves around youthful beauty and adaptability, subjects them to the male gaze and popular demand, which determine their market value. Thus, women's career longevity in AV depends on others—in this case, male AV users who judge their appearance, performance, and personality—whereas men's career trajectory is based on their potency alone. Said differently, AV actresses' labor precarity is much more complex and mediated by multiple factors. AV actresses' work is arranged by their talent agents, paid by video makers, and evaluated by consumers. Meanwhile, male actors' work is directly provided and paid for by AV directors. It is much clearer who their boss is. As such, it is virtually unthinkable for them to go against a director's commands and stop their sexual performance, even if they sense their partner's unwillingness to engage in it. They risk losing their job if they disturb AV production. "Our job is so trivial," Yamaguchi said. "We are exchangeable and expendable." He understands AV actors' positionality, AV directors' responsibility, and AV makers' authority. He also understands talent agencies' difficult task of supplying AV actresses as well as AV actresses' physical and psychological conditions. Worrying too much about others, however, negatively impacts his sexual performance. He instead focuses on his assigned job: the completion of sex scenes. To this end, he tries to flatter the actress so that she feels good about herself and follows his lead on camera; by so doing, he helps the director as much as possible. "In that sense," he confessed, "I would say I'm involved in the [AV] industry's plotting and assisting in coerced performance."

While admitting that male actors are enablers of coerced AV performance, Yamaguchi was ambivalent about the outcome of this seemingly problematic event. In his thirty-five-year AV career and appearances in more than 10,000 videos, he claims to have encountered only a handful of women who were noticeably reluctant to perform. "Women are much more adaptable than men," Yamaguchi said, "So, nobody knows which one will turn out to be a problematic case until it actually happens." His view aligns with other business insiders' observations. Sakai, a veteran talent agent introduced in the previous chapter, also stressed women's adaptability as crucial to untangling knots on set. Nakano, a female talent agent and former actress, reinforced this view in chapter 2. Despite her emotional turmoil the day before her first AV shoot, she was "proud of herself" for admirably managing to deliver what she promised. But women's adaptability is an acquired characteristic often out of necessity, not an innate trait. They are socialized to adapt to a given social environment and perform emotional labor, disguising their mental distress with seemingly joyful attitudes. Women know how to fake it until they make it, despite the psychic consequences.

It is unknown what exactly happens behind their public façade, especially when structural violence is normalized under the guise of women's "adaptability." Being part of the production side, male business insiders—like producers, directors, actors, and talent agents—are members of the masculinist coalition known as the *AV mura* (the AV village). There is a tacit understanding that the entire village lives off of AV actresses, their most valuable commodity. The "rules of the AV village" strictly forbid any male staff or performers to personally get close to these valuable assets and damage them. If a man transgresses this line, he is likely to be punished, even physically beaten. Yamaguchi and the other male actors I interviewed insisted that they must obey these rules and focus only on their own performance. They keep their heads down and remain loyal to their director-bosses. They never reveal to AV actresses how male business actors cooperate among one another to deliver adult videos to the world. It thus takes a village, embedded in AV infrastructures, to persuade women into performing in adult videos. Structural violence against women in the AV industry is therefore perpetuated not by legally bounded contracts and conducts but by socioculturally practiced customs and codes.

## "IT'S BETTER FOR A VIDEO MAKER TO LET A *TANTAI* ACTRESS GO"

The more I learned about the business of AV, the more I came to see that video makers, especially leading companies, function as the capitalist owning class in the industry. They own the means of production and hire everyone else—talent agencies, video directors, and AV performers—to work for them. They also own the commodities and accumulate capital. Nonetheless, they largely remain detached from the production side by outsourcing everything with the exception of casting, budgeting, and marketing. Agreeing with director Suzuki's wishes for top-down reforms, I felt it would be video makers, if anyone, who could initiate any necessary changes since they were at the top of the ecosystem in the "AV village." I approached several video makers for an interview, but my requests were declined; they were highly concerned about how they would be represented amid the heightened critique and scrutiny due to the politicization of the forced performance issue. Toward the end of my fieldwork in 2018, however, I lucked out: thanks to video directors and former producers I met, a handful of employees at a major video maker and owners of small video production companies agreed to talk to me confidentially.

By way of an introduction from Honda, the former AV producer and director featured earlier in this chapter, I met Watanabe Shinya, a thirty-six-year-old chief of casting at Stardust, a leading Japanese AV maker. Watanabe is an early example of a new breed of AV workers who got involved in the industry after graduating from college. (Older generations tend to have no college degree or have worked elsewhere before.) He began his AV career in the mid-2000s when the industry was growing rapidly. By the mid-2010s, several leading companies involved in sex-related commerce—AV, sex toys, and modeling—collectively held an information booth at a job fair at Waseda University, a top private university in Japan, to recruit young creative talent. These companies, including Stardust, presented themselves as innovative "content creators" in the new digital economy, which was at the heart of the Japanese government's growth strategy at that time. Along with advancements in information technology, the Ministry of Economy, Trade, and Industry and the Agency for Cultural Affairs alike attempted to nurture the content industry, systematically promoting animation, gaming, and other media arts. In this sociohistorical context, AV makers presented themselves as part of this developing field and attracted a new breed of college-educated elites like Honda and Watanabe.

In the industry, college graduates at video makers are known as *seifuku gumi* (literally, those who are in uniform, meaning elites in suits and ties). *Seifuku gumi* mainly work out of office buildings, engaging in such intellectual labor as programming, casting, marketing, and other desk work that determines video sales and trends. They are full-time, salaried employees with full benefits. They are not only physically distanced from the AV production line. They are also socioculturally distanced from the line workers—street scouts, talent agents, and video directors, who have less prestigious backgrounds and engage in physical and emotional labor to secure raw materials and produce commodities.

Dressed in a dark business suit, Watanabe politely greeted me as I entered a meeting room at Stardust's sleek seven-story office building in central Tokyo. He introduced himself as a casting chief and video producer, someone who liaisons between video directors and talent agencies to produce marketable videos. His main job is to create storylines for *tantai* actresses—from their AV debut to "graduation" from exclusive model contracts with Stardust—and hire directors to produce videos that support them. His company aims to create AV idols and sell a series of their videos, not just a single video, to users. In this way, video users will enjoy actresses' character development based on their storylines and escalating sexual acts over time. At the same time, the company profits from loyal video users, the theory goes. Watanabe oversees this kind of creative, intellectual labor, which is crucial to both AV production and promotion. It comes down to a casting director's hunch to predict whether a new model can make it and how long she will last. Watanabe judges a new face's appearance, tolerance for publicity campaigns, and eagerness to perform a wide range of sexual acts. It is not easy for him to assess anyone's future success, however, even though he has been in the business for more than a decade and a half. Despite many unknown factors, he is in the position to determine contractual terms and present them to his company's executive board for approval.

Contract making is, after all, based on the *appearance* of an actress's marketability rather than the *actuality* of it since it deals with future events.[11] "It's my job to create a nice package and make it marketable," Watanabe said. "In a word, marketability itself is a product." Keeping his company's profit-driven goals in mind, he develops storylines based on interviews with a few dozen women a month, newly recruited and supplied by talent agencies as *tantai*-class models. He also conducts his own thorough inspection through interviews and test screenings. "I'm always thinking of a storyline and marketing strategy I could come up with while interviewing and observing a woman," Watanabe said. The more novel the storyline, the better the chance that her videos will sell. In this pursuit of novelty, he asks personal questions about her sexual experiences, boyfriends, and hobbies. After a roughly half-hour interview, he brings her to another room for a test screening, leaving her agent behind. While explaining this step, he opened his laptop and turned it to me. On the screen, a topless young woman held her breasts up with her hands.

Watanabe explained that he asked her to do this to assess whether her breasts were implants. Based on his instruction, the woman in the screening test then took off her panties and showed her backside. The camera shot her at long range and gradually moved to capture her breasts and hips in close-up. Watanabe was checking her body line and body parts from different camera angles.

To my surprise, the interaction between Watanabe and the woman was very business-like throughout the screening test. It seemed like a doctor examining his patient to provide an accurate diagnosis. In contrast to a medical exam, however, Watanabe examines a woman's body to assess her commodity value and make a business deal. I commented that the woman on Watanabe's computer screen demonstrated no sign of shyness or embarrassment. Watanabe explained, "All girls who come for an interview are able to take off their clothes without hesitation." He added that these women are easily desensitized to being uncovered on set. It eventually becomes his job to remind them to cover their private parts and show shyness if they want to maintain their market value. He also shared his own experience dealing with nudity. "I was a bit nervous seeing naked bodies when I first started this job in my early twenties, but I soon found myself completely desensitized. I no longer feel anything. It's just like dealing with vegetables," he laughed. His remarks convinced me that the emotions naked bodies evoke are a social construct; therefore, feelings like embarrassment and nervousness can be undone in a different social setting such as an AV film set.

Gazing back at his computer, Watanabe noted that the young woman on the screen, from the southern Japanese island of Kyushu, succeeded in getting an exclusive model contract with Stardust for a total of three videos. According to him, her appearance is B-class, but her plain and simple personality inspired him to come up with a unique storyline for her: an unsophisticated girl, working at a local souvenir shop for tourists, meets a city boy and enjoys sexual adventures with him. Watanabe's explanation suggested that a casting team's package proposal for an exclusive model contract strongly influences whether the board will approve it. Watanabe's team determines the contractual terms, including the performance guarantee and the number of videos to be made.

During exclusive model contract making, a subtle power dynamic plays out between AV makers and talent agencies. Exclusive model contracts are uniquely distinctive: only a handful of top-tier actresses are offered them. Moreover, only a dozen of the wealthiest AV makers, who can afford to own special labels to showcase their top models, offer these prestigious contracts. An exclusive model contract typically binds a model to performing in AV once a month so that the video maker releases her videos monthly up to the number she is contracted to produce. The maker guarantees high-quality videos and publicity campaigns, featuring the model exclusively, in exchange for the highest possible pay for the top model. For an AV maker, committing to an exclusive model contract for multiple videos is costly when the model does not become a breakout star. At the same time, it is also a lost opportunity if a video maker turns her down and loses a great business opportunity to a competitor.[12] As such, talent agencies who supply highly marketable top-ranking models have great bargaining power, especially when they receive offers from numerous video makers. Obviously, AV makers want to make a small "investment"—minimal wages and videos to contract—for maximum return. Meanwhile, talent agencies want to secure the largest possible performance guarantee and video slate to produce so that they can stabilize their models' income and their own commission fees. This is the turf where different interests are subtly played out and fought over.

The power dynamic on this turf is historically contingent on the supply and demand of AV actresses. In the past, when adult video DVDs sold millions and yet the supply of quality models was scarce, talent agencies had much more leverage. Video makers offered more lucrative exclusive model contracts, such as a few million yen per performance for ten to twelve videos. Today, with video sales declining because of streaming and the supply of young would-be models increasing, even a leading video maker like Stardust can no longer afford such lucrative contract packages. The highest-selling label at Stardust contracts six videos per model on average nowadays, and lesser labels can offer only three at most. Pay for performers has also been cut by roughly 30 percent from the early 2000s. Like their competitors, Stardust increasingly commits to the so-called debut-video-only deal, meaning an exclusive performance contract limited to just the model's first video. These cuts reflect changing consumer behaviors and shrinking AV sales. For example, Watanabe's company estimates a total of 5,000 video sales for a *tantai* debut video and only half or less for the same actress's second video. "Most video users still buy *tantai* models' debut videos to check new faces. Otherwise, they just enjoy online adult content for free," said Watanabe. Debut video sales are also declining today. "Bootleg copies are up for free on the internet, even on the same day the original videos are released," he lamented.

Changing the subject, I asked him to give his perspective on the Tokyo district court case where a talent agency sued a woman who requested premature termination of an exclusive performance contract (as I discuss in chapter 1). Watanabe lowered his voice. "I shouldn't say this out loud," he said, "but I would honestly feel a little bit relieved if I learned that our exclusive model, who performed in a couple of videos, says she wants to quit without completing the rest of her contracted videos. I would say to her, 'Please, go ahead.' It wouldn't occur to me at all that we would need to charge her a penalty fee." This is not simply because Watanabe is a nice person but because it best serves his company's profitability. He went on:

> As far as profit making goes, it's better for a video maker to let a *tantai* actress go as soon as possible. Otherwise, we need to continue paying her the same amount of money for her appearance in the rest of the contracted videos. I think it is the talent agency that is in the position to be frustrated about the [damage done by] the cancellation of an exclusive model contract.

Watanabe's comments suggest his well-sheltered position at a leading AV maker and the power imbalance between AV makers (the employer) and talent agencies (the employee). It is not overtly hierarchical, but the risk of damage is not equally distributed either. Watanabe's sense of relief itself manifests his company's greater privilege in the stratified AV ecosystem. Just like AV directors, who do not have to get their hands dirty to secure a supply of AV actresses, AV makers can afford to pay talent agencies to do the "dirty work," making them responsible for supply failures (actresses) or cleanup of the messes actresses make. Talent agencies' frustrations about damage control and the use of penalty fees are indicative of their structurally vulnerable position in relation to wealthier AV makers. The capitalist owning class, in this case influential AV makers, will simply take advantage of the existing infrastructure favorable to the protection of their economic interests.

The diversity in size among AV makers, however, complicates a simplistic view of the class-based power dynamism between the employer and the employee. While a handful of large video makers can afford profitable *tantai* actresses whose performance guarantee could be over 800,000 yen (US$8,000) per video, most small makers instead hire affordable second- and third-tier models. Ishii Yoji, in his mid-forties, is an AV director and owner of Blue Sky, a company he established in 2004 to specialize in outdoor scenes, peep shots, and exhibitionism. Initially working in AV distribution, he realized how profitable it would be to produce adult videos at the turn of the twenty-first century. But he soon became aware that Blue Sky could not compete against larger, wealthier makers. Producing low-budget videos, his company had to find its own niche. "So, we use external beauty like outdoor scenes—mountains, riversides, and hot springs in snow—to compensate for what we lack," Ishii said. His company also maximizes the value of its videos quantitatively, displaying multiple sexual acts featuring multiple models in a video. Ishii's experience handling non-*tantai* models is thus quite different from the larger makers' exclusive relationships with top actresses. Outdoor filming requires lowering his expectations for an actress's appearance and performance in exchange for more challenging and demanding shoots. In the outdoors, sunburn, bug bites, and unpredictable weather are inevitable. It also takes longer to get to a shooting location. According to Ishii, a workday easily stretches to fifteen to twenty hours, including a commute to a location outside Tokyo. Nonetheless, his production budget is roughly half that of a large AV maker. To lower production costs, Ishii's company hires a *kikaku tantai* actress for 400,000 to 500,000 yen (US$4,000–5,000) or a couple of *kikaku* actresses for 80,000 to 150,000 yen (US$800–1,500) each.

Small video makers like Ishii's face a double challenge today: budget cuts due to fewer DVD sales and flexible labor accommodations based on the industry's new guidelines. Ishii used to pay actresses much more than what he does but has had to cut back to accommodate declining video sales. In addition, he faces much stricter guidelines in the wake of the AV Human Rights Ethics Committee's new rules for standardized contract forms, cancellation policies, and product recalls.[13] The Committee, established in 2017 in response to the politicization of forced AV performance, mandated the use of a standardized form of contract whereby the full performance guarantee is disclosed and a cancellation policy with no penalty fees is spelled out. The Committee also created a "five-year rule" through which former actresses can request to recall videos released more than five years ago. Ishii generally welcomes these reforms implemented at the beginning of 2018, but he is also frustrated by unexpected outcomes small makers need to absorb.

In the past, AV makers typically charged talent agencies last-minute cancellation fees to cover the damage to an AV production budget, including studio bookings, makeup artists, and production crews. As it turned out, talent agencies inflated these penalty fees and passed the cost along to their actresses—who, as the Tokyo district court case exemplified, would be coerced into performing to avoid paying the exorbitant fees. The AV Human Rights Ethics Committee, which consists of legal scholars, criminologists, and lawyers appointed by major AV makers, proposed a standardized performance contract to free AV actresses from any cancellation or penalty fees. This seemingly positive change for AV actresses has negatively impacted Ishii's small business. Two film shoots canceled recently within the span of a few months put his company under the burden of paying for the damages. He is now afraid of having more frequent cancellations. Ishii raised his voice. "The Ethics Committee's guidelines are based on large makers' exclusive model contracts, not taking into consideration small makers' needs."

Ishii laments the lack of more nuanced industry guidelines about new cancellation policies. The AV Human Rights Ethics Committee simply made an announcement that actresses should be free of any penalties or fees related to cancellation, suggesting that video makers and talent agencies figure out how to make up the lost revenue. While a prestigious video maker can pressure a talent agency to cover costs, a small maker cannot do the same. "Smaller makers struggle to secure a stable supply of cheaper actresses under less favorable shooting conditions and, therefore, need to maintain good relationships with agencies," Ishii explained. As a result, he has had to accept unacceptable business deals and pay the price. Recently, a *kikaku tantai* model he hired for 400,000 yen (US$4,000) did not show up at the appointed start time. So he contacted her agency and learned that she had responded to none of their calls. He was offered a substitute, which he took to avoid a costly last-minute cancellation. Receiving the substitute a few hours later, he was disappointed that she was not even close to the booked actress in terms of appearance and performance quality. He assumed that the agency had sent a *kikaku* actress who was available on such short notice. In his mind, he was ripped off. Moreover, he found out later that the model he originally booked slept in and felt too embarrassed to pick up the phone; meanwhile, her agent was reluctant to do anything about it. Under the new AV Human Rights Ethics Committee rules, actresses can quit any time for any reason without repercussions—so the agent was afraid of angering the actress and losing her.

The power dynamic between AV makers and talent agencies is not monolithic. While AV makers are at the top of the industry's ecosystem, there are hierarchies among AV makers themselves. While larger and wealthier makers can afford "investment" in top-class actresses, publicity campaigns, and strategic marketing, smaller makers must seek alternatives and attempt to maximize their profits with limited profit margins. From smaller makers' perspective, the fundamental problem that AV actresses suffer from roots in the corrupt relationship between major video makers and talent agencies. "A talent agency and video maker share a common interest in persuading a pretty girl to become a highly profitable *tantai* actress," Ishii said. The fewer restrictions she imposes on her publicity and sexual performance on camera, the more profitable she is. He inferred that talent agencies persuade their top-class models to remove restrictions as much as possible even though the models prefer lower publicity to protect their confidentiality; video makers produce and promote their products relentlessly, even if it puts actresses under higher risk of identity reveal. Ishii suggested that greedy agencies and makers take advantage of naïve women and bind them to exclusive model contracts. Ishii insisted that women must be free of this kind of contract bondage.

Admitting that small video makers may put non-*tantai* actresses in demanding shooting conditions for much less pay, Ishii welcomed some regulations to protect workers' rights. Commenting on the 2018 reforms in the AV industry, like other business insiders I met, Ishii admitted that the new rules and policies have brought some good changes that would protect actresses. By the same token, he was skeptical about the industry's loose definition of forced performance and its response to it through self-regulated cancellation policies. "It doesn't make any sense that an actress, who has signed a performance contract, is responsible for nothing. What's the point of making a contract if she freely fails to deliver what she has agreed upon without any consequences?" Ishii said, shrugging his shoulders. "Honestly," he continued, "I'm confused by the notion of forced performance, which can be essentially anything and everything based on AV actresses' subjective perceptions." To elaborate this point, he shared his observation of how AV actresses casually weaponize the term to tease—and potentially challenge—him as director and, by extension, his company. Due to the nature of sometimes harsh, demanding outdoor shoots, he insists that he has been accommodating actresses' bodily needs flexibly by trading what's written in the script for what they would be willing to do. If an actress shared that she was experiencing genital discomfort, for instance, he would substitute other sexual acts for intercourse. But, he says, it has become increasingly difficult to make such changes, as if calling off production is the only option to completely avoid problems. "No matter how much I try to take actresses' needs into consideration, they tease me by joking, 'Isn't that forced performance?' I feel anything can be taken as 'forced performance' nowadays," he sighed.

While listening to Ishii, I recalled Watanabe's comment: "Better for a video maker to let a *tantai* actress go as soon as possible." The haves—major AV makers like Stardust, who sport expert legal knowledge and plenty of capital—can swiftly adapt to the industry's one-size-fits-all rules to "protect" actresses especially when expensive *tantai* actresses are past their peak. In contrast, the have-nots, who are less equipped financially and juridically, struggle dealing with upper-handed talent agents and non-*tantai* actresses. This struggle, which essentially trickles down to AV actresses at the bottom of the industry's food chain, is not a sign toward social justice but a byproduct of finding the middle ground within the self-regulating industry.

## "AN ALLIANCE OF MIDDLE-AGED MEN TO . . . PROTECT THEIR VESTED RIGHTS"

During my 2018 interview of criminologist Kawai Mikio, who serves on the AV Human Rights Ethics Committee as an intellectual advisor and board member, he acknowledged that these changes won't solve problems completely but believes they are better than nothing. "Policy changes are a result of adjusting differences of opinion and finding a middle ground," Kawai said. "Finding a middle ground is a good Japanese convention, though it is often criticized for its leniency toward the industry's business interests rather than victims and vulnerable populations." From his scholarly perspective, Kawai reminded me of the ways that the issue of forced AV performance emerged and how ineffective policy making would be if nobody complies. In his view, large video maker *seifuku gumi* elites like Watanabe constantly recruit new bodies and strategize their marketing to promote video sales amid declining video sales. On the one hand, AV has gained more mainstream currency, attracting many young women to perform. On the other hand, sex work is still stigmatized, causing inner conflicts and mental distress among those who engage in porno. It is within this context that, as Kawai stressed, the issue of forced AV performance became politicized as a threat to young Japanese women in the mid-2010s.

Situating the larger picture of forced AV performance in this sociohistorical context, Kawai summarized three main problems AV actresses bring to the AV Human Rights Ethics Committee for consultation: the most common involves performance guarantees; the next, requests to recall old videos; and finally, the rarer cases of actual forced performance. Kawai, who has investigated some guarantee-related issues, blames customary practices surrounding how the most valuable *tantai* actresses are paid. The video maker and the talent agency, on behalf of the actress, agree on a performance guarantee, which the maker pays to the agency. In other words, the maker simply pays the agreed sum of money and leaves the agency to take care of paying a "fair" share to the actress; the specific amount she'll be paid is not noted in the contract.[14] In an extreme case reported to the Committee, Kawai said that a *tantai* actress, who used to be a television celebrity, was paid 1,000,000 yen (US$10,000) without being notified of her full performance guarantee, which turned out to be 50,000,000 yen (US$500,000). "Only 2 percent of what she earned!" Kawai exclaimed, as his eyes widened.[15]

Inadequate compensation aside, Kawai pointed out that actual forced AV performance itself was rare; nonetheless, upset actresses loosely used this politicized notion to recall their videos. According to him, what really bothers AV actresses is not sexual performance itself but their treatment on sets, which, as I discuss in chapters 2 and 3, quickly deteriorates as their commodity value declines. "In the beginning, when they are most valuable," Kawai said, "they are treated well, like a VIP. But soon [they are] treated like a disposable commodity. As a result, they come to realize that they are being exploited." He thinks these disgruntled actresses retrospectively claim that they were forced to perform. My interview with Sato Jun (in chapter 2) reinforced this point in that she became resentful when she learned about her unexpectedly early call time that involved internal ejaculation. Reflecting back, she angrily said to me, "I couldn't stop thinking that I was, after all, a disposable commodity to them," and confessed that she could have "filed a legal case against [her] agency regarding this incident if it actually happened as it was intended."

Another related issue that the AV Human Rights Ethics Committee handles today is the internet, especially easy access to free sample videos. "Nobody, including the video makers themselves, predicted that old videos would remain in cyberspace for so long and so ubiquitously," Kawai stressed. This situation puts both current and former performers under high risk of identity reveal—but these performers, who have already released their images and copyrights to AV makers, can do nothing about the situation juridically. Kawai hypothesizes that some actresses claim that they were the victims of forced AV performance in order to officially demand that video makers remove their videos from the market—something video makers can request from their distribution companies. From this unofficial business practice, Kawai assumes that the label "forced performance in AV" is not only misleading but also weaponized by some actresses. The women's support group members I interviewed, however, felt that a "forced performance" claim is the only "weapon" available to AV actresses; otherwise, they have no better option to stop the endless circulation of their videos and protect themselves.

For Kawai as well as the AV Human Rights Ethics Committee, implementing new self-regulation rules in the AV industry would be the first step toward complying with the imperative to protect the human rights of AV actresses. The use of a standardized contract form is designed to disclose the full amount of a performance guarantee to AV actresses in hopes that the contract-making process becomes more transparent. In addition, the five-year rule, through which actresses can request the recall of videos released more than five years prior, is one solution for the problem of identity reveal (especially for former actresses) in the internet age. However, Kawai admits that the new rules are, after all, "designed to minimize damage on the industry's side." For example, as Watanabe, the *seifuku gumi* elite, describes above, video makers profit most from newly released videos, not older ones with little market value. So the five-year video recall rule won't affect AV makers' profit margins. As for the full disclosure of performance guarantees, talent agencies get around potential business losses by arranging with video makers to pay "consultation fees" under the table and disclose the rest as the full amount of the performance guarantee in the contract. "There is always a secret pathway to break free from policies and regulations," Kawai said. "So, what policy makers can do is to find a balance of enforcing rules without letting them [go] underground."

Kawai further explained that Japanese legislative reforms are never especially radical because reform officers, who have top-down policy ideas, ask those involved if they can handle new policies on the ground. This is because, according to him, uncomplied policies are no good. Practicable ones are necessary, even if they are not the most ideal to victims and vulnerable populations. Policymaking is one thing, law enforcement is another. Kawai points out that law enforcement in Japan does not take the issue of forced performance seriously, a viewpoint he has gained through his connections with senior officers at the Japanese National Police Agency and his criminologist network. Unlike national security issues, public safety, and criminal cases, civil affairs like sexual commerce, economic exploitation, and social discrimination are located near the bottom of the Agency's priority list, he said, slightly above parking and traffic law enforcement. As a result, it comes down to the industry's own self-regulation to deal with these women's problems.[16] Thus, Kawai stressed that policy changes in Japan's AV industry are destined to be neither radical nor proactive.

Meanwhile, women performers are recruited, hired, screwed, profited from, and circulated throughout different compartmentalized segments of the industry: scouts, talent agencies, AV directors, male actors, video makers, distribution companies, and video users. "It is an 'alliance of middle-aged men,' to safeguard their customary business practices and protect their vested rights in profit seeking," Kawai said. This is factual. There are a few women working in the AV industry but there are literally zero women at the leadership level of decision making for the industry. Indeed, the "AV village" in Japan is largely parallel to a kinship system in which women are exchanged.[17] In her 2005 article, "Stopping the Traffic in Women," Kathy Miriam points out that the exchange of women is not simply about the symbolic transfer of rights but also about politico-economic power relations. "Women's 'sexual energy,'" Miriam argues, "is *appropriated* by johns, pimps and traffickers for the latter's profit and pleasure, analogously (although not perfectly) to the way in which (according to Marxist theory) the worker's 'energy' is appropriated by the capitalists for the latter's profit."[18]

Here, it is important to reach beyond a radical feminist or Marxist binary thinking that largely limits the concept of domination to a particular individual's or group's *power over* subordinated others, such as men's and capitalists' power over women and the proletariat. In Japan's AV industry, as with Japanese society at large, domination is more discursively diffused across lines of gender, class, age, division of labor, and even business sizes, among other factors. There is no black-and-white split between domination and subordination within this ecosystem. Rather, a pecking order among male AV production staff emerges from the matrix of job title, educational background, the type of work performed, and the size of the company these industry men belong to—with younger male actors taking their place at the low end of the hierarchy. In this way, power dynamics are subtly played out and constantly (re)configured. At the same time, structural inequalities enable the haves—those enjoying the privileges of bourgeois masculinity—to legally exploit the have-nots unless the have-nots are overtly violated. Such systemic violence remains perpetuated, invisibly.

Kawai's remarks—"an 'alliance of middle-aged men to protect their vested rights'"—further opened my eyes to the men in and outside Japan's AV industry. The AV enthusiasts I observed at Amatsuka's fan event at the beginning of this book are also middle-aged men who do not exist outside this pecking order. The next chapter sheds light on these male fans, revealing another layer of structural violence embedded within the infrastructure of (involuntary) consent to precarious labor in contemporary Japan's widening disparities.

# 5

## THE MALE FAN

"It's gonna be aerial combat," warned Daigo, a participant on a 2018 round-table about the issue of forced performance in the Japanese AV industry. Daigo worked in adult content distribution for more than a decade before depression and overwork caused him to quit. He still has friends and former colleagues in the industry and keeps up with what's going on in the business. Forty-five years old and single, he is also a big AV fan. His allusion to aerial combat—*kūchūsen* in Japanese—seemed an apt way to describe the issue of forced AV performance: a fight among insiders and outsiders alike about the industry, to win a war of ideas rather than improve AV performers' lives on the ground.

*Mainichi Shimbun* newspaper reporter Nakajima Miki invited me to fa-cilitate the roundtable, which consisted of four male AV fans she connected with through Twitter—each of whom spend, on average, 10,000–20,000 yen (US$100–200) a month on adult content DVDs and fan events. I quickly learned that the participants already knew one another through Twitter, where they disguise their identities using *ura* (hidden) accounts. The social media platform is their main communication hub and a virtual kiosk for fan events. In their late thirties through late forties and casually dressed—T-shirts and sweaters, jeans or slacks, and comfortable sneakers—these men shared how their AV viewing practices shaped their beliefs, values, and viewpoints related to the industry.

Like AV actresses, AV users often remain unknown to the public. I was taken aback and puzzled throughout the roundtable discussion: despite the common perception that AV users' voracious sexual appetites turn women into disposable commodities, the AV fans in front of me seemed vulnerable, even timid. I later discovered that most loyal AV fans are middle-aged men—late thirties through early fifties—who came of age during the so-called *Shūshoku Hyōgaki* (Employment Ice Age), circa 1993–2005. They live precarious lives with little job security and financial resources. The roundtable participants, as well as other male fans I interviewed, were often in poor physical and mental health; just like Daigo, their unwellness tended to be driven by work-related stresses. Most remain single without ever having had serious partners—in many cases, no dating or sexual experience at all. These male fans, who have failed conventionally hegemonic corporate masculinity—the middle-class masculinity built on lifetime employment and seniority system—are the very backbone that sustains the Japanese AV industry today.[1]

In the digital age, declining sales of adult videos have created new opportunities for AV fans to directly interact with AV idols through fan events. Male fans can easily seek information about their favorite actresses and connect with other fans through social media. For men lacking both wealth and wellness in mainstream Japanese society, buying and watching adult videos is not simply about transient sexual pleasure. It is a sustaining feature of their everyday lives. Attending fan events is a way for them to embrace romantic fantasies with their idols, connect with fellow fans, and fulfill their lives through modest spending.

Looking beyond the AV industry, this chapter explores the relationship between AV fandom in Japan and the precarious labor conditions typically experienced by male AV fans. Many have given up looking for full-time employment and continue to tread water in a flexible labor pool. Like AV actresses, whose involuntary consent to sexual labor results in social stigma and discrimination, male AV fans are subjected to nonregular employment options that undermine their dignity and social status. Indeed, AV actresses and male AV fans face many parallel struggles in gender-specific ways. To unpack such connections, I provide an overview of male fans' perspectives on forced performance in AV and then in-depth, personal stories from several AV fans about their experiences working in sweatshop-like corporate office settings and having nervous breakdowns. Their stories illuminate why, despite their ongoing financial struggles, they continue to buy expensive DVDs—many of which they admit to not even watching—and show up at fan events for their favorite actresses. Their involuntary consent to precarious labor conditions is key to understanding individual men's (and women's) struggles and suffering as symptoms of structural violence.

Japan's insecure labor market and exploitative working conditions are the root causes of young women finding work in AV after migrating to the city, as well as middle-aged men (and women) finding nonregular work. Unstable and even stigmatized jobs have become the best and often *only* option available to many in the wake of the Employment Ice Age and the series of labor deregulations that have occurred since the mid-1980s. Nonetheless, as the 2015 forced AV performance legal case also revealed (see chapter 1), the fallacies of liberalism create an ideological smokescreen, as if precarious life is a personal "choice." This pitfall, I argue, reduces pervasive structural violence to an issue of individual consent, rendering invisible social suffering—the symptoms of structural violence—experienced by both AV actresses and their male fans.

## "ALL THAT MATTERS TO [AV] USERS IS OBSCENITY"?

Similar to AV actresses who fear having their identities revealed more than anything, anonymity is everything for men who are addicted to watching adult videos. Even in Tokyo, a city that epitomizes anonymity, these men go by nicknames or *ura*, hidden Twitter handles and accounts. All four participants, for instance, would use only their incognito names for the roundtable: *Supagon, Daigo, Araki*, and *Harry*. Afraid that their neighbors will guess what is in their packages, these men typically purchase adult entertainment DVDs from the Amazon Japan store rather than through other online adult video shops; Amazon packages are generic and discreet enough to avoid social scrutiny. Their concerns echo the notion of sex as something shameful, dirty, and secretive.

In Japan, adult videos are often hidden in the back corner or segregated from other products at video shops, where users quietly select titles. And, as Daigo explained, most DVD sales are now made at fan events held in Akihabara, the largest electronics retail marketplace in the world and the mecca of so-called *otaku* geeks. "It doesn't make much sense holding events in regional cities," Daigo said. "Nobody [would come] to such an event because they are afraid of others' eyes on them." Supagon, who is originally from the Tohoku region, the northern part of the main island of Japan, said, "It was just like that in the area I'm from. It's a small world. Everyone knows everyone else. You would feel shame if someone sees you attending an AV actress's event. . . . Only when I came to Tokyo did I start attending fan events."

Although such public shaming shapes a certain behavioral pattern among AV users, what individuals get from watching AV is as varied as their individual fetishes. Supagon is, for example, in love with his favorite actresses. His first AV love was with Sakura Yura, who retired from AV a few years ago but continues to act in non-AV mainstream films. "I couldn't believe my eyes when I first saw her at a fan event nearby where I live now. I had never seen such a pretty girl in the world. I simply fell in love with her, whether she was an AV actress or not." Like Supagon, who likes young and pretty *tantai* actresses, Araki (not his real name), forty-eight years old, is fond of *tantai* actresses with beautiful and clear voices. He confesses that he fetishizes the female voice and thinks this is because he used to be fanatic for the J-pop group Morning Musume, a female singing and dancing unit founded in 1997 that won numerous music awards. Araki said he would typically spend 100,000 to 200,000 yen (US$1,000–2,000) a month on the group's CDs and went to its concerts all over Japan. He piled up huge debts as a result. He switched to AV idols when Morning Musume reshuffled their lineup in 2007 and lost many of their enthusiastic fans thereafter. He now spends roughly 10,000 to 20,000 yen (US$100–200) a month on adult videos and attends AV fan events, enjoying more up-close and personal encounters with his idols at much smaller venues than the concerts he used to frequent. Unlike the other roundtable participants and video users, who favor popular *tantai* idols, Daigo prefers *namanamashii kōi* (a seemingly unstaged raw act), which nameless *kikaku* actresses perform in scenes and genres like SM, hidden camera sneak-peeks, the so-called *shirōto mono* (amateur genre), and *chikan* (unsolicited touches and molestation on public transportation). "I'm not interested in *tantai* actresses at all since erotic sexual acts per se, not actresses' appearance, are what arouse me," Daigo elaborated. "If an actress I know acts in a scene, it becomes obviously fiction to me. If a nameless woman does the same thing, it looks much more realistic even if the scene was performed by a *kikaku* actress."

I was intrigued by these men's different motivations and viewing practices. I asked whether they project themselves on the male actor while watching, so as to vicariously experience sex with their favorite actresses. The men who are in love with *tantai* actresses more or less agreed that they do get sexual pleasure vicariously, whereas Daigo, who likes kinky scenes and situations, told us that he gets off watching a scene where a woman on a train has her breasts groped over her clothes, for instance. I sensed from my observations that these men were not comfortable discussing such details about their preferences among themselves, even though they were open to talking about AV in general.

Delving into their AV viewing practices, the roundtable participants shared that they routinely watch adult videos before going to bed. "It's a part of my routine. It's like brushing my teeth," Supagon responded immediately. Daigo jumped in, saying, "It makes the most sense that men 'do that' (implying masturbation) at night so that they peacefully fall into sleep afterward." He emphasized the stress relief function of AV viewing. "It's like a 'nightcap,'" Daigo laughed, and joked about his loss of sexual stamina once he hit his forties. Araki, in his mid-forties, shared experiencing the same age-related decline and use of AV as stress relief. It was interesting to me how these men presented their behaviors to two women at the discussion table (a newspaper reporter and a field researcher) and how they nonchalantly referred to seemingly heavy use of AV as simply one of their habits—oral hygiene or having a drink before bed—rather than as a stimulus for sexual satisfaction. AV viewing is thus routinized in their everyday life.

One other trait that the roundtable participants shared was their preference for Japanese adult videos and Japanese actresses. Harry, twenty-two years old and the youngest panelist, joined the conversation. When he was younger, he said any sort of adult content, including *yōpin* (Western pink films and more generally Western adult content), aroused him; but he recently became more exclusive with Japanese AV because he thinks Japanese actresses are prettier and Japanese videos are more creative. "Western porn is like watching an athletic event such as professional wrestling," Harry said. Western porn actresses, as he sees it, take off their clothes and have sex immediately without showing any hesitation or shyness. As I discuss in detail in chapter 2, the wide range of realistic fictions in Japanese AV enable him to engage in scenes more deeply. The other participants agreed, saying that they prefer Japanese AV over Western porn, which they observe lacks subtlety in plot and performance. "Maybe our preference is related to race," Harry said. "Japanese men tend to like the dark hair, petite body types, refined skin, and reserved femininity of Japanese women." Others nodded. Their claim about Japanese AV's aesthetics—subtlety, hesitation, and reserved femininity—speaks to exactly what AV fans cherish and AV actresses produce: the pornographic illusion.

Beyond their AV preferences, these male fans also shared their observations about the changing nature of AV idols over time. Pointing to Iijima Ai and Akane Hotaru, once-popular AV idols in the late 1990s and the 2000s, respectively, who often appeared on mainstream television programs as personalities, Harry noted that they are quite different from contemporary idols like Sakura Mana and Toda Makoto. Iijima and Akane both died in their thirties (in 2008 and 2016, respectively) and were known for their activism in the promotion of condom use and the raising of awareness about HIV/AIDS.[2] "Although Sakura and Toda are not activists," Harry explained, "their messages reach a wide audience probably because of their aptitude for writing." He alluded to their public reputations. Unlike Iijima and Akane, whose "retirement" activities evolved into influential sex education, Sakura and Toda, still AV actresses today, are already known for their smart blogging about a wide range of topics from fashion and cinema to opinion pieces. Daigo elaborated further, comparing the earlier AV idols with today's: Iijima, who eventually became a major figure in Japanese mainstream society, was a *yankī* (literally Yankee, meaning young delinquent) with a troubled early life as a runaway and rape victim (she also repeatedly participated in *enjo kōsai*, or paid dating, and admitted to having an abortion); Sakura and Toda, on the other hand, both appear to lack such baggage. "They are from normal-functioning families and also well educated," Daigo said, commenting that Sakura is quite intelligent, having graduated from an elite five-year professional engineering school.

The participants concluded that women with backgrounds similar to Iijima and Akane considered AV performance as an opportunity to escape from desperate circumstances and gain fame. "In that sense," Daigo summarized, "AV actresses in the past were inferior to ordinary women." Agreeing with Daigo, other participants expressed the belief that today's AV actresses are mostly just ordinary women. Their tone of voice communicated that they were proud of the currency and "citizenship" AV actresses have recently gained. Although they did not spell out why they were so supportive of "ordinary women," it seemed to have to do with a sense of guilt about watching "pitiful women" on screen. As I will detail shortly, all participants except Daigo confessed that they would not be at ease watching AV if their favorite actresses involuntarily performed in adult videos as self-harming acts. "The supply [of AV actresses] has become much more diversified," Daigo said. "It might have become easier for women to cross the threshold [into AV]. For that matter, AV actress as an occupation may have become more casual and accepted in society." Supagon added that he could wholeheartedly support what his favorite actresses enjoy doing.

The casualization of AV performance as a job has been concomitant with the advancement of information technology. Like business insiders in the AV industry, roundtable panelists believe that increasing numbers of young women, who are exposed to free online adult content and AV idols in social media, have become wannabe AV idols. Their view is largely based on AV actresses' voices and anecdotal stories. In AV debut videos, new *tantai* actresses typically introduce themselves to the audience and answer interview questions at the beginning of the video to give a sense of who they are and set the tone for their pending performance. Following these "self-introductions," Supagon reports that many actresses express a desire to engage in so-called idol activities, including a variety of media appearances, offline events, and interactions with fans. According to him, free online videos have contributed to the production of these wannabe AV idols and, by extension, the increase in labor supply. To illustrate this point, Daigo shared an anecdote about young girls he met through his former AV distribution job who he said confessed to secretly longing to become AV idols at a young age.

While this trend may have increased the labor supply of AV performers and reduced the psychological guilt of AV viewers, today's AV actresses are subject to AV makers' higher expectations in appearance, personality, and performance for less pay. Plastic surgery and breast implants are options to enhance physical beauty. *Shiofuki*, or vaginal female ejaculation—for which Akane was known for two decades ago—is one of many acts that AV actresses are expected to perform nowadays. Yet despite this demand for higher specs and more specialized performances, AV actresses' wages have been declining in recent years. "The irony [of this trend]," Daigo stressed, "is that young girls [I met] obviously watched free online videos since they were prohibited from purchasing adult content as minors. And just like them, most people watch AV for free nowadays and as a result, the market is shrinking." Daigo cynically continued, "Even my younger colleagues in the industry rarely paid for adult videos. So, it is extremely competitive even if wannabe AV idols dream of fame and money."

Roundtable participants brought up AV viewers' responsibility for the shrinking market and other issues such as labor exploitation. "There are many economically illiterate viewers," Supagon murmured. "They simply think things online are free without taking into consideration the labor process behind it." I asked what makes certain people literate and others illiterate. Hesitating, Daigo hypothesized, "It must come down to whether or not you have the moral sense that you are not supposed to grab and go without paying for the commodity." To him, it is about morality. All four participants agreed that, like careless consumers who enjoy cheap sweatshop goods, most video users today—including wannabe AV actresses—want a free product. The dialogue heated up when the panelists discussed users' accountability regarding forced performance in adult videos. Daigo pulled the trigger by posing a rhetorical question. "What's the user got to do with the issue? If an actress claims that she was forced to perform in AV, it is indeed a serious problem in the production, but not on the user's end. All that matters to male users is whether or not the video is erotic, right?" Others at the table seemed unsure of how to respond.

Breaking the silence, Daigo said again, "I just wonder if users would still remain loyal to so-called clean, legitimate videos if video makers rigorously self-regulate and end up undermining obscenity." He added that he is specifically concerned about the user like himself who prioritizes obscenity over fairness in the labor process. With still no noticeable reactions from other panelists on the table, Daigo spoke about other sweatshop products such as Nike athletic clothes, reminding the others that consumers can do only so much. He then tied the point back to general attitudes among AV users: commodities are made available in the market only when they clear a labor standard. Supagon finally spoke. "Can we go back to the earlier point? I do not completely agree with Daigo [that] all that matters to users is obscenity. I personally feel unease to indulge myself in the fantasy world if I come to know [that the workers] are exploited with low wages and harsh working conditions." Daigo interrupted before Supagon could finish. "AV actresses' performance guarantee is very low if you are concerned about that." Supagon responded, "Well, it's not necessarily about wages per se but rather the working environment in general. If workers are coerced against their wishes, it's a violation of human rights."

This is the departure point to shift focal awareness from AV-specific labor exploitation to precarious labor more generally in contemporary Japan. "Speaking of that [workers being coerced against their wishes]," Daigo followed up, "it happens not only in the AV industry but also in any other workplace. I think it is the essential nature of work that one has to compromise one's wishes." Arguing against AV exceptionalism about involuntary consent at work, Daigo shared his sister's experience as an example. According to him, his older sister recently found a sales representative job after numerous unsuccessful attempts on the job market. On the first day of work, her employer asked if they could put her cell phone number on her business card. Although she was reluctant to use her private phone for work, she could not say no. She was afraid of losing her job. Ever since, however, she has been troubled by the thought that a stranger could pick up her card on the street and abuse her personal information. Caught between needing a job and this stressful business card dilemma, she ended up suffering from depression. Daigo made an analogy here between his sister and AV actresses in terms of the difficulty of saying no. "These women might never make those who are in no need of a job understand why they cannot say no clearly," Daigo said. His sister also found out it was mandatory to attend the company's annual weekend trip, even though she did not feel like going. As her mental health deteriorated, her family and friends advised her to quit; however, she was reluctant to walk away because the job paid well. "There must be so many women whose mental state is similar to my sister's at any given workplace." Everyone at the table nodded.

Gaining consensus from the roundtable participants, Daigo made another point about involuntary consent. For him, an AV performance job is no different from any other, based on his belief that it is "the essential nature of work that one has to compromise one's wishes." The Japanese term for work, *shigoto*, literally means "to serve the superior," which is vernacularly understood as the toil one has to do for a living. From this commonsensical understanding of work, Daigo suspected, "AV performance is differentiated only because it requires women to have sex on camera." Regarding what he sees as AV exceptionalism based on an artificial distinction between involuntary sexual labor and other forms of work, Daigo reiterated that the issue of forced AV performance remains "equivocal." For wage workers, consent to subjection to the employer's commands and orders is assumed to already be folded into the labor contract—but for sex workers, consent cannot be treated the same way due to, as discussed in chapter 1, the legal need to procure consent for the "sex part" of the work, specifically. Legality of such sexual consent is, however, gendered. It is applied only to female AV performers.

Beginning with my own comment about the relationship between involuntary consent and young women's tendency to avoid confrontation, the discussion moved to gender difference in the (in)ability to say no. "I definitely think that men cannot clearly say no, either," Supagon jumped in. Daigo agreed and commented that there are many Twitter postings from men who complain about their bosses or company presidents, demonstrating that salarymen also suck it up to avoid confrontation at work. Nakajima Maki, the *Mainichi Shimbun* reporter at the table, joined the discussion to share stories about notoriously forceful female sales representatives attempting to sell young, reserved Japanese men an expensive Christian Lassen sea life painting. These representatives would try to shame the men, "Come on, aren't you a man? Can't you make up your mind right now? You will never be able to make any important decision in your life, will you?" Comparing this example of an art purchase to AV performers' decisions, Nakajima pointed out that men tend to excessively react when they have their pride hurt, whereas women cooperatively respond when they are told how pretty they are—and it is suggested that they "share" their beauty with their admirers. "The psychological mechanism [through which] men and women reach a compromise is different when they cannot say no, I guess," Nakajima said. "Men would say, 'I can [do that],' to prove himself, whereas women say, 'I will [do that],' to serve others even if both men and women end up doing things against their wishes." The participants shared Nakajima's view on gendered differences in psychological manipulation and involuntary consent.

The talk lasted for more than three hours. During the extended dialogue at the end, the participants remained open and respectful to one another. Moreover, their differing opinions regarding Japanese AV seemed to derive from their sexual preferences and moral stances as consumers. For example, Supagon, who admires AV idols and values nobleness, projected an idealistic moral standard when discussing labor rights and policies. Daigo, who consumes erotic content and sees things cynically, instead expressed sarcasm toward moral righteousness. This conversation helped me understand these men's different values, ethics, and perspectives on adult videos, labor processes, and consumer accountability. Perhaps most significantly, however, they would all come to agree that they deeply care about both adult videos and AV actresses in their own ways. Later, my extended interviews with panel participants and other male AV fans would deepen my understanding of men's involuntary consent to precarious labor and its consequences manifested in gendered ways.

## AV AS A LIFELINE FOR A HAVE-NOT MAN

"I wonder if the politicization of forced AV performance, after all, aims at dismantling the AV industry itself," Supagon said two weeks after the roundtable discussion. "[I'm] seriously worried about that as an AV fan." Supagon is one of seven ordinary fans I interviewed who came of age during Japan's Employment Ice Age, involuntarily have accepted their own precarious lives, and found AV as a lifeline.

On a late Sunday afternoon in March 2018, we met at a quiet coffee shop in Shibuya, the bustling hub of youth culture in Japan, which he could easily access from his shared three-bedroom apartment in Yokohama, about half an hour away by train. In person Supagon is tall, muscular, and handsome—not necessarily what one would expect a shy AV fan to look like—and thirty-eight years old. Just like the last time, he was wearing an off-white casual shirt, blue jeans, and sneakers. And just like at the roundtable discussion, he was quiet and thoughtful, looking for words before he spoke. His utterances, however, tended to be short and abrupt. I felt I was compelled to ask for examples and details to fill in gaps between what I heard and what he possibly meant.

" '[You're] seriously worried' . . . why would you feel that way?" I was puzzled as to what exactly he meant.

Supagon folded into himself.

I pressed him: "What happens if the AV industry vanishes?"

"I will lose *yoru no okazu* (literally night snacks, or nighttime pleasure)," he said. "Something important in my life . . . will be . . . gone." He was serious.

"Come on! Isn't it just a fun pastime?" I teased him.

"Well, my life will be no fun!" He grinned.

"Seriously?" I laughed, playfully.

"It's a big deal. . . . It's one of the three basic human desires."

"Do you think other men share the same sensitivity? Or, is it peculiar to you?"

"I'm not completely sure, but I guess . . . all men are more or less the same." He stiffened his shoulders.

"So, AV is indispensable to your life, not simply additional, correct?"

"Yes . . . especially when you don't have access . . . to real women," he explained, smiling shyly.

Uncertain what he meant, I asked what kinds of intimate relationships he'd had.

"I've never had any girlfriend in my entire life." His voice was flat and emotionless.

I always assumed that watching adult videos is entertainment and not much more. It can be, however, essential for someone like Supagon, who has never had a romantic partner.

I asked when he began watching adult videos and how his relationship with

AV has evolved. To my surprise, he said that he hardly watched adult videos until he left his hometown to go to college at age eighteen. This did not mean that he was disinterested in pornography; he kept his sexual interests hidden from his family and even close friends. Raised in a rural, conservative community and three-generational household—construction worker father, part-time working mother, two younger siblings, and grandparents—he long believed that those who are prematurely sexual are looked down on for precociousness. To avoid such prejudice, as an adolescent he refrained from engaging in dirty jokes, reading pornographic magazines, or watching adult videos. He instead focused on his studies and athletics in school. His hard work paid off when he was admitted to a Japanese national university in the neighboring prefecture. In 1998, around the time the adult video industry took off in Japan, Supagon lived alone in an apartment for the first time. "I liked [watching AV], but it was not my preoccupation," he said. He had other things to devote himself to. In college he studied electronic engineering, a growing field driven in part by the rapid expansion of Microsoft Windows. Besides his schoolwork, he enjoyed gaming and betting on horse racing. Overall, he felt he enjoyed his college life though he did not have much of a social life.

After graduation, Supagon took a sales job in Osaka. But being far away from his hometown while struggling to adjust himself to work that required good social skills, Supagon damaged his health. (In his own words, *karada wo kowashita*—literally, [he] has broken his body, or [he] has had his body broken).[3] Despite his perfect health in the past, his work-related stress caused chronic fatigue, insomnia, and feverishness; he felt under the weather much of the time. As a result, he quit his job and went back home to stay with his family again. During the following four years, he worked for a local IT company near home and seldom watched adult videos. While visiting the annual Tokyo City Cup for horseracing, he stopped by a few adult video shops to purchase several titles, something he was too embarrassed to do in his hometown.

Supagon's life changed drastically in 2008, when he was transferred to his company's Tokyo office. He moved into his current rental place, a three-bedroom apartment in Yokohama, and resumed watching AV in his room. He soon became a big AV fan.

"AV is . . . now *seikatsu no ichibu* (a part of my everyday life)," he said in a monotone. "Along with daytime work and weekend horse racing, AV watching in the night is . . . built in."

I asked for details. "What is your typical day like?"

"I usually come back home around 10 p.m. after eating out on the way home from work. I spend about three to four hours a day checking social media and playing games. I then watch an adult video for half an hour to an hour until I fall asleep. I also spend two to three hours a day checking AV news and following actresses on Twitter."

"That means you spend most of your free time on AV-related matters, doesn't it?"

"More than half of my spare time [on AV] a day. . . . That's why I'm seriously worried if AV disappears."

I wondered why such a tall, good-looking man with a good education like Supagon would stay in "love" with AV actresses rather than strive to find a life partner. Feeling the question could be too personal, I asked, hesitantly, "Do you feel AV satisfies your love interests?"

"Better than . . . no girlfriend . . . or nothing," he said abruptly.

"Have you tried to find one?"

I'd pressed a button. "No opportunity [to meet a woman]."

Supagon's reluctance to satisfy his desire for love somewhere other than through AV was, I suspect, related to his current job situation. "I don't think I can afford marriage with my annual income anyway," he said. Explaining how sexual entertainment is woven into his everyday life, Supagon confessed that he preferred watching AV to other commercially available sexual services. He did not deny that he had enjoyed having sex in exchange for money, but he also found it unsustainable financially. His first sexual experience took place at a pink salon, where male customers get oral sex for 5,000–8,000 yen (US$50–80), when a boss from his Osaka company headquarters took him to a commercial establishment. A few weeks later, after he won money at a horse race, he visited a so-called soap land, where men pay a few hundred thousand yen (US$300–600) to have sex. Although he enjoys the soap land service, he can afford it only occasionally. By contrast, AV is so affordable that he can enjoy watching and masturbating every day.

Supagon's modest aspiration is indicative of the pecking order that is manifested in Japan's stratified world of sexual entertainment. He describes it as follows:

> Wealthy IT millionaires can buy hours to take out AV idols for dates and satisfy their sexual interests. Middle-class salarymen in my age group are mostly married with kids. They might secretly watch AV and visit soap lands

occasionally for enjoyment. They still fulfill their lives at home. But lower-class people like me are rarely promoted to regular employment. A pay raise is out of the question. There is no guarantee whether a contract will be renewed every six months. Contract workers are flexibly hired and fired, if necessary, for labor equilibrium to protect regular employees. We are a release valve.

I appreciated Supagon's frankness to show his vulnerability even though it undermined his masculinity. This could not have been easy. I asked how he would define the middle and lower class, and what it means for him to be a contract worker. He said that middle-class people are full-time employees who make an annual income of over 5,000,000 yen (US$50,000) that comes with health insurance and job security. Lower-class people, on the other hand, are nonregular employees who make less than 3,800,000 yen (US$38,000) and lack social security and a safety net. As a contract worker without job and financial security, Supagon self-identifies as lower class. "For a lower-class person who cannot afford marriage, dating an AV idol is a dream within a dream," he joked. His remarks suggested that wealthy and middle-class men have the option of whether to marry, but lower-class men do not. Similarly, different kinds of access to AV idols are demarcated by class lines. Wealthy men can pay great sums of money to date AV idols, whereas lower-class men can access their idols only vicariously, mainly through adult video purchases and fan events.

Being one of the have-nots, Supagon uses AV actresses for multiple purposes: to maximize the cost-benefit value of adult videos and to make his life more livable. For that reason, he classifies AV actresses into three different categories that occasionally overlap. The first is the actress he watches to receive sexual pleasure. The second is the AV idol he enjoys interacting with at fan events. The third is the one he follows and connects with through social media. He sometimes finds an AV actress through her Twitter account and then goes to her offline events and/or watches her videos. There are several entry points and patterns in how he engages with AV actresses, their videos, and events. Nonetheless, he stressed that he would go to an offline event only when he knows who the actress is and anticipates it being a fun experience. Otherwise, it is too costly—purchasing two or three DVDs and traveling to the event site—to find himself unentertained. He juggles with his limited time and money to maximize what he gains out of his "investment." For that reason, he said he "studies" an actress online first.

"Who are the actresses you fantasize about most for your sexual pleasure?" I asked.

"New girls, those who made their AV debut within the last two years."

"Fresh girls?"

"Fresh ones," he laughed.

"Who are the ones you go to see?"

"Girls with a pretty appearance, nice personality, and friendly attitude, who I observed on social media."

"Do you follow some actresses for more than two years?"

"Sure. The more I get to know them, the less I come to watch their videos, though."

"Is that because they become stale to you?"

"They become more like my friends and relatives."

I was puzzled. "Feeling closer to them, do you become unable to watch their videos due to a sense of guilt, a loss of sexual interest, or something else?"

"I do watch them, but only occasionally . . . otherwise, I prioritize new faces," he laughed.

I have repeatedly heard from male AV fans that they fantasize about new faces and use them as a masturbation tool. But these men cannot do the same with a woman they perceive themselves as getting to know well and beginning to respect. This seems another example of the male AV fan experience that is neither monolithic nor static. Their perception of particular actresses can change over time as their sense of a relationship with the actress transforms. A male fan can use adult videos and sexual fantasies about actresses for multiple purposes too. AV actresses can be sexual objects to be consumed, idols to be admired, and "friends" to be connected with through social media. The diachronic and multilayered nature of fans' AV experience challenges such a sweeping generalization that AV objectifies women and manifests male dominance and female subordination.

The AV enthusiasts I met in Tokyo were struggling with low incomes and single status, perpetually—indicators of how uncertain their lives had become. They were also symbolically knocked off the corporate ladder that arguably still remains the benchmark of hegemonic masculinity in Japan. So-called Japanese-style management once provided male workers with lifetime employment, full benefits, and a seniority-based salary system. But amid the prolonged economic stagnation that overtook the country following the burst of the early 1990s bubble economy, lifetime and even full-time employment have increasingly become unattainable. Male AV fans of Supagon's generation, who came of age during the Employment Ice Age, face a different world wherein social disparities are growing.

### A LIFE-ENHANCING SENSE OF CAMARADERIE

"I'd locate myself at *chū no ge* (literally beneath the middle, or the lower-middle class),"[4] Araki, a forty-eight-year-old full-time office assistant for a woman accountant in Tokyo, shared with me. I interviewed him alone three weeks after the roundtable. During the group discussion, Araki was interrupted several times by Daigo and did not seem to be able to express himself fully. His answers tended to drift away from the main topic, causing his interlocutors to wonder where he was going. Daigo would often dismiss him, saying, "That's nothing to do with what we are discussing." Indeed, Araki characterizes himself as a clumsy person who is constantly scolded by his female boss at work; the type of person who takes things too literally, whose answers to questions can miss the point. Yet he was far more eloquent during our one-on-one conversation at a Shinjuku coffee shop than at the roundtable talk.

Although he could still go off-topic for long stretches, I sensed that Araki tried to answer my questions sincerely. "What do you mean by the lower-middle class?" I asked, seeking his definition of the class category. "It means that you have regular Monday through Friday work days that come with a monthly salary, health insurance, and social security. If you are a nonregular worker, social security and welfare might not be covered even partially." He discussed other personal resources that keep him from "feeling *himoji* (starving to death or being really hungry)." He lives with his retired father, who rents an apartment for them in Saitama, a Tokyo suburb. "I don't live in luxury but I'm not desperate, either. I have a little bit of money to spend on my hobbies," Araki said. Turning fifty in a couple of years, he is also concerned about his future. "I am worried, what if I become unable to work or lose my father's financial support?" He continued:

> I have made up my mind to simply hang in there to survive even though a very unstable life is ahead of me. This is the conclusion I eventually reached after experiencing all sorts of difficulties in my life. One thing I am absolutely certain of is that I have no wealth. Nonetheless, my recent experiences have made me think that it will still be okay to live.

Araki shared an episode that reminded him of his financial struggles. During a workshop he recently attended with other men his age, the workshop moderator asked the participants to raise their hands if they earn as much as or more than their age times 10,000 yen a month. In the case of forty-eight-year-old Araki, this would be 480,000 yen (US$4,800). Unlike most other attendees, who were proud of their administrative positions and high earnings, he couldn't raise his hand. These men surely benefit from Japan's seniority system—but not Araki, who had changed occupations several times in the past.

Graduating from a Tokyo college with a degree in economics, Araki took a sales representative job at a Japanese pharmaceutical company in 1993. After completing three months of company training in Tokyo, he was transferred to a branch office in Aomori, the northernmost prefecture on the Japanese main island. He knew very little about the people and communities in the region. There, everybody knew everybody else, he explained, and would remain aloof from strangers like Araki. Not knowing how to connect with local people, including medical staff, doctors, and potential clients, he immediately faced communication difficulties. Araki admitted that he was not good at socializing and made few friends while in college, though he went to school every day. Moreover, he hardly received any proper training or mentoring as a new employee beyond the centralized three-month training. He was only told to work like *gamushara ni* (working like mad) to learn his job quickly and produce sales. Although he did everything he thought he was expected to do—drinking with doctors at bars after hours, playing golf over the weekend, and cross-dressing for entertainment at an end-of-the-year party—none of his social gestures seemed to help him make sales. "Honestly, I was clueless. Everything was new to me. I tried reckless things, but it resulted in no progress," Araki sighed, gazing downward.

Being constantly pressured to work harder and longer over the course of eight months, Araki finally snapped. He began missing appointments and wound up being badly scolded and harassed as a "loser" and "useless human" in front of people by his boss and broker. He said that his body still remembered those days vividly—he couldn't stop feeling his pager constantly vibrating at his waist, even when it was shut off completely. "It was creepy and sickening," Araki added. His mental health situation became unstable. Araki said, "*Ki wo yanda* ([I] became mentally ill)."[5] To take his mind off his problems, he started pachinko gambling and became addicted, piling up a 3,000,000 yen

(US$30,000) debt to a credit loan company. Araki explained that he tried other forms of entertainment such as hostess club visits, but he found himself most at ease when he was alone. He went back to pachinko parlors again and again where he felt free of his work-related stresses and depression. He finally succumbed to reality when his older sister told him to quit his job and come home.

Although he moved back to Tokyo and started living with his family, life was not much easier there. Even though his father helped repay his debt, he couldn't stop pachinko completely and resumed borrowing money once again from a loan company. "It is a shameful story," Araki said. He was still under a lot of pressure—his father continually asked when he would find a new job—and he wanted to escape into pachinko. Meanwhile, for almost an entire year, he couldn't even make the first cut on jobs he applied for. He lost his confidence and hope for the future. During this period, Araki developed a stutter and avoided conversation both inside and outside his home. While his father relentlessly lectured him about what it meant to be an adult citizen, he remained silent and internalized his shame. He felt he could not speak back to his father, as he financially depended on him. Araki admitted that he felt as driven into a corner at home as he did in society.

He spoke frankly about what it was like to be in such a circumstance. "I was empathetic with domestic violence news on television due to my sense of alienation."

"Were you empathetic with the offender or the victim?"

"The violence itself is unknown territory to me," Araki said. "But I started to see the thin line, whether or not I would actually cross it. Frustration can manifest itself outwardly in a harmful act against others, and also inwardly in a self-harming act." His voice was sincere.

"Could I ask about your case?" I suspected he had tried to harm himself, not others. I was nervous about his reaction and at the same time confident that his answer would be sincere.

"I attempted self-harm several times. I overdosed on cold medicine once in Aomori, attempting to commit suicide. I regret it, it was a thoughtless act."

"What happened after that?"

"I woke up with a horrible headache after an entire day of sleep. The body's self-healing power took care of it, expelling toxicity out of my system. I saw bodily fluids all over the place on the bathroom floor, though I didn't remember anything," he recalled. "I didn't think I would talk about these kinds of things today," he added.

"Are you all right?" I felt bad and decided to stop there.

"I'm fine. The past no longer bothers me. I now know that I used to be thoughtless. I tried other things like hanging myself. But I couldn't find a tree of the right height. In hindsight, I guess I didn't look for it seriously. I ended up attempting to choke myself while holding a towel tightly. But I couldn't bear the pain in my strained arms and released them. I was nothing but a coward." Distancing himself from the past, he recounted one scene after another without emotion.

"Forgive my rude question, but I wonder if you hadn't really given up on life yet," I said, nervously looking into his face.

"Indeed, there was a bit of a feeling that death would not be the only option I had. It was not out of hope, though. In my mind, it was *amae* (my weakness or self-doubt) not to be able to consummate anything, I used to think."

"*Amae* (weakness)?" I felt his internalized self-criticism keenly and sympathized with his suffering.

"It was about my self-centered attitude. I simply wanted to escape from things in front of me without thinking of other people's feelings my thoughtless acts might affect. I was selfish. I began seeing through it once I met a group of Morning Musume fans in the late 1990s. They helped me put things in perspective."

"How has your perception changed, then?" I asked.

"I came to the conclusion that nothing would change even if you hit rock bottom and made bad choices. Life goes on. I now think, so what if I fail. I can always keep death as my last resort."

Araki's stress-driven depression and tendency toward self-harm haven't gone away, however. For his second job, he worked full-time as a secretary for the president of an electronics company in Akihabara, which had over 150 employees. Like everyone employed there, he worked from 8:30 a.m. to 7–8 p.m. Monday through Friday, and from 8:30 a.m. to 6:30 p.m. on weekends—with only the first three days of the new year off. He no longer suffered from suicidal thoughts but still repeated self-harming acts. Whenever he made errors at work, he banged his head against the office wall so hard that he hurt his neck. He also started dozing off during work hours, for which he was scolded. He finally saw a doctor, who specialized in insomnia, and was diagnosed with severe depression. His anti-depression medication, however, made him even sleepier, which led to major errors at work and more self-harming acts. This vicious cycle got worse.

Despite the hardships he experienced at work, however, he said he handled his situation differently this time. His lifeline lay in his fandom for Morning Musume, a Japanese female singer idol group that made its debut in 1998 and cultivated superfans, most of whom were men. He became a big fan of the group at age thirty when their 1999 single "Love Machine" became a massive hit. According to Araki, at his age he was late to becoming an enthusiastic follower of a Japanese idol group. Thanks to the internet, he connected with other fans over thirty who encouraged him to attend concerts, follow the group all over Japan, and support them in any possible way. As a result, his financial trouble shifted from pachinko gambling to idol group fan activities. His debt doubled from 100,000 yen a month to 200,000 yen (US$2,000) in order to finance his travels throughout Japan, including transportation, lodging, dining, and sightseeing on top of concert tickets and goods purchases. To make the trip, he sometimes took unpaid leave from the electronics company. Despite the financial strain, he said that he couldn't live without his commitment to the group, as he was stressed out constantly at work.

After working this job for nearly a decade, Araki resigned from the electronics company in 2000, right at the turn of the twenty-first century. Relieved from the work-related stress for a short while, however, he had to find another job fast to repay his growing debts. Araki took an office job at a temporary employment agency in Shinjuku; his job was to match job seekers with potential employers and required a daily quota of at least 100 to 120 calls. His new job was no easier. On the third day, Araki was asked whether he could transfer to a branch office in Fukuoka, Kyushu, the southern island of Japan. He could not afford to lose his job again and had no other choice but to accept the transfer. Although he tried to convince himself that his work would essentially be the same no matter the location, he soon found he was mistaken. Arriving at his new office, work started immediately with no time to find a place to live. He ended up staying at a hotel for the first two weeks and working between 8:30 a.m. and 10:30 p.m. every day. His day started with a morning company meeting and ended with an evening meeting in which his boss berated every one of the underperforming employees, including Araki. After a long day with two 60-minute breaks—for lunch and supper—he came back to his hotel (and later, a provided apartment) around 11 p.m. to take a shower and sleep. Going to bed around 1 a.m., however, he kept waking up around 4 a.m. and couldn't go back to sleep.

Unsurprisingly, his lack of sleep negatively impacted his performance. He couldn't think and speak logically. His boss constantly scolded him for his nonsense and singled him out at the morning and evening meetings. Even though he was constantly tired and ill, he refrained from using the company sickroom, where employees take a temporary rest. He was afraid of being thought of as a loser who failed to manage his health. He could not quit his job so soon and return home only to embarrass himself. Meanwhile, he quickly learned there was high turnover at his office. He witnessed two or three new employees like him quit every week. One day into his fourth week, Araki finally called the office and took a day of sick leave. He did the same thing the following day. He then stopped calling and simply stayed at home all day long. Looking back, he told me that he was deeply depressed. Still waking up at 4 a.m. on a sick leave day, he turned the television on even though he rarely watched TV. He had no appetite and no energy for anything except lying down. This happened around the same time the company was facing several lawsuits over their labor exploitation, including a case of *karōshi* (death by overwork). As a result, Araki was politely asked whether he would like to continue working for the company or quit and return to Tokyo. He didn't know what to do. To him, neither option seemed ideal. Meanwhile, he was hit by more self-doubt.

"It occurred to me numerous times," Araki said, "that I shouldn't have existed in this world. I was already over thirty and had built nothing but a sick body. I felt my existence would only cause of trouble for others—my family, company, and friends."

I was at a loss for words.

"It was my fellow Morning Musume fans, the only contacts I had left, who convinced me to quit and head back to Tokyo." Araki paused. "I was saved by the sense of companionship and belonging." (A few years later, Araki realized that the harsh working conditions he experienced were not peculiar to his company when a newly coined term, *burakku kigyō* (literally black company, a sweatshop-like workplace in any given business field), won the 2013 *gendai yogojiten* word of the year and gained wide currency in Japan.[6])

Araki sounded relieved but also subtly animated. Stressing the importance of his fan friendships, he explained that what he received from them was the kind of support that he could not get from his colleagues at work. With his colleagues, Araki was so afraid of being labeled as a failure that he could not complain about his work or show his vulnerability openly. By contrast, with his fellow fans, he could frankly talk about his occupation and laugh it off.

"How did you build such strong bonds?" I asked. In the back of my mind, I was thinking of his friendless college and work life.

"We used to talk a lot about Morning Musume over drinks. Each one has his own favorite member to speak highly of. We seriously discussed each member and also the unit as a whole, to think through how to maximize the group's ability while highlighting individual members' strengths, all night long sometimes. [Eventually] we all came as one to chant, 'Morning Musume, the Best!' holding each other's shoulders and singing their hit songs together. We shared the sense that we enjoyed ourselves afterward more than [during] the concert itself."

Araki's description of idol fans reminded me of the roundtable discussion among AV fans. At the table, AV enthusiasts frankly shared their different sexual preferences, viewing practices, and moral standards. At the same time, they seemed to hold a strong sense of trust based on the shared belief that they genuinely care about adult videos and actresses. Such a profound sense of trust, despite differences in ages, occupations, and values, creates a safe space for those who feel socially marginalized to bond together.

"One night," Araki continued, "I was drinking with some fan friends who I knew for over fifteen years. I told them that I was suffering from diabetes. Acting a bit self-destructive, I said, 'I won't change my diet or lifestyle. I'll eat and drink as much as I want. Death is inevitable, anyways.' One of them shot back, 'My life won't be the same without you. It'll be no fun. Please take care of yourself and cure the disease, will you?'"

Pausing suddenly, Araki's tearful eyes caught mine. "Excuse me." He looked down.

Araki's circle of friends tends to be limited to those who share a similar lifestyle. In the normative life course scenario, men his age are married with kids, affording little time and money for personal hobbies like following idols. "Fandom is," Araki said, "a prerogative of single men."

Like Supagon, Araki has never had a romantic partner. His first sexual experience took place at a soap land. Also like Supagon, Araki's work-related acquaintances in Aomori invited him to join their visit to a sexual entertainment site; he was twenty-three years old and a virgin. Since then, he has never visited another soap land. He has only visited pink salons for oral sex a couple of times, again under peer pressure. He is not very interested in sexual services.

"It simply did not occur to me that I would want to use commercial sex," Araki said. "I guess I was preoccupied with fan activities surrounding Morning Musume. Watching adult videos alone was good enough to satisfy my [sexual] needs."

"Can an idol singer be a sex object for you?"

"Not really, though I understand others might sexually fantasize about an idol."

"What kind of role does an idol play in your life, then?"

"An oasis."

"Oasis?"

"I have never been in love nor had opportunities to meet women. I have a female boss who constantly scolds me at work. So, she is certainly not my love interest."

"Are you frustrated about the situation?"

"I used to be when I was still in my early forties and thinking of marriage."

"You have changed since then?"

"I came to realize that it was too late to realize my dream."

"What do you mean?"

"If I rush into looking for a marriage partner now, I feel she would be more like a caretaker than a wife. I would feel sorry for that woman."

"Is that why you go for female idols?"

"I'm into idols. But it's not really for salvation. It's not comfort or healing, either. Idols are an oasis that enriches my life. Without them, I would have been locked at home, passively waiting for the time to pass away alone."

Araki's remarks reinforced the notion that idol fandom brings single men together whose masculinity is similarly marginalized in mainstream Japanese society. These men in similar situations, largely due to their age, class, and marital status, get together to temporarily free themselves from social expectations. This seemingly temporary bonding has a profound effect on their quality of life. In Araki's words, idol worship is neither a dead end nor a salvation. It is more proactive. Far from what they endure in their workplaces and their families for that matter, as Araki's narrative demonstrates, the male bonding they experience through AV idol worship is invaluable to secure safe, supportive spaces in their otherwise lonely, stressful lives.

## SELF-ACCEPTANCE, THE PATH OF BELONGING

"Those idol fans who hang out in Akihabara have very little experience with women," uttered Shimada Noriyuki, a forty-three-year-old adjunct history lecturer at a Japanese national university in Tokyo. His tone clearly implied his distance from such men and scorn for them as well. I met him at an Amatsuka Moe fan event and interviewed him at a family restaurant of his choice weeks later. While admitting to being part of the fan event scene, Shimada distanced himself from the Akihabara crowd by referring to them as *otaku* and "those people in Akihabara." *Otaku* are known as persons who are obsessed with computers and particular aspects of popular culture to the detriment of their social skills.[7] "Those men," Shimada continued, "have neither financial resources nor communication skills. They rarely can afford to go to hostess clubs or the like. They can last only a few minutes in conversation with women, anyways. Bunch of losers!" He laughed hysterically.

Yet, while sipping a glass of water, Shimada admitted that he was blown away by the *otaku*'s enthusiasm—in his words, *sugoi na otaku tte* (they are admirable, the *otaku*)—when he attended an AV fan event for the first time in the mid-2000s. This was about the same time that Shimada's life swiftly changed overnight. Graduating from college in 1997 amid Japan's Employment Ice Age, Shimada decided to pursue a master's degree in history at the national university where he currently works. Earning the degree in 2002, he stayed at the university as a researcher. To supplement his salary of 150,000 yen (US$1,500) a month as an academic researcher, he took a contract-based curator position at a history museum and also an adjunct lecturer position at a high school affiliated with his university. A couple years later, his work and life began to fall apart.

At that time, he was on the right academic track in Japan and had a girl-friend he was thinking of marrying. A vicious downward cycle, however, began with what he claimed was a false accusation of stalking made against him by a female coworker at the museum. According to his side of the story, she was a "crazy girl" and a type of person in great need of attention. He told her not to bother his junior friend, who confessed to Shimada that he suffered from her bullying. As a result, Shimada said he received fierce resentment from her, being accused of harassing and stalking her. Soon after, his yearly contract at the museum was not renewed, ostensibly for budgetary reasons. Around the same time, he had more trouble at the high school he taught. According to Shimada, he was falsely accused of sexual assault out of jealousy; his colleagues did not like him because he was a good teacher, worked hard, and even provided supplementary lectures after school. He assumed that he stirred up feelings of resentment among regular full-time instructors because of his work ethic; as a result, they spread a rumor that he sexually harassed female students during the supplementary lectures.

"It was of course a total lie that somebody made up, but I was immediately fired without any investigation." He was still angry. He seriously considered suing the school but refrained after consultation with his friends in academia. In consideration of his future employment opportunities, they thought it would be wiser for him to remain silent in the long run than possibly win small compensation money out of the legal suit and create lifelong enemies. "No matter what the truth is," Shimada stressed, "I would be blacklisted as a troublemaker within the small world of schools affiliated with my university. [Then] it becomes impossible to find any job." For this reason, he grudgingly accepted a dishonorable discharge without appeal. This was not the end of his agony. Shimada's serious girlfriend also left him during the "false accusation." He thinks the incident triggered the breakup even though he sensed that she had already fallen out of love with him. He was frustrated about her unsympathetic attitude when he was struggling with the accusations. The more he complained about her lack of understanding and asked her to provide necessary emotional support, the further her heart drifted away from him.

I felt a vague sense of uneasiness while listening to Shimada. I wasn't sure where the discomfort came from. I simply assumed that he was suffering from a persecution complex. But transcribing his interview later, I realized that something about his condescending attitude, accusatory tone of voice, and one-way, machine gun-like chatter kept me from believing everything he said. I wondered why he looked down on *otaku* in Akihabara while he was also part of that scene. How coincidental was it that he experienced a series of women-related troubles, from stalking to sexual assault to the loss of his serious girlfriend?

As he shared more about his background with me, however, I began to understand that he failed to receive necessary support at a vital time in his life due to his dysfunctional family upbringing. He has lost both of his parents. In his family, he still has his older brother, who he refers to as *kuzu* (a waste or a good-for-nothing). His father did not acknowledge his brother as his legitimate son, assuming that his wife became pregnant by her former boyfriend. He didn't allow her to raise him at home, letting her parents take care of him at their place. Meanwhile, his father died of cancer in his forties, after which Shimada's mother brought the older brother back to live with the family and spoiled him out of guilt. His brother turned out to be a troublemaker with huge financial debts for gambling and hostess clubbing. His mother repaid his brother's seemingly endless debts and eventually used all her savings set aside for Shimada's college education. While the family was spiraling into darkness, his mother died in a car accident. Shimada was left alone to take care of his "useless" brother.

Facing a series of problems at work and in his private life, Shimada's health deteriorated. He said that his mind tried to understand everything going on in his life, but his body told an honest tale. "*Karada ga okashiku nacchata* (Literally, my body went wrong). I couldn't get up all of sudden one day. I was surely suffering from deep depression." (Shimada seemed irritable while sharing this part of his story.) At that time his leg would become swollen like a balloon when he walked to a convenience store a block away, he said. It took him two days to recover. This repeatedly happened, limiting his mobility. He suffered from this reoccurring symptom out of unknown causes. He became bedridden for two years when he finally learned that the root cause was kidney failure. Without proper medication, his kidney condition still cuts off his blood circulation and increases his blood sugar level uncontrollably.

Left alone with his brother and losing two of his jobs, his health, and his girlfriend all at once in the mid-2000s, Shimada had to adjust his life accordingly. He used to go to the gym to work out regularly, but now he goes only for rehabilitation. He had several hobbies in the past, but he pretty much gave up all of them due to his financial and health-related concerns. He used to enjoy traveling, especially to Kyoto for his archival research. He also enjoyed drinking with his friends or alone at hostess clubs in the past. "My private life almost entirely changed. I came to focus on one thing, and one thing only: AV fan activities," he said. Shimada began attending events in Akihabara around 2010. Nowadays, he spends most weekends at fan events. He used to "escape" to Kyoto to get away from his stressful everyday life in Tokyo; he now escapes to Akihabara for the same reason. He only recently joined the *otaku* crowd in Akihabara, the crowd he would have stayed away from completely if his life hadn't become so "derailed."

Despite Shimada's professed distaste for the *otaku* crowd, he nevertheless enjoys a sense of belonging with them, a feeling that he claims he cannot get at work. His work relationships are always hierarchical and political in terms of who are his allies. By contrast, he refers to the relationship he develops with other fans as *furatto* (flat—neither hierarchical nor political), regardless of differences in age, status, and educational background. Fans rarely talk about their occupations in detail. They only make fun of their work. Nobody brags about their wealth or success. He feels at ease due to everyone's respect for boundaries, which allows him to avoid nosiness and yet share something in common; this is the "flat" aspect of their relationships that he appreciates. Like Araki, Shimada feels closer to his fan friends than his work colleagues. He sends text messages to his friends daily and they also check on him. Even though the text messages are brief and trivial, he still feels a sense of oneness with his fellow AV idol enthusiasts.

He particularly appreciates his fan friends' kindness. He shared an anecdotal story about one friendship. He received a ride offer to a fan event that took place in an inconvenient location from central Tokyo; a friend arranged for Shimada to ride with him and another fan. The day of the event, he was running late and texted them to go without him—but both insisted on waiting for him. Due to the delay, all three missed the important opening speech from their favorite AV idol, but nobody even mentioned it. "They were so cool, and I was very touched by that," Shimada said. "There is a good amount of distance [between us], as we don't even know one another's real names, occupations, and private lives. But we all share the sense that we are there together for our favorite idol," he added.

Like Supagon and Araki, Shimada highlighted two meaningful aspects of AV fandom. For one, a favorite AV actress, who creates the opportunity for them to come together. She not only tries to understand fans' secret fantasies and acknowledge their support but also expresses her personalized appreciation (remembering their names, referring back to previous conversations, and saying kind words—recall Amatsuka Moe's efforts from the introduction). Second, AV fans build and enjoy a sense of camaraderie through what Shimada refers to as *mitomeau*, accepting one another as they are. "In such a safe space, I feel at home and enjoy myself, although I did not used to think that I would be part of *otaku* circles," Shimada laughed.

Fan activities are the backbone of Shimada's current life. But his budget is quite tight. "It's not an ideal thing to do," he lowered his voice, "but I resell DVDs as soon as I get an event ticket." Usually, event attendees are required to buy three DVDs to get a ticket in. It costs almost 10,000 yen (US$100) to purchase three DVDs at the regular price. Akihabara video stores, however, set what is known as an "Akihabara price," providing a slight discount compared to other shops. A DVD with a retail price of 2,980 yen (roughly US$30) is sold for 2,458 yen (nearly US$25) at the Akihabara price. Shimada takes advantage of the special price, then brings what he has just purchased to a used video shop to resell for 1,600 yen (US$16) if the buyback place has yet to stock the title. He is willing to take a train to find a buyback place outside Akihabara so that he has a better chance. In this way, Shimada spends only 3,000 yen instead of 10,000 yen (US$100) for each event ticket. "I sell DVDs," Shimada said, "without watching or even opening them. If it's open, the value of the product drops significantly." Understanding the economics, he added, "It is such a rude deed since actresses work hard to produce adult videos, but many justify it as a way to minimize damage."

Shimada did not mention how much time it would take to save 7,000 yen (US$70) every week, waiting in line for hours for the video stores to open and hopping from one store to another in different areas of the city to resell what he has just purchased for the best prices. Nonetheless, it is easy to predict how much it means for him to save nearly 20 percent of the monthly wages he earns from his contract-based lectureship. Shimada insisted the frequent event-goer winds up owning too many videos to possibly watch them all. A fan like Shimada buys DVDs not necessarily to watch them but to obtain an event ticket. For financially struggling fans, the buyback service is the best option, even if it is time consuming. This is the downside of the face-to-face sales method that AV makers require AV idols to do to sell DVDs to their fans. It is unpaid, extra work for the idols and a financial burden for some fans. The reselling practice of DVDs quickly drops the product's market value, as used DVDs circulate widely soon after. The devaluation of adult videos feeds back into the intensified labor process—longer hours AV actresses work for less pay.

"On average, how much per month do you spend on DVDs?" I asked Shimada.

"Including transportation, dining, and other miscellaneous costs, about 100,000 yen (US$1,000). But then I get about 60,000 yen back from reselling items. So, about 40,000 yen on average."

Although AV fans in general seem economically constrained, Shimada had an especially keen awareness of his financial limitations. Despite his higher educational background and the symbolic honor to be referred to as *sensei* (teacher) in society, his income was less than that of other fans, who are non-regular employees with college degrees like Supagon and Araki. As an adjunct college lecturer, he makes only 1,800,000 to 2,400,000 yen (US$18,000–24,000) a year, whereas Supagon, a computer engineer, and Araki, a secretary of a certified public accountant, make nearly 3,000,000 yen (US$30,000) and 3,600,000 yen (US$36,000) a year after taxes, respectively. Shimada spends disproportionally more—a quarter of his monthly earnings on his event-going—than the other two.

Economic differences aside, Shimada aligned with Supagaon and Araki's sensibility about objectification of his favorite AV idol: the better acquainted with their favorite actress through fan events, the less able they are to treat them as sex objects. Shimada admitted that he used to watch Amatsuka videos nearly every single day at the beginning of his fan phase. He enjoyed the voyeuristic excitement of thinking that an admirably pretty girl does *konna koto* (this kind of [dirty] thing)."[8] He has, however, stopped watching her videos almost completely after frequenting her events and getting to know her as a person.

"It might sound odd to you, but I come to feel guilty about fantasizing," Shimada said. "It's like the awkward sense that occurs when you imagine jerking off to your own sister or your best friend's girlfriend. All Amatsuka enthusiasts I know say that they don't masturbate to her," he added.

"Is that out of a sense of guilt, or simply a loss of sexual interest after binge watching?" I asked, curious.

"She is still attractive to me, greatly. She has such a pretty face with a nice, slender body and small but nicely shaped breasts. She has a great personality, too. I would beg her to make love with me every night if she was my girlfriend. Here, I feel an ethical dilemma as her fan. I'm supposed to watch her videos, but I don't. Upon the occasion that she asks my thoughts on her new video, I manage to respond with something like, 'I have to watch it once again.'"

Shimada reflexively explained that *shitashimi* (translated into familiarity, friendliness, and intimacy) and masturbatory pleasure do not go hand in hand. His sense of *shitashimi* overwrote his sexual interest in her almost completely when Amatasuka shared her "secret" plan to step away from an AV idol unit with him a few years ago—a sign to him that she thought of him as special. Shimada explained that Amatsuka knew he never missed the unit's concerts and always positioned himself in the front row to shout her name loudest even if he lost his voice; she whispered her plan in his ear and asked him to keep it secret when she shook his hand at a fan event. "It comes down to her trust in me. Since then, my sense of guilt overwrote my dirty mind," Shimada said. "I don't want to pollute her with my dirty imagination."

I thought his logic interestingly complicates a sexual double standard. In a masculinist binary thinking that divides women into either promiscuous or pure (and therefore worthy of protection and respect), Amatsuka, an AV actress, is already "polluted." But a male fan's sense of *shitashimi* with a "contaminated" woman obscures such classification. An AV actress with dignity can possibly ascend to the "worthy of protection and respect" category when, through her personality, she generates audience empathy and demonstrates what her fans perceive as integrity. The irony I found there is that the AV actress gains a particular kind of respect or admiration because of, not despite, her already "polluted" and "contaminated" image. In other words, it is not inherited values in particular actresses but what fans project on her that yields idol worship.

An idol thus becomes invaluable to the fans themselves. Like Supagon and Araki, Shimada's interaction with AV idols is indispensable to his well-being. So is his friendship with other male fans who share the same values. He stressed that he goes to fan events so frequently because he gains vitality more than anything. "I admit," Shimada said, "that I feel physically tired when I go back home late night after going to events and hanging out with other fan friends. But I also feel full of energy that helps me to finish up my preparation for my lecture the next day. Otherwise, I have very little energy with my messed-up body and exhausted mind." His remarks echo Araki's and other fans' experiences—gaining support and energy necessary to keep going. With this safety net of camaraderie, as well as idol worship, men I met in Akihabara have come to better accept their lives. For them, the AV industry provides what they cannot receive at home, at the workplace, and in mainstream Japanese society at large.

## EMBODIED MANIFESTATIONS OF STRUCTURAL VIOLENCE

Back in mainstream society, the AV fans I met identify themselves as lower-middle or lower class based on their income and nonregular employment status. Indeed, their lives might be only slightly more secure than those of Japan's *andākurasu* (underclass) who, by definition, earn 1,860,000 yen (roughly US$18,600) or less yearly on average.[9] The Japanese underclass numbers nearly 10 million, comprising almost 15 percent of the entire work force. More drastic, however, has been the rise of nonregular employment. According to 2022 government statistics, 37 percent of the nation's labor force is now nonregular.[10] Nearly 70 percent of these workers are women; 32 percent are men.[11] The poverty rate among them is 38.7 percent, and it jumps to nearly 50 percent among the female underclass.[12] Of the male underclass, 66.4 percent have never married.[13] Hashimoto Kenji, a Japanese sociologist, explains that the rise of this underclass was concomitant with the late 1980s' restructuring from lifetime employment to flexible labor. Along with the burst of the bubble economy in the early 1990s, the following decade witnessed the bleakest job market in modern Japanese history, at the turn of twenty-first century and beyond. The first generation of those who came of age amid such bleakness is now in their late forties. Most AV fans belong to this generation and face economic austerity and uncertainty.

The job situation for this generation is no better today and unlikely to improve in the near future. The harsh reality in Japan is that workers who fail to find or keep a stable job will most likely fall into the underclass. It is rare that a contract or "gig" job will turn into a full-time occupation. Moreover, Japanese corporations continue to gradually replace full-time regular employees with contract workers to cut labor costs. Even many college graduates struggle today to find full-time jobs that come with benefits and job security.

This is exactly the situation wherein involuntary consent to precarious labor is structurally incited in the name of personal "choice." The consequences of such structural violence are manifested in embodied psychological and physiological disorders among nonregular workers. The symptoms may vary from person to person depending on one's bodily construction, adaptability, familial support, and perhaps most crucially, economic security. Supagon, Araki, and Shimada have all experienced fatigue-induced depression, though they expressed their symptoms differently. Araki referred to his situation as *ki wo yanda* (he suffered mentally). Supagon described his case as *karada wo kowashita* (he ruined his health). Shimada felt that *karada ga okashiku nachatta* (literally, his body went out of control). Interestingly, they described their symptoms in neither active nor passive voice. Instead, they used middle-voice Japanese expressions—the expressions that I discussed in chapter 1—, as if their disorders were simply things that happened to them and they need to cope with.

This is, I suspect, exactly the voice one would use to accede to involuntary consent. Like most AV actresses who end up resigning themselves to engage in stigmatized sex work, these men had no better choice but to accept unfavorable offers, such as a short-notice transfer to a remote office, an overloaded work schedule, or an honorable discharge in the slim hope of a better job opportunity. They were not forced to accept these difficult offers. Once accepting them, however, they face the irreconcilable gap between involuntary consent and its unacceptable consequences—exploitative work, excessive stress, and mental breakdown—which results in embodied symptoms of disorders. In other words, their mental and physical distress is, I contend, manifestation of structural violence, triggered by involuntary consent and fueled by labor exploitation.

The rise of work-related mental illness validates the view that seemingly personal suffering is, rather, a larger social problem. "Japanese-style fatigue-induced depression" is a new pathology, arising in the context of the country's prolonged economic recession and broken lifetime employment system. In her 2012 book *Depression in Japan*, medical anthropologist Junko Kitanaka argues that depression in Japan is understood to be "not only a pathology of the individual brain but . . . rooted in the Japanese culture of work itself."[14] Social understanding of depression is, as Kitanaka points out, gendered too. Men's depression tends to be associated with work-related stress and treated accordingly, whereas women's depression is largely unrecognized or trivialized as simply excessive stress from relationship problems due to their assumed economic dependency.[15] This sexist understanding of mental health issues justifies prioritizing men's disorder, which is perceived to be socioeconomically more important than women's "relationship problems."

While the male AV fans I met did not use medical terms to name or describe their suffering, as their narratives demonstrate, their physical and mental health problems have been closely intertwined with economic upheaval and social marginalization in the wake of Japan's Employment Ice Age. For those who cannot keep up with Japanese corporate masculinity, or what sociologist R. W. Connell calls "hegemonic masculinity,"[16] the AV subculture may provide what they need: self-acceptance, intimacy, and a sense of belonging. Purchasing adult videos and going to fan events can be a "lifeline," an "oasis," and a source of pleasure for those socioeconomically marginalized men at the intersection of gender, class, and age. To put it differently, their "marginalized masculinities"[17] prime them to become loyal customers of the AV industry.

Being loyal to the AV industry, however, does not necessarily mean that they invest in the industry per se. Their allegiance is, rather, a method to support their favorite AV actresses and secure a space wherein they are accepted as who they are, as part of an alternative community based on camaraderie. In exchange for moderate spending, male fans receive idealized, hermetically sealed perfection in the AV idols that they lust after (or in many cases fall in love with), in physical appearance, personality, and hospitality. Nevertheless, these men are rarely aware of how much tireless sexual and emotional labor—and often, mental distress—an actress endures behind the scenes to sustain the pornographic illusions and cater to their male fantasies. In this way, men make their lives livable at the cost of women's unpaid, invisible labor. Discovering such a haven, thus, still depends on the pornographic illusions video makers stage for AV actresses to produce.

AV makers, who own the means of production, capitalize on AV actresses and their fans' enthusiasm, as both are willing to go the extra mile to promote the industry's output. Actress-fan bonding, which is the backbone of DVD sales, is a recent development, concurrent with AV makers adopting a face-to-face, personal selling method in the digital age. AV makers reap massive profits from a socioeconomically marginalized population—young women and middle-aged men—who struggle with an unforgiving labor market and deflated economy. Although AV fans lack social standing, they still benefit from the bourgeois patriarchal politico-legal systems that protect sexual entertainment (but not women's sexual labor). As AV sales continue to decline, the triangular and mutual yet asymmetrical relationship among AV makers, fans, and actresses remains intact.

The male-centered adult video industry, deeply embedded in bourgeois, masculinist politico-legal systems, operates according to the logics of liberal contractualism in a democratic society like Japan. By signing a contract, AV actresses become independent contractors—while, in practice, they are trivialized as "girls" due to their gender, age, and social standing. Like AV actresses, AV fans, who have involuntarily consented to their nonregular employment status, are emasculated as second-class citizens due to their lack of normative middle-class markers such as marriage, fatherhood, and job security. And like AV actresses who accept structural violence as part and parcel of their employment options, the AV fans I met also live with such violence, keeping their insecure, precarious lives private. In this respect, the lived experiences of AV actresses and fans alike unfold through a paradoxical liberal premise. The premise—individual autonomy, freedom, and equality under the law—makes involuntary-ness invisible within *involuntary* consent to structural violence and treats subordination as if *by free choice*.

The Japanese AV industry, nested in a liberal democratic society, is, after all, a microcosm of paradoxical liberalism wherein not only liberty but also violence is experienced in the space of neither-overtly-forced-nor-completely-voluntary resignation of the self. It is this in-between space where the have-nots are in the position to accept unfavorable (and even unacceptable) conditions and enter contractual relationships. In the relationships, the haves, who gain the upper hand, can legally violate consent givers. The covert power dynamic is further complicated in the triangular relationship among AV actresses, AV fans, and the AV industry, and obscured or distorted by pornographic and political fictions. Just as the pornographic illusion of free expression justifies AV as a harmless fiction, political illusion of free choice is the fertile ground for a legal fiction of liberal contractualism: where willful subjects freely consent to structural violence and democratically perpetuate structural inequalities. This is a part of the story about AV production and consumption that usually goes untold. By unfolding the ways that different social actors—AV actresses, talent agencies, video makers, AV fans, and the Japanese public—(ab)use, leverage, and negotiate pornographic and political illusions, this book is a modest attempt to ethnographically provide a glimpse of the inner workings of liberal reasoning behind involuntary consent to structural violence.

# EPILOGUE

In April 2022, Japan lowered the legal age of adulthood from twenty to eighteen. This was historically significant. The definition of an adult had not changed in more than 140 years, since the Meiji Civil Code decreed twenty as the legal age. The impetus behind the change was, officially, (1) to enhance the active participation of Japanese youth in civil society; (2) to respect their self-determination; and (3) to align with global standards.[1] This change in the law also aligns with Japan's efforts to produce self-governing citizens and (re) structure the Japanese nation-state, which is rapidly aging and needs manpower to maintain its global competitiveness. Regardless of political motivations, the change has considerably expanded freedoms and responsibilities for new consumer-citizens. These new adults are now eligible to apply for a ten-year passport, serve on a jury, and make contracts without parental consent. While Japanese minors (those under the age of eighteen) still cannot make contracts without their legal guardians, the new adults—now younger than ever—have gained new freedoms at the cost of age-related legal protections. The changes, which did not come with much systematic education, support, or a transition period, have heightened concerns about young adults becoming easy targets for fraud, scams, deception, and exploitation.

What does this change have to do with contract making in Japan's AV industry? Simply put, it broadens the legal gray areas through which the industry operates, as I discuss throughout this book. Though contracts are, by definition, enforceable by law, the sexual exception to this legal paradigm often falls through the cracks. As the 2015 Tokyo district court ruling states, it is illegal to coerce individuals to perform sexual acts against their will. This means that an AV performance contract essentially becomes null and void if the performer, at any age, says no to performing a sexual act. Only a handful of performers, however, understand the implications of this ruling, and even fewer act on what they are legally entitled to do. New adults who are interested in AV work are left alone to navigate this ambiguity.

The recent change in the legal definition of adulthood echoes turn-of-the-twenty-first-century Japanese legal reforms in many ways. In 2002, with little preparation, the Japanese government implemented the so-called *Shihō Kaikaku*, or legal reforms intended to transform the national consciousness into one in which citizens would view themselves as active self-governors rather than passive recipients of government by the state. In reality, however, these nominally self-governing citizens became "independent contractors" with severely eroded rights as workers. In 2022, the Japanese government deployed similar logic when lowering the age of adulthood in the name of active social participation by self-governing youth; millions of eighteen- and nineteen-year-olds have now become new adults, losing their rights as minors. The bottom line is that these legal changes forcibly expand self-determination, whether or not citizens demand it. Changes are executed no matter how well citizens are prepared for the legal ramifications of their new responsibilities as "free" subjects. Such liberal violence—universalizing liberal assumptions of autonomy and freedom under the rule of law—leaves the socioeconomically marginalized in an especially vulnerable place.

As with the 2015 Tokyo district court ruling and the rhetoric of young women as victims of forced performance in AV, the change in Japan's age of adulthood has once again set off alarms about young Japanese women being manipulated into signing dubious contracts, among other concerns. The Japanese Cabinet Office's website issued a special alert regarding talent and model contracts on March 28, 2022, a few days before the new rule went into effect. The alert informed that the National Consumer Affairs Center identified more than 8,337 cases of young people (most in their twenties) reporting problems with talent and model contracts since 2011.[2] Of those reporting, 70 percent were women. "Young women are easy targets," the website stated. This heightened alert has enabled activists and women's support groups to mobilize legislators across different political parties to unanimously pass legislation to protect new adults from being preyed upon by Japan's AV industry. This resulted in an expedited measure, the Adult Video Appearance Damage Prevention and Relief Law, which went into effect on June 23, 2022, an exceptionally speedy outcome within Japan's bureaucratic bill-making process.

The new law assumes that, once given enough time and measurement of protection, AV performers will make free choices—before, during, and after filming and even video release. It mandates that performance contracts be made a month in advance of shooting and that no videos can be released in the four months following filming. AV performers can also freely terminate their contracts for one year from the date a video is released, regardless of their age and gender, and can halt sales and distribution of their videos.

The "AV Prevention and Relief Law" is, as Yamai Kazunori, a central proponent of the bill and a member of Japan's Constitutional Democratic Party asserted, "revolutionary" because it could be "a powerful weapon" to finally protect these victims.[3] In an interview with a regional Japanese television news outlet, Yamai stressed the severe consequences that performing in adult videos potentially cause: "One's life could be destroyed completely by having to face severe discrimination at school, the workplace, and in marriage once a person's identity is revealed. Even suicide could be a result." Yamai also noted that because of the COVID-19 pandemic, single mothers, students, and young adults who have lost their part-time jobs are now seeking higher-paying jobs. Under these circumstances, he claims, many have been "deceived into performing in adult videos." But he also corrected the "forced performance" label as misleading since physical force was usually not involved. He said he has come to believe that the larger issue here is *social discrimination*, not merely discrete victimization within the AV industry. He noted many cases where young women were involved in brainwashing and manipulation, later realizing that their consent was given involuntarily out of persuasive recruiting tactics and socioeconomic circumstances. Though Yamai does correctly identify the fundamental problem (i.e., structural violence), his "revolutionary" solution and "powerful weapon"—punitive measures taken against the AV industry—is incompatible with solving it.

The AV industry is, I argue, an easy target for such seemingly just punishment—a convenient scapegoat that deflects attention away from the fundamental problem of structural violence: precarious labor market, gender inequality, and sexual double standards. The law does not address the fact that AV actresses remain at the mercy of gender and sexual discrimination, both inside the AV world and in mainstream society. Labor in Japan is increasingly uncertain and precarious for all. This is especially true for women, who more than ever turn to seemingly lucrative work in AV and other sex-related entertainment industries—work based entirely on catering to heterosexual men's fantasies. The work is not only demanding but also short-lived. Stigma attached to the work and social discrimination against the sex worker lingers long after "retirement." The legal frame does not target such structural vulnerability built into the business. It instead pressures individuals, including vulnerable new adults, to protect themselves against manipulation by unscrupulous business practices.

Without an in-depth understanding of structural violence, AV actresses' experiences are narrowly confined to the AV industry and an either/or binarism. Toda Makoto, an influential adult video actress, spoke out against the new law due to its lack of nuance. When the bill was crafted in May, Toda posted a lengthy, highly critical essay on her Twitter account, expressing discomfort about the current depiction of the AV industry and the misrepresentation of AV actresses.[4] The bill, she argued, conveniently overlooks what the AV industry has been doing to improve working conditions for performers while ignoring what AV actresses, the target group of such legal protections, think and do. Toda is also critical of how the law assumes that many actresses are involved in illicit sexual acts and, even worse, are forced to engage in such acts against their will. This misrepresentation, she claimed, has negatively affected her own mental health. Depicting AV actresses as if they are more in need of psychological treatment than other workers is a form of "occupational discrimination," she wrote. "Any sweeping generalization is problematic. Neither are all actresses victims nor free agents," she continued. "What hurts and what empowers differs from person to person. And, a person's answers could differ from one moment to another."

Lived experience is ambivalent, messy, and contradictory at times. So is the social practice of consent, particularly with the multiplicity of meanings that Japanese notions of consent harbor. In her tweets, Toda used the Japanese word *nattoku*, among other similar expressions for consent such as *dōi* and *shōdaku*. Unlike *dōi* and *shōdaku*, which connote more unilateral, superficial acts—simply agreeing or approving of others' ideas or proposals—*nattoku* implies multilateral, comprehensive understanding of a given situation and acceptance of others' proposals. In one of her tweets, Toda wrote, *nattoku shite hataraite iru*, meaning that AV actresses like her understand the circumstances well enough to make their own decision to continue working. *Nattoku* consent is intersubjective, not self-contained, and takes external conditions into account.

The culturally specific meaning of consent in Japanese vernacular language is quite different from the one in English, for example. The *Oxford English Dictionary* defines "consent" as "permission for something to happen or agreement to do something," as if the giving of consent is a completely self-contained process. Against this hegemonic Western conceptualization of consent, wherein the consenting subject is the causal agent who makes things happen, the meaning of Japanese consent, *nattoku*, is lost in translation. Consent in Japanese is, by definition, always already compromised. *Nattoku*, as I discuss in chapter 1, manifests in the middle voice: neither active nor passive but reflexive and reciprocal, blurring rigid distinctions between cause and effect, the subject and object, and consent and coercion. Involuntary consent is, therefore, ubiquitous. And yet, it may remain latent for some time before it is manifested in expressions like *shite shimatta* ("I regretfully did x") or through embodied suffering upon encountering social discrimination, relationship problems, and mental health issues.

As I argue in this book, the AV contract negotiation process involves gendered power structures and cultural logics, both of which are downplayed in the universal, liberal principles of autonomy, freedom, and equality under the law. When dominant negotiators—consent seekers—maneuver vulnerable consent givers into accepting someone else's ideas, requests, or offers, the socioeconomically subordinate—namely, women, young adults, and gig economy workers—often struggle to outright reject these offers, whether out of peer pressure or economic necessity. They may feel that they must accept such offers involuntarily or deal with the repercussions of nonacceptance. Once such consent is given, moreover, they may feel obligated or pressured to deliver what they promised, even if they later realize it is not feasible. They may complete the sexual acts they are being pressured to perform, even though they are, in theory, free to say no at any time. With such negotiations, consent givers' *nattoku* (understanding of the situation and the other party's offering) can lead them to consent to things that they did not realize they were signing up for. Unsurprisingly, those who give involuntarily consent, and even those who are deceived into consenting, often blame themselves first for their (mis)judgement and the disappointing, sometimes painful results of a dream gone sour.

Sexual labor contracts are also sociolegally muddled. Legally, the age of consent for sexual activity is thirteen in Japan. But the age at which a person can contract to perform sexual scenes on camera, or legal adulthood, is now eighteen. Nevertheless, regardless of age, a woman can cancel her sexual labor contract at any point she feels coerced. Even if she, the contract signer, understands this legal ramification, acting on it is another question. In this wide-open gray area, customary practice plays a larger role in the making of a contract than legal enforceability. The process of negotiating a contract is always intersubjective and compromised. Furthermore, the symbolic effect of the contract does not end at the delivery of consented-to sexual performance. A woman's video release may extend well beyond the realm of contractual-legal obligation, entering a socioeconomic and cultural sphere in which her pornographic images may forever circulate and damage her reputation. The temporospatial effects of a discrete AV performance contract has infinitely expanded to the virtual world due to unprecedented technological advancements over the last fifteen years. In the digital age, when any image becomes instantly ubiquitous and eternally present in cyberspace, to what extent should an AV performer's consent be held responsible for social discrimination that she faces years after the contract itself expires?

Sexual exceptionalism in contract work, legal ambiguity about sexual commerce, and the digital economy have all made it more difficult than ever for consent givers to predict the unknown effects of signing a contract. For these reasons, the AV actresses I met almost unanimously raised red flags about casual entry into AV employment. Yet they do not completely argue against working in AV either. Imai Haruka, the twenty-eight-year-old *kikaku tantai* performer introduced in chapter 2, reflected:

> I think everybody changes once they have stepped into this [AV] world. It is such a drastically different environment for an ordinary woman who has experienced no particular prejudice or discrimination. With overwhelmingly enthusiastic support and harsh criticism all of sudden [coming at her], she will be either empowered through the experience [to overcome] difficulties or completely defeated and crushed.

The AV actresses I interviewed often repeated the phrase "*nobody* forced me to," implying that they understood the situation before they made their own decisions within their limited structural standpoints. Many women "choose" AV performance because it is more lucrative and rewarding than other work;

others feel it is a stepping stone leading to other business opportunities. In this context, AV work becomes the "best" option even though it comes with the greater risk of identity reveal and social discrimination in today's digital age.

Nested in mainstream Japanese society, the AV industry is, after all, deeply underwritten by bourgeois, masculinist logics of liberal contractualism, free speech, and the sexual-moral economy. I argue throughout this book that these sociolegal and cultural infrastructures render involuntary consent illegible, perpetuating systemic inequalities in both the free market and liberal democratic society. On paper, consent comes to be regarded as a rational choice made by an autonomous individual. But this is a legal illusion. Since the possibility of consent is always already compromised in everyday life, sexual contracts in the AV industry rely as much on the political illusion of choice— the fantasy of unencumbered, enthusiastic choice—as on the pornographic fantasy of adult videos as "harmless" entertainment.

# ACKNOWLEDGMENTS

As a cultural anthropologist, I'm always intrigued by people and their stories. An inquiry into their experiences and narratives entails two-way communication processes. Throughout the course of my seven-year journey writing this book, I have received invaluable guidance, wisdom, and inspiration from many people. First, I wish to thank people working in the Japanese adult video industry—performers (especially actresses), scouts, talent agencies, video directors, producers, distribution companies, and AV Human Rights and Ethics Committee members—and AV fans. Without their open-minded willingness to share their stories, this book would have never been written. My gratitude extends to newspaper reporters, human rights activists, lawyers, case workers at women's support groups (Light House and PAPS [People Against Pornography and Sexual Violence]), legislators, and scholars who spoke to me about their perspectives on the issue of forced performance in adult videos. My special thanks go to Kozai Saki, Amatsuka Moe, and other AV actresses who want to remain confidential. I am grateful for their rapport and willingness to share their narratives and life histories, which have helped me see things that are often invisible even though ubiquitous in everyday life.

Ethnographic book projects take time to conduct fieldwork, analyze data, and write fine-grained portrayals of lived experiences. It can be costly. I am grateful to the organizations that provided financial support for this process. The Japan Foundation Research Fellowship generously funded my initial fieldwork in 2015. The University of Kansas's sabbatical leave allowed me to revisit my research site and complete my fieldwork in 2017–2018. The Social Science Research Council (SSRC)-Abe Fellowship enabled me to sit down and write my entire book manuscript in 2020–2021 during the COVID-19 pandemic. Besides these major grants, institutional support from the University of Kansas, including the General Research Fund, Level II Strategic Initiative Grant, and numerous research travel grants, enabled me to continue my research and writing during summer breaks over the course of this project.

If financial support helped build a foundation for the field-based ethnographic study, my academic peers in the US and Japan enriched this book and helped it grow to full maturity. I would like to thank constructive comments and suggestions at several institutions. My thanks go to Colby College, Dickinson College, Ohio State University, Sophia University, Tsuda University, University of Hawaii, University of Kansas, and Wellesley College. My special thanks go to Alex Hambleton, Andrea Arai, Aya Kitamura, Ayu Saraswati, David Slater, Laura Clark, Yasuyuki Motoyama, Hajime Miyazaki, Hideko Abe, Keiko Nishimura, Love Kindstrand, Patrick Galbraith, Risako Gen, Shawn Bender, Sachiko Horiguchi, Shunsuke Nozawa, Satsuki Uno, Satsuki Takahashi, Stephanie Metzger, among others.

At the University of Kansas, many people helped me in various ways. I wish to thank Kathy Porsch for her tireless support with grant writing, Alesha Doan for her mentoring, and Japanese friends, including Maki Kaneko, Michiko Ito, Ayako Mizumura, Utako Minai, and Yuka Naito, for their emotional support and fun times. I also wish to thank Hannah Britton, Ayesha Hardison, Ann Schofield, Nick Syrett, Stacey Vanderhurst, Joan Nagel, Brian Donovan, Katie Rhine, Allan Hanson, Brent Metz, Megan Greene, John Kennedy, Kelly Chong, Xiao Faye, Kyoim Yun, Maya Stiller, Sherry Fowler, Elaine Gerbert, Maggie Childs, Amanda Snider, LaGretia Copp, Abby Barefoot, Aster Gilbert, Mie Takikawa, Mio Yoshizaki, Marcy Quiason, Melinda Chen, and Mariah Stember. My gratitude goes to Bill Tuttle, Mary Fry, Patrick Suzeau and Muriel Cohan for their enduring friendship.

Outside the University of Kansas, I'm grateful to Lieba Faier, Gabriella Lukács, Allison Alexy, Sachi Schimidt-Hori, Christine Yano, Kazuko Suzuki, Akiko Takenaka, Jason Karlin, Martin Manalansan, Nicole Constable, Jesook Song, Srimati Basu, Ilana Gershon, Abel Valenzuela, and Bill Tsutsui. Beyond the academic circle, I would like to thank the following individuals: Takeshi Ai, Oka Megumi, Kanajiri Kazuna, Miyamoto Nobuko, Taguchi Michiko, Kudo Shinji, Ito Kazuko, Akatani Marie, Kaname Yukiko, Mizushima Kaori, Kurumin Aroma, Marica Hase, Sugimoto Takamichi, Matsui Saburo, Tsukio,

Kawana Mariko, Tameike Goro, Nimura Hitoshi, Takaoka Tetsuya, Kawai Mikio, Yamaguchi Takashi, Hirota Taizo, Shida Yoko, Yagami Rei, Saegusa Susumu, Namikata Aki, Usui Kiyoshi, Tsujimaru Kohei, Tao Masahide, Takaoka Terumasa, Nakajima Miki, and many AV actresses and actors who wished to keep their identities unrevealed.

An academic book becomes fruit when nutrition and care is given. I am extremely thankful to Sherrie Tucker and Nichole Rustin for our weekly writing group meetings. Their timely feedback, insightful comments, and caring friendship supported me throughout my book writing. Fun conversations were precious supplements, particularly during the COVID-19 pandemic. I am grateful for Giang Nguyen, Haruka Nagano, Karisa Shirai, among others, who kept me on course—and accountable—throughout our many early morning writing club sessions. I also would like to thank Sara Appel, who provided superb editorial service for my book draft. Her attentive work and developmental suggestions significantly improved the finished work. I am extremely grateful to Marcela Maxfield, my editor at Stanford University Press, who steadfastly believed in this project and provided excellent editorial advice. I also wish to thank the anonymous reviewers of the manuscript whose suggestions for revision helped improve it. Lisa Wehrle's copyediting resulted in a more readable book. The earlier version of chapter 1 in this book has been accepted for publication in *Current Anthropology* under the title "Involuntary Consent: Contract Making in Japan's Adult Video Industry." I wish to thank Laurence Ralph, editor of *Current Anthropology*, for granting his permission to publish it.

Last, but most important, I thank my family. My parents, Yusaku and Tomie Takeyama, have never questioned what I devote my efforts to. They continue to believe in and support me in any possible way even though they do not always know what I have been working on. I am fortunate to have an "in-house" proofreader in the name of my father-in-law, Bill Steele, whose deft touch as an editor helped improve the final product. My best friend and life partner, Will Steele, is still the best choice I have made in my life. With him, any trivial things, and certainly challenging times, are turned into adventurous journeys to enjoy. Though this book concerns the *illusion* of choice, I am confident that this relationship isn't fantasy, and if it is, I hope it lasts forever. If my husband was my choice, I feel as though I'm the chosen one by our sixteen-year-old cat Charcoal, who has been my companion and secret mentor throughout my professional academic career. His free-spirited nature and wandering ways lifts my spirits.

# NOTES

**Introduction**

1. Throughout this book, I use the words "model," "performer," "actress," and "talent" interchangeably, as Japanese AV scouts and talent agencies often present "modeling" opportunities to young women. Modeling is inclusive (or vague) enough to function as a euphemism for sex work, including AV performance. Agencies that specialize in mainstream modeling are themselves often vaguely referred to as *tarento jimusho* (talent agencies) and *purodakushon jimusho* (production offices). Accordingly, AV models are also referred to as *AV joyū* (AV actresses), *sekushī joyū* (sexy actresses), and *"adaruto" moderu* ("adult" models).

2. Galbraith and Karlin 2012; Lukács 2010; Aoyagi 2005.

3. An average AV production budget is today set around 2 million yen (US$20,000).

4. *Asahi Shimbun*, 2015, "AKB Total Sales Number One," December 10, http://database.asahi.com.www2.lib.ku.edu/library2e/main/top.php.

5. In 2015, Amatsuka won both the DMM Adult Award for Best New Actress of the Year and the Sky Perfect TV! Adult Award for New Actress of the Year.

6. In Japanese society, such jobs are referred to as *hi-sēki koyō* (nonregular employment), including *kēyaku* (literally contract work, meaning fixed-term employment); *haken* (dispatched work from a temporary labor agency); and *pātotaimu* (part-time and temporary work), as opposed to *sēki koyō* (regular, full-time employment with benefits including employee rights, lifetime job security, health care, and a seniority wage system). See Cook 2016, Gagné 2020, and Takeyama 2016 for the discussion of changing selfhood, masculinity, and adulthood in contemporary Japan.

7. Act on Punishment of Activities Relating to Child Prostitution and Child Pornography, Act No. 52 (May 26, 1999).

8. In 2018, the Japanese content industry generated 10 trillion yen (US$100 billion). Of this, 2.6 trillion yen came from digital content. The industry has grown. However, Japan's content industry growth rate hasn't kept pace with the other leading countries. Between 2019 and 2023, the global growth rate has been estimated at 8.2 percent whereas Japan's is expected to grow only 6.6 percent. *Nihon Keizai Shimbun*, 2020, "Digital Content: 2.6 Trillion Yen in 2018," February 12, https://www.nikkei.com/article/DGXMZO55528690S0A210C2EE8000/.

9. *Gijutsu rikkoku, chizai rikkoku* in Japanese. This has been done under the Koizumi Junichiro administration (2001–2006), known for its insistent implementation of a series of neoliberal policies.

10. To promote a network society and protect intellectual property, the state passed the Basic Act on the Formation of an Advanced Information and Telecommunications Network Society in 2000; it also put the Intellectual Property Basic Act into effect in 2003 and passed legislation to promote the creation, protection, and exploitation of content in the following year. To respond to these state initiatives and protect copyrighted videos that generate royalty revenues and licensing fees, the AV industry established the IPPA (Intellectual Property Promotion Association) in 2010.

11. The association consists of 290 AV makers and 3,300 rental and sales shops as of 2022. IPPA homepage, https://www.ippa.jp/organization/ (accessed October 31, 2022).

12. In Japan, there is a very narrow window for new high school and college graduates to receive regular full-time employment. If they miss this once-in-a-lifetime opportunity, they usually have no other choice but to take temporary employment jobs, often ending up working at so-called *burakku kigyō* (black companies, meaning sweatshop-like workplaces).

13. During Japan's economic growth period (mid-1950s through early 1990s), major Japanese corporations provided their male employees with a package of lifetime employment, seniority wages, and full benefits. They also trained their new employees thoroughly. Their heavy commitment to job training and security has been known as Japanese-style management. But they no longer offer such trainings. In these precarious labor times, they now limit the number of new employees while simultaneously retaining the once-in-a-lifetime job-hunting system first established in the mid-1950s.

14. The "Izanami Boom," which did not redistribute wealth to workers and citizens, was consequently short lived. Once the 2008 global financial crisis struck, market competition became even more fierce and working conditions worsened, fueling a profit-supremacist environment and widening economic disparities.

15. Sōmushō Tōkēkyoku (Statistics Bureau of Japan), "Rōdōryoku Chōsa: Chōki Jikēretsu Dēta (Survey of Labor Power: Long-Term Chronological Data)," chart 9(1), "The Number of Employees by Age Group (10 Years) and Different Employment Status (Since 1984)," https://www.stat.go.jp/data/roudou/longtime/03roudou.html (accessed July 20, 2022).

16. Sōmushō Tōkēkyoku, chart 9(1).

17. See Benner 2002; Curtin and Sanson 2016.

18. Council of Judicial Reforms, 2001, Opinion Brief, "21-seiki no Nihon wo Sasaeru Shihō Seido [Judicial Systems that Sustain Japan of 21st Century]," https://www.kantei.go.jp/jp/sihouseido/report/ikensyo/index.html (accessed on September 10, 2019).

19. Annually, they work on average ten to eleven hours a day with one day off per month.

Japan Animation Creators Association, 2015, Animation Creators Survey Report (Tokyo: JAniCA, 2015), 44, http://www.janica.jp/survey/survey2015Report.pdf. Also see Kim and Ikegai 2006: 186.

20. Kim and Ikegai 2006: 186; Yagi 2006: 56; Tēkoku Dēta Banku (Tēkoku Data Bank), 2020, *A Trend Survey about Animation Creation Industry*, https://www.tdb.co.jp/report/watching/press/p201002.html.

21. Meanwhile, 8.7 percent of the male workforce were nonregular workers in 1989, gradually increasing to 11.1 percent in 1999, 17.8 percent in 2009, and 22.4 percent in 2019. For details, see Sōmushō Tōkēkyoku, chart 9(1).

22. A twenty-four-year-old elite employee of Dentsu Advertisement Co., Takahashi Matsuri, who graduated from the University of Tokyo and worked in the digital advertisement section, took her life in 2015. Mita Labor Bureau, a Tokyo Office, identified the cause of her death as suicide by excessive overwork. A woman employee of NHK, Sato Miwa, who was a journalist, passed away at the age of thirty-one from overwork in 2017. Unlike married women, who can play the "gender card" to avoid overtime and fulfill their household duties instead, these single women may feel particular pressure to say "yes" to extra work, especially in a short-staffed workplace. Young women are also, as labor lawyer Kawahito Hiroshi stresses, vulnerable to power and sexual harassment at work (Fumoto Sachiko, 2016, "*Karōjisatsu wa Taningoto dewa nai* [Death by Overwork Is Not the Issue of Others]," *Nikkei Style*, August 12, https://style.nikkei.com/article/DGXMZO10151500R01C16A2000000/).

23. Men's nonregular employment has significantly increased, from 9.4 percent in 1993 to 17.8 percent in 2005, during the Employment Ice Age. Sōmushō Tōkēkyoku, chart 9(1).

24. Hashimoto 2018: 8.

25. *Omoshiro so* in Japanese.

26. *Kotowaru riyū ga nakatta* in Japanese.

27. *Tada nantonaku yattemiyō kana* in Japanese.

28. *Okane ga hoshikatta* in Japanese.

29. *Yūmē ni naritai to omotta* in Japanese.

30. *Shitsuren shite jibōjiki ni natteita* in Japanese.

31. Asad 2003: 59. Also see Neu 2018 for the discussion of liberal violence.

32. See Suchland 2015 for the similar cases in the former Soviet Union and Eastern Bloc.

33. Yagi 2006: 53.

34. *Nuku tame no dōgu* in Japanese.

35. Contract and legal compliance are used to justify adult video making as a business transaction in the digital economy, where worldwide circulation of pornographic images has the potential to generate staggering scales of cyber traffic and copyright revenue too.

36. Archard 1998; Fried 2015 (1981); Gilmore and Collins 1995; Popova 2019; Wertheimer 2003.

37. Male actors have been subject to consent giving only recently. The Japanese legislature now requires all AV performers to sign a month-in-advance contract, due to concerns over COVID-19. The age of adulthood was also lowered from 20 to 18 in 2022, the first such lowering in more than 140 years.

38. Spivak 1987: 207.

39. Pateman 1988: 149. Also Stanley 1998: 2.

40. Fischel 2019: 4.

41. Fried 2015: 1–2. Similarly, sociolegal scholar Hugh Collins argues that the legal frame of the contract ignores relational aspects of contract making, such as how contractual terms were negotiated, how a contractual relationship fitted into a prior relation between the parties, and how performance of the contract would serve the interests of the parties (Collins 1999: 15–16).

42. Frug 1985: 1131; Hadfield 1995: 338; Held 1987: 111–13; Stanley 1998: 2; Sullivan 2000: 113. Linda Mulcahy contends that the legal premise that autonomous citizens freely give consent or refusal manifests "masculine ideals of the discrete arms-length transaction between strangers." Contractual exchanges, in this view, are the "mere expression of economic relationships: a callous cash nexus divorced from intimacy" (Mulcahy 2014: 4).

43. Pateman 1988: 39.

44. Catharine MacKinnon, for example, states, "Little girls may not consent [to sex]; wives must. . . . The result of us falling into parallel provinces: good girls, like children, are unconsenting, virginal, rapable; bad girls, like wives, are consenting, whores, unrapable" (1983: 648).

45. Robin Morgan famously argued that "pornography is the theory and rape is the practice" (1977: 169). In her 1984 article, "Not a Moral Issue," Catherine MacKin-

non similarly asserts, "Pornography, in the feminist view, is a form of forced sex, a practice of sexual politics, an institution of gender inequality (325). MacKinnon also claims, "Woman through male eyes is sex object, that by which man knows himself at once as man and as subject"; as it is linguistically reinforced, "Man fucks women; subject verb object" (1982: 538; 541). For other anti-porn scholarly and activist work, see Barry 1979; Brownmiller 1975; Dworkin 1981; Dworkin and MacKinnon 1988; Griffin 1981; Lederer 1980; Rich 1980; Russell 1998.

46. In her 1984 article "Thinking Sex," Gayle Rubin, for example, criticizes the anti-porn regime's claim that sex is a natural force (e.g., sexual essentialism). Claiming that sex is a social construct rather than a biological entity, Rubin proposes deconstructing social norms. From this perspective, sexual exploration is a way to practice this deconstruction (277). Within a normative sexual value system, "sexuality that is 'good,' 'normal' and 'natural' should ideally be heterosexual, marital, monogamous, reproductive, and non-commercial" in contrast with "bad sex," which is defined as "homosexual, unmarried, promiscuous, non-procreative, or commercial" (280–81). Thus, sex work, which belongs to "bad sex," has the potential to problematize or even subvert such a value system.

47. Allison 1984; Assiter and Carol 1993; Califia-Rice 1980, 1994; Carol and Kennedy 1994; Dodson 1987; Duggan and Hunter 2006; Rich 1983; Rubin 1984; Vance 1984.

48. Berg 2021: 35.

49. Berg 2021: 35. Meanwhile, Berg writes that directors and video makers have the "ability to rehire, give this person a good referral, or not" (63).

50. Berg 2021: 63.

51. Doezema 1998: 38, 41.

52. Appel 2019: 138–43.

53. Appel calls this a form of "nation-fetishism" (Appel 2019: 145).

54. Appel 2019: 144.

55. Strictly adhering to general rules and regulations, however, does not prevent corruption. Sylvia Tidey ethnographically reveals that adherence to the superficial forms without taking into consideration their meaning ends up reproducing wrongdoing that the rule of law intends to overcome (Tidey 2013: 195).

56. I conducted a total of ninety-eight in-depth interviews, with twenty female and nine male AV performers, three recruiters, twelve talent agents, six directors, six video-maker employees, four distribution company employees, seven male fans, and numerous lawyers, activists, case workers, newspaper reporters, and others. I also analyzed the discourse surrounding the issue of forced AV performance in the mainstream press. Despite my initial struggle to secure interviewees due to the controversy surrounding "forced performance in AV," people in the adult video industry gradually opened up as I developed a rapport with them. My interviewees, especially talent agencies that tend to be the target of AV bashing, said that they were

worried about their distorted image in the mass media and asked me to share their voices, though they did not expect me to gloss over problems in the industry, either.

57. See Ivy 1995 for a discussion of the 1990s national project of building a new consciousness in a late-capitalist consumer context.

58. Ivy 1995: 59.

59. Fassin 2012: 4.

60. It was 1981 when the first "adult videos" appeared in Japan. The Tokyo-based Japan Video Motion Picture Company released two titles, translated into English as *A Woman in a Dirty Magazine: Take a Peek at Her Deep Secret* and *White Paper on Office Ladies' Vaginas: Heated Secret Garden*. At the time, only a small number of people—5.1 percent of the population—owned the home videotape recorder (VTR) required to watch these movies. Tanemura Takashi,2014 "Bideo (Video)," http://tane mura.la.coocan.jp/re3_index/6H/hi_video.html.

61. Ownership of VTRs rapidly increased to 33.5 percent by 1986, 53.0 percent by 1988, and 71.5 percent by 1991 (Chūo Chōsasha, "Taikyūzai no Henyō [Transformation in Durable Consumer Observed through Statistics]," https://www.crs.or .jp/backno/old/No614/6141.htm (accessed March 3, 2020). Nobody had imagined that this new home electronic appliance would become one of the so-called Three Sacred Treasures—must-have durable goods of modern Japan—within a decade. The Three Sacred Treasures in post-WWII Japan shifted from a black-and-white television, dishwasher, and refrigerator in the 1950s to 1960s to a car, air conditioner, and color television in the 1970s, and then VTR and other appliances such as hot plates and coffee machines in the 1980s. Along with the widespread use of the VTR, rental video chains swiftly opened up all over the country. (See Alilunas 2016 for a similar development in the US.) The roughly 500 video rental stores that existed in 1984 had proliferated to more than 13,500 by 1990. These numbers are based on a survey of JVA, Japan Video Software Association, http://jva-net.or.jp/report/joiningshop.pdf from the home page of JVA: http://jva-net.or.jp/ (accessed February 29, 2020). By then, all rental shops carried each title in two different video formats—VHS and Betamax—as a fierce format war raged between Sony (Betamax) and Matsushita (VHS). Ultimately, VHS won the battle. What is little understood are the reasons for the VHS victory. To address the mystery, an urban legend illuminates the significant role of adult videos. It goes like this: since most small-scale porn video makers couldn't afford Betamax, which had better picture quality, more adult video makers used VHS, producing a wide variety of titles in this cheaper format (Nakamura 2015: Kindle Location 59 of 2434). Increasing numbers of consumers—mainly fathers, husbands, and single men—also bought the cheaper VHS-formatted VTR so that they could enjoy watching a range of adult videos at home; and retail shops helped further by giving adult videos away to buyers of VHS players as "gifts." Whether the legend is true or not, however, the birth of the adult video industry is imagined to be

closely related to the emergence of new technologies and the spread of rental video shops in the 1980s.

62. Japan's Penal Code, Article 175, prohibits distributing, selling, or publicly displaying an obscene document, drawing, or other object. The penalty for breaking the law includes "imprisonment with work" for up to two years and a fine of up to 2,500,000 yen (about US$25,000). While the definition of obscenity has been well outlined—any public display of genitals must be covered up—enforcement has often been arbitrary, capricious, and selective.

63. *Asahi Shimbun Digital*, 2017, "9 Men and Women Arrested for Selling DVDs without Mosaic," September 21, https://www.asahi.com/articles/ASK9P42C6K9PPT IL00Q.html.

64. At the dawn of the AV industry, video makers and wholesalers created a lucrative distribution system that relied on pricing adult videos—an unprecedented commodity—very high. The retail price of an adult video was about 15,000 yen (US$150). Video makers solicited preorders from rental video shops and had wholesalers deliver copies based on the order. Selling to wholesalers, AV makers earned 60 percent of the retail price, or 9,000 yen (US$90) per title. Wholesalers then resold the videos to rental shops for 12,000 yen (US$120) per copy after adding a 30 percent commission fee (Nakamura 2015: Kindle Location 113 out of 2434). Shops charged customers 700–1,000 yen (US$7–10) per title for a two-day, one-night rental. In the mid- to late 1980s, a typical producer of adult videos sold an average of 2,000 copies per title. According to nonfiction writer Nakamura Atsuhiko, who has studied the AV industry in Japan for the last two decades, the estimated profit margin (before taxes) for a maker was a high 60 percent (Nakamura 2015: Kindle Location 145–51 out of 2434). This meant that a maker yielded a profit of 150 million yen (US$1.5 million) per year from new titles alone, never mind ongoing sales of back titles (Nakamura 2015: Kindle Location 151 out of 2434). Of course, adult video makers did not publicize their annual sales, and therefore the real figure remains unknown.

65. Especially younger generations, who have easy access to free content online, spend much less money on AV and other cultural products. According to a white paper by the Ministry of Internal Affairs and Communications, 94.6 percent of people in their twenties own smartphones, followed by 90.4 percent of those in their thirties, 81.4 percent of teenagers, and 79.9 percent of those in their forties (https:// www.soumu.go.jp/johotsusintokei/statistics/data/200529_1.pdf [accessed February 5, 2021]).

66. Over the past fifteen years, the Japanese AV industry has drastically transformed along with the advancement in information technology and the distribution change to on-demand streaming—where subscription prices are much cheaper, if not free. With DVD sales, adult video makers earn 60 percent of the retail price, whereas with internet streaming, they make only half of this. In the early years of

the new millennium, AV makers allegedly treated the on-demand streaming service as secondary to DVD products and agreed to release video content in exchange for modest broadcasting fees. By the mid-2010s, however, on-demand streaming had rapidly outgrown the original DVD sales. As a result, AV makers have struggled with shrinking revenue in their main profit-making domain.

67. Declining sales, especially DVD sales, have pressured AV makers to cut production expenses while still maintaining quality in order to survive in the hypercompetitive content industry. Inevitably, the industry has solicited everyone, including performers, to work harder for less money. Most full-time employees at video production companies enjoy labor protections, whereas gig workers—directors for hire, assistant directors, staff, and AV actors alike—are not safeguarded from long, intensive work hours for less pay.

68. *Shūkan Post*, 2012, "Study of Businesses Catering to Human Desires: Adult Video Industry, the Declining Business Field," *Shūkan Post* 44 (17): 152–55. The mass media have reported that adult video in Japan is a *shayō sangyō* (declining business field). Video makers, especially the small ones I interviewed, lament the rapid changes in digital technology and viewership that have made survival itself their ultimate business goal.

69. Iijima's influence across AV and mainstream worlds was indicative of the fruitless turmoil that the "rental versus sales" battle generated in the 1990s adult video industry. The battle over the distribution format mattered only to AV makers, who were ultimately subject to end users' desires. Consumers began to actively engage in the selection of adult content and access methods. Meanwhile, a few AV idols went beyond the industry's internal battle, gaining nationwide fame in the mainstream media.

70. Like Iijima, Komuro Yuri, a former photogravure idol, and Morishita Kurumi, a Lolita, gained nationwide fame and successfully transitioned to second careers after their "retirement" from adult video. Komuro, who maintained top-selling AV performer status for nearly four years after debuting in 1996, went on to work as a theater actress, singer, essayist, and sexual advisor. Morishita, who made her debut in 1999 and stayed popular for nearly 10 years, became a writer and actress.

71. The actresses in the 1980s were not necessarily well compensated despite their contribution to AV. Video makers tacitly agreed, like a cartel, to cap women performers' guarantees at between 200,000 to 300,000 yen (US$2,000–3,000) per title. After their talent agencies deducted commission fees, performers received only a quarter to half this amount. But Muranishi Toru, a director at leading AV producer Diamond Motion Pictures, whose success story was recently depicted in the Netflix series *The Naked Director*, broke this de facto cartel by offering female performers significantly more money. An outlier in the AV industry, Muranishi "bought out" women directly from street scouts and raised their guarantees significantly, to the

extent that he paid up to 1,000,000 yen (US$10,000) per video to his best-selling performers, who included Kuroki Kaoru, among other porn stars like Matsuzaka Kimiko, in exclusive contracts. In his 2016 biography, *The Naked Director: Muranishi Toru*, he said that he paid generously to induce street scouts to bring fresh women to him first (Motohashi 2016). With the large buyout payments and guarantees, Muranishi was able to recruit a new crop of extremely beautiful young women with high potential—all the while circumventing talent agencies. Muranishi's bold move eventually resulted in increasing women's performance guarantees throughout the industry. By the same token, however, performers themselves never organized a union or an advocacy group to collectively negotiate their pay and work conditions. They have acquiesced to the price and contractual terms set by the video makers, no matter how much profit their videos make.

72. Coates 2014; Wong and Yau 2014. Aoi Sora, a moderately popular Japanese adult video actress, for example, became a superstar in China after her pornographic work was introduced to the Chinese market through informal networks of pirated DVDs and file sharing in the late 1990s. She is now a transnational celebrity, establishing her status as a "teacher" and "goddess" among urban middle-class youth in mainland China, Hong Kong, Taiwan, and South Korea.

73. The rapid growth of the adult video business in the 1980s was concomitant with Japan's so-called AV boom. Several women performers became famous in Japan, their stardom fueling the popularity of adult videos. They contributed not only to refining AV genres but also drawing Japanese mainstream attention to adult videos. In the 1980s, *Forbidden Relationships*, the 1986 video debut of former stripper Kobayashi Kaoru, sold a record 50,000 copies and led to the boom of the *bishōjo* (pretty girls) subgenre. Her popularity with a mainstream viewership helped adult video gain popularity too (*Shūkan Asahi Geinō*, September 19, 2019, 47). Matsuzaka Kimiko, who first appeared in the 1989 adult video *Discovery of the Big Boobs*, gained fame for her H-cup-sized breasts and fired up a *kyonyū* (huge breasts) boom. Around the same time, a prolific performer known as Toyomaru gained legendary fame for her apparent excessive sexual drive. In videos with eye-popping titles such as *The Sucking Power of Pussy: The Most Obscene in History* and *Empire of Blooming Promiscuity*, she let loose unfiltered orgasms on camera and inserted anything and everything into her vagina. In magazine interviews, she openly spoke about her instant sexual arousal and daily masturbation even after having multiple orgasms during a porn shooting. Toyomaru helped transform *inran* (excessive promiscuity) into a subgenre. But it was Kuroki Kaoru who became a national icon for adult videos. Altogether, these AV stars played a significant role not only within the booming industry but also by bringing AV to the attention of the mainstream Japanese public.

74. In 2008, one of the largest AV makers in Japan launched a new label, MUTEKI (meaning *invincible*), to specialize in *gēnōjin debyū* (celebrity debuts). Suzuki

Shoko, a Japan Record Awards–winning singer in the idol duo Wink, appeared in a MUTEKI video in 2009 (engaging primarily in soft-core pornography). Kozai Saki, a former model and public figure, also made her debut with MUTEKI in 2011. Other celebrities, such as well-known members of female idol groups, television stars, and photogravure models, were increasingly recruited to AV performance in the 2010s. These professional career paths also set the bar for other actresses.

75. Largely because of free speech laws and neoliberal economic policies, the AV industry has been the most legally protected sector among all sex commerce in Japan. The industry has grown significantly since its emergence in the 1980s. It enjoyed nearly unrivaled prosperity in the early 2010s, generating an estimated US$5 billion a year, churning out some 35,000 video titles—DVDs and online—aimed mainly at a male heterosexual audience. To put this in perspective, the US porn industry's online video sales are estimated at US$2.8 billion, serving a population of more than twice Japan's (Futrelle 2012). Though Japan's AV industry sales peaked at the beginning of 2010 and have been declining ever since, the industry demands that young, inexperienced actresses perform in adult videos, two-thirds of whom are replaced annually (Nakamura 2012: 16). More than 150 adult video talent agencies, most located in the Tokyo metropolitan area, are believed to supply 2,000 to 3,000 fresh female actresses to the business each year to meet the growing demand (Nakamura 2012: 16).

76. Ebisu Muscats, Sexy-J, me-me, Marshmallow 3d+, BRW108, Pinky, Kuhn, Vitch Vitch, Kiss, OFA☆21, Milky Pop Generation, and Honey Popcorn, to name a few.

77. Nakamura 2012: Kindle Location 349 out of 2966.

78. In her essay, Suzuki metaphorically expresses what it is like to live a life as an ex-performer who got involved in adult video for trivial reasons but ended up destroying her future: "It was no big deal at all for my 19-year-old self to make an AV debut. It was like kicking a pebble with my foot to clear the discontent and frustration of adolescence." More than ten years later, she still suffers from the pebble she kicked one day that continues to bounce back to her, her parents, and her boyfriends. "The pebble occasionally hit my face, causing a bloody nose and dizziness in the head," she confesses.

79. Suzuki Suzumi, 2020, "The Price of 10,000,000 yen, the Performance Guarantee, for My Debut Video," Bunshun Online, January 30, https://blogos.com/article/432936/?p=2.

80. Kawana Mariko, 2018, Facebook, March 18. Kawana writes: "I am so sad and depressed about the fact that 15 years of my self-devotion to write great mysteries are spoiled by four years as an AV actress long ago."

81. See Bourdieu 2004 for symbolic violence.

## Chapter 1

1. Nakamura 2015.

2. Tomohiro Osaki, 2015, "Landmark Ruling in Favor of Victimized Porn Actress Paves Way for Others to Quit, Lawyers Say," *Japan Times*, September 30, https://www .japantimes.co.jp/news/2015/09/30/national/crime-legal/landmark-ruling-favor-vic timized-porn-actress-paves-way-others-quit-say-lawyers/#.XE3A989KhTY.

3. These terms were used in the titles of reports and inquiries in early 2016 by Miyamoto Setsuko, then representative of the victim-support group PAPS (People against Pornography and Sexual Violence); Ito Kazuko, the lawyer and head of human rights activist group Human Rights Now; and Ikeuchi Saori, then a member of Japan's House of Representatives.

4. The Office has appointed April, the beginning of the Japanese school year, as the campaign month to prevent sexual violence against women, highlighting the issue of forced AV performance and so-called JK business—meaning *joshikōsei* (high school girls) involved in sexual trades such as "sugar daddy" dating and *enjo kōsai* (other compensated dating).

5. The *Japan Times*, for example, uses the term "forced performance in adult videos," whereas the Human Rights Now report refers to it as "coerced filming of adult pornographic videos." See *Japan Times*, 2018, "Japanese March in Shibuya Calls for End to Sex Crimes against Young Women," April 20, https://www.japantimes .co.jp/news/2018/04/20/national/crime-legal/japanese-march-shibuya-calls-end-sex -crimes-young-women/; Human Rights Now 2016.

6. *Oxford Dictionary of English*, 3rd ed., 2010.

7. Nietzsche 2003 [1913]: Kindle Location 740 of 2433.

8. In his 2017 award-winning book *Chūdōtai no Sekai (The World of Middle Voice)*, Japanese philosopher Kokubun Koichiro states, *kyōyō wan ai ga jihatsuteki demo naku, jihatsuteki demonai ga dōi shiteiru to iu chūkanteki na Ishi*: "Non-forced but also non-voluntary consent is ubiquitous. Nonetheless, it is rendered nonexistent in such dichotomous views as consent vis-a-vis coercion and activity vis-a-vis passivity" (Kokubun 2017: 158).

9. In Japanese, *'hanashi dake demo' to iware te tsuite itta*.

10. In Japanese, *'toriaezu sain wo' to iware te ōjita. Toriaezu*, which is casually used in various situations, can be interpreted multiple ways: for the time being, for now, and first of all. The term can also simply be a space holder, without meaning anything specific.

11. Macpherson 1962.

12. Osaki 2015.

13. Osaki 2015.

14. Human Rights Now 2016.

15. Osaki 2015.

16. PAPS is a nonprofit organization, established in 2009, to advocate for victims of sexual exploitation, connecting victims to necessary legal services and other social resources. According to the organization, the first call they received from a victim was in 2013, and it involved trouble caused by forced performance in AV.

17. Human Rights Now 2016: 3. The report is based on its own investigation, which included hearing from victim-support groups such as PAPS and victims themselves.

18. Ikeuchi Saori, 2016, "Pursuing Sexual Violence and Human Rights Violations against Women" (blog), March 11, http://www.saori-ikeuchi.com/proceeding/av.

19. Sex workers rarely go public for help when they are in trouble, partly because they know how dismissive police officers and legal professionals can be even if they are trapped in contract bondage or experiencing other forms of abuse. Studying the politico-legal grayness of the sex industry in Japan, anthropologist Gabriele Koch has made similar observations, stating that "go[ing] to the police would entail exposing [sex workers] themselves to unwelcome scrutiny"; and in court, for the most part, "claims by sex workers are voided on the basis that they entered into an illegitimate 'prostitution contract' (*baishun keiyaku*) by engaging in sex work" (Koch 2020: 160).

20. Fassin 2012: 4.

21. Bumiller 2008: 37.

22. Catharine MacKinnon reminds us of the masculinist logic of sexual consent, in which little girls are not supposed to consent to sex. Based on this assumption, good girls are "unconsenting, virginal, rapable" whereas bad girls are "consenting, whores, unrapable" (1983: 648). In this way, only "rapable" good girls become worthy of protection. Bumiller (2008) also argues that expressive justice expands punitive measures while also doing little to actually help the victim.

23. For more information, see https://withnews.jp/about.

24. NHK's *Kurōzu Appu Gendai* [Today's Close-Up] broadcasted the program on July 25, 2016. For more information, see https://www.nhk.or.jp/gendai/articles/3843/index.html.

25. NHK's description of the problem included the wording "deceived with sweet words," or more specifically, as the documentary put it, "Women are coerced, or deceived with sweet words, into performing in adult video, AV."

26. The US has historically exercised its hegemonic power as "world police" of global security issues like human trafficking. Its annual report ranks countries based on their compliance with the US standards outlined in the Trafficking Victims Protection Act (TVPA) of 2000 and promotes the Act's criminal justice model: prosecution, protection, and prevention. The 2017 report ranked Japan tier 2, a country whose government does not yet fully comply with the TVPA's minimum standards but makes significant efforts toward the goal.

27. US Department of State 2017: 227.

28. Bernstein 2010.

29. Macpherson states that this self-possessive quality is grounded "in its conception of the individual as essentially the proprietor of his own person or capacities, owing nothing to society" (Macpherson 1962: 3).

30. Pateman 1988: 59, 151.

31. Pateman 1988: 149.

32. The Japanese phrase *uru uranai wa watashi ga kimeru* is derived and modified from women's self-determination over their reproductive health: *umu umanai wa watashi ga kimeru* ([I ]decide whether or not to give birth).

33. In Japanese, *sekkusu wāku wa jiyū ishi*.

34. Osaki 2015.

35. Osaki 2015.

36. I learned later from business insiders that Kozai brought her legal representative upon making an exclusive management contract with her agency; therefore, they believed her forced performance claim was "bogus." Kozai admitted that she asked her lawyer-acquaintance to attend the signing since she needed to make sure that she could continue her weekend modeling job.

37. Entwistle and Wissinger 2006: 782.

38. Entwistle and Wissinger 2006: 786, 788. Also note Witz, Warhurst, and Nickson's (2003) notion of "aesthetic labor" in freelance work, in contrast with "emotional labor" in corporate settings.

39. *Honban* means both a real shooting (in contrast to a trial run) and real hardcore sex (in contrast to *giji*, imitation sex).

40. *Shūkan Bunshun*, 2016, "Ninki AV Joyū Jitsumē Kokuhatsu: 'Kyōhaku, Sennō, Kakoikomi Jigoku' (Popular AV Actresses' Accusation: 'Threatening, Brainwashing, Isolation Hell')," July 14, 126.

41. *Shūkan Bunshun* 2016: 129.

42. *Shūkan Bunshun* 2016: 129.

43. *Shūkan Bunshun* 2016: 129.

44. MacKinnon points out that "what conditions make [what happened] reasonable—is one-sided: male-sided" (MacKinnon 1983: 654).

45. MacKinnon 1983: 650.

46. MacKinnon 1983: 652.

47. MacKinnnon 1983: 653 (emphasis mine).

48. Thanks to widespread internet use and exposure to pornographic videos, AV actresses today are much more familiar with AV than those who started their performance career before the emergence of smartphones and tablets in the late 2000s.

49. Diet Cabinet Office 2017: 7.

50. Diet Cabinet Office 2017: 17.

51. Diet Cabinet Office 2017: 20–21.

52. Diet Cabinet Office 2017: 23–25.

53. Diet Cabinet Office 2017: 26.

54. Diet Cabinet Office 2017: 26.

55. This remark, *kakugo wo kimeru,* echoes what Kozai's fortune teller stressed as a form of self-determination.

56. Reinforcing her view, Kondo's Japanese landlady commented, "The Japanese don't treat themselves as important, they spend time doing things for the sake of maintaining good social relationships, regardless of their inner feelings" (Kondo 1986: 81).

57. Kondo 1986: 81 (emphasis original).

58. See Kondo 1990 on the sociocultural construction of selves in Japan. Also see Bachnik and Quinn 1994, Kuga 1999, Lebra 2004, and Rosenberger 2011.

59. Council of Judicial Reforms, 2001, Opinion Brief, "21-seiki no Nihon wo Sasaeru Shihō Seido [Judicial Systems that Sustain Japan of 21st Century]," https://www.kantei.go.jp/jp/sihouseido/report/ikensyo/index.html (emphasis mine).

60. Derrida 1999: 66.

61. Pateman 1988: 152.

62. If sexuality is, as MacKinnon writes, "relational, specifically if it is a power relation of gender, [then] consent is a communication under conditions of inequality" (MacKinnon 1983: 652).

63. Collins 1999: 15–16.

64. Frug 1985: 1131; Hadfield 1995: 338; Held 1987: 111–13; Sullivan 2000: 113.

65. Mulcahy 2014: 4.

66. Mulcahy 2014: 4.

67. Mulcahy 2014: 4.

68. Pateman 1988: 39.

69. He states, "Violence with a clear subject-object relation is manifest because it is visible as *action,*" as easily captured in language: "subject-verb-object, with both subject and object being persons" (Galtung 1969: 171).

70. Cheryl I. Harris argues that the legal logic of what is valuable and which rights merit the protection of the law is deeply embedded in structural inequalities. While Harris discusses the legal protection of white privilege as a form of *property* in the US, her anti-racist critique applies to the protection of gender, sexual, and class privileges in many other societies as well (Harris 1993: 1730, 1742). Despite the popular perspective of property as a thing a person possesses or a right of a person with respect to a thing, Harris points out that property may consist of "rights in 'things' that are intangible or whose existence is a matter of legal definition" (1725).

71. Harris 1993: 1725.

72. Marx 1990 (1976).

73. See Pateman 1988: 57–58.

## Chapter 2

1. Das 2008: 284. For example, as Lisa Rofel points out while analyzing the Chinese revolution of the 1940s and 1950s, expressing "bitterness" may not simply involve complaining about the past but may be a means through which to interpret one's life in a new way or see oneself as a new person (Rofel 1999: 140). In other words, projecting bitterness might function as a method to overcome hardship and experience feelings of empowerment.

2. Women who perform in adult videos are referred to as simply *ēbui joyū* (AV actresses). Within this, there are three rankings. The most rarefied are the *tantai joyū* (or simply *tantai*) actresses, who have exclusive performance contracts with specific video makers. *Tantai* performers' videos are released only once a month as "luxurious" commodities, to maintain their "freshness" and extend their market value as long as possible. Only a few dozen, flawlessly beautiful women—like Amatsuka Moe, featured in this book's opening vignette—attain this prestigious status. Other women, who may have *tantai*-level appeal but want to be free from exclusive performance agreements that limit money-making opportunities to once a month, become *kikaku tantai*. Their agents freely book performance offers from multiple video makers, allowing the actresses to appear in miscellaneous videos. The more videos they appear in, the more money they can earn. *Kikaku tantai* performers, however, occupy only about 10 to 20 percent of the entire actress pool for adult video. The rest belong to the *kikaku* category. Within this category, performers play supportive roles or appear in omnibus without credits.

3. Participant observation conducted at PAPS office between December 2017 and March 2018.

4. *Morahara* and *pawahara* (abbreviations of Japanese English for moral and power harassment, respectively) refer to forms of harassment during which a dominant individual humiliates a subordinate in front of others, tearing down their dignity, morality, and self-worth in either the domestic sphere or in a public space like a school, workplace, or neighborhood. Both *morahara* and *pawahara* largely gained their recognition in the 1990s and 2000s after *sekuhara* (sexual harassment) won the 1989 Word of the Year, by Jiyū Kokumin Sha, an influential publisher who annually publishes neologisms, and raised social awareness for other forms of assault. With these types of harassment, the powerful generally make degrading remarks about the powerless's simple errors, negligence, or mistakes based on moral claims, as if their behavior is rooted in the person's morals and personality. *Morahara* and *pawahara* were often used in the context of the so-called *burakku kigyō* (as I discuss further in chapter 5) to describe how Japanese work environments have become exploitative, toxic spaces, not only socioeconomically but also morally and mentally.

5. Yasuda 2018: 107.

6. Yasuda 2018: 107.

7. Yasuda 2018: 179.

8. Yasuda 2018: 95.

9. Yasuda 2018: 145.

10. Alexy 2020; Hendry 2019; Ronald and Alexy 2011; Sugimoto 2010.

11. Rubin 1984: 280.

12. *Tantai* actresses are closely "cared about" (read: monitored) in order to not be snatched by other agencies. Other actresses are also banned from exchanging their contacts or getting together after hours in the name of "protection of privacy," which is, as I learned from AV talent agents, a smokescreen. AV actresses, who try to avoid trouble with their agencies, follow the rules and avoid seeking help from fellow actors. Thanks to social media, only recently have AV performers found ways to connect with one another in private and discuss their work.

13. Yasuda 2018: 94–95.

14. For fake ejaculations, an assistant director inserts fluid that looks just like semen into the actress's vagina as soon as the male actor pulls out, so that the camera captures the fluid coming out, as if the man came inside of her.

15. Bourdieu 2001: 2.

16. Scheper-Hughes and Bourgois 2004: 1. Sociologist Jane Kilby elaborates on the "slipperiness" of violence, claiming that violence exists as a binary: "material and symbolic; structural and abstract; collective and individual; visible and invisible; legal, extralegal and illegal; brutal and subtle; sporadic and everyday; and spectacular and banal" (Kilby 2013: 263).

17. "*Giji* (fake sex)," pretending to have sexual intercourse on camera, is differentiated from hardcore "real sex," which is referred to as *honban* in Japanese. Under Japanese obscenity laws, which forbid genital display without *mozaiku* (literally mosaic, meaning fuzzing out), fake sex can be presented realistically on the screen. Though obscenity codes evolve based on what law enforcement deems a disturbance of *kōjo ryōzoku* (public order and moral decency), it is still illegal to produce such explicit videos within Japan and sell them on the domestic market.

18. Fischel 2019: 4.

19. During my interview, actresses told me that their readiness to perform sexually can differ from moment to moment, depending on their own body and mental conditions as well as their chemistry with other performers on set.

20. Bourdieu 2001: 2.

21. Galtung 1969: 171.

22. Ramsay 2010: 238.

23. Cited in *Excite News!*, 2016, "Sakura Mana, Amatsuka Moe, Kawana Mariko et. al., AV Actresses, Fight Back to the United Nation Report on 'Human Rights Violation in Adult Film Making,'" May 1, https://www.excite.co.jp/news/article/Litera_2203/.

24. *Excite News!* 2016.

25. Allison 2013: 32; Brinton 1992; Lukács 2020: 9–10; Takeyama 2016: 8. Chizuko Ueno writes, "70% of Japanese women of productive age have now joined the labor market, which exceeds that of the USA and the EU in number, but nearly six out of ten women work at low wages [under] irregular conditions" (Ueno 2021: 15).

26. Hochschild 2003.

27. Kozai Saki's unscripted interview in the beginning of her debut video, *RACE QUEEN* (introduced in the previous chapter) is another example. Her puffy face with drained eyes (a trace of her crying) showed on the screen while she was asked whether she was ready to shoot.

## Chapter 3

1. The IPPA homepage states that they require AV makers and talent agencies alike to comply with business guidelines, including the use of a standardized form of contract. https://www.ippa.jp/tekisei/ (accessed December 20, 2020).

2. Those who have come out to their families almost unanimously share that their families, especially parents, never understand what they do; siblings generally accept that they make a living in the AV business but never bring up the topic again.

3. A sexual practice mainstream society would consider shameful and deeply marginal may lead some to adopt this kind of smokescreen. In what Gayle Rubin calls the sexual value system, she writes, "good," "normal," and "natural" sex is presumed to "not involve pornography, *fetish objects*, sex toys of any sort, or roles other than male and female" (Rubin 1984: 281, emphasis mine). Individuals who partake in such acts are, Rubin argues, "subjected to a presumption of mental illness, disreputability, criminality, restricted social and physical mobility, loss of institutional support, and emotional sanctions" (279).

4. He would also not forget to tell her, I'm sure, how competitive and time-consuming it is to pursue fame in mainstream showbusiness, where newbies are often charged for voice, dance, and modeling lessons instead of earning anything.

5. "Delivery health" is a commodified sexual service delivered at a designated time and place.

6. Cabinet Office 2017: 22.

7. Cabinet Office 2017: 22.

8. Originally, most agencies hired street scouts to recruit potential AV performers, until street scouting was banned in Tokyo under the 2005 City Ordinance Against Disturbing the Peace. But some agencies still secretly rely on scouting to recruit top-class actresses. A scout usually approaches a young woman on a busy street in Tokyo metropolitan areas, especially Shibuya, Shinuku, and Ikebukuro, and escorts her to a nearby talent agency. There he receives either a one-time "buyout" payment—usually a few hundred thousand yen in cash—or a "lifelong" rebate—15 to 20 percent of the commission taken out of the actress's performance guarantee as long as a new

title of hers is released every month. More specifically, the agency distributes 15 to 20 percent of this performance guarantee to the scout, 20 to 50 percent to the actress, and the rest to the agency itself.

9. In his words, *"Iyada to iuno o muriyari nejimageru koto,"* literally forcing an unwilling object to bend.

10. Larkin 2013: 328.

11. In his words, *"Kane de damarase te hatarakase te iru."*

12. Some newly launched agencies, who have few well-paid *tantai* actresses, disclose the full amount of a performer's guarantee, splitting half each between the office and the performer. But most others continue the agencies' conventions.

13. *Saikopasu no otoko* and *hattatsu shōgai no onna*, in his own words in Japanese.

14. In agents' eye, scouts are reckless, bold, and potentially dangerous due to their alleged connections to underground gangs like the *yakuza*.

**Chapter 4**

1. Based on his experiences, he gives public lectures today on how to communicate more effectively and has published popular books on the topic.

2. Their remarks reminded me of the defensiveness of the fortune teller, discussed in chapter 1. When Kozai Saki, who came out as a victim of forced AV performance, accused the fortune teller of being part of the brainwashing efforts made by Kozai's talent agency, the fortune teller told Japanese weekly magazine *Shūkan Bunshun* in its July 14, 2016, issue that all the actresses she met had "already *kakugo wo kimete ita* (resigned themselves to AV performance)." In her own words, "I have never pushed them. Nor have I intended to be involved in brainwashing them, ever" (*Shūkan Bunshun* 2016: 129). She stressed not only that these women's resignation was a form of self-determination but also that her influence was none to minimal.

3. Mainstream Japanese often perceive the AV industry to be recession-less, even though the nation faced a prolonged economic hangover after the burst of bubble economy in the early 1990s. People in the business, however, tell me that the industry has experienced recessions too; this is simply not obvious because overall profits have remained greater than losses.

4. Nakamura 2015: Kindle Location 148 out of 2434. With video makers reliably nabbing 60 percent of retail sales, according to Nakamura, this meant they would earn about 54,000,000 yen (US$540,000) per video title and 32,4000,000 yen (US$324,000) after the price reduction. In both scenarios, releasing ten video titles monthly equated to annual sales of multibillion yen (multimillion USD), easily affording the purchase of office buildings in Tokyo for those behind the distribution.

5. *Shukan Post*, 2016, "1990-nendai AV wa Rentaru Zensē kara Serubideo no Jidai e (1990s AV Shifted from the Age of Rental to Sales Videos)," July 28, https://www.news-postseven.com/archives/20160728_432624.html?DETAIL.

6. *Suki shibari ni suru* in Japanese.

7. Rubin 1984: 307.

8. Rich 1980.

9. Nakamura 2012: 16.

10. Only recently have some popular male actors published books on "sex education," sexual communication, and sex and health, and have organized fan events for their mostly female fans (see Hambleton 2016).

11. Tsing 2000: 141.

12. For the *tantai*-class model, there is no previous record since she must be new and fresh, meaning no experience performing in AV. In the AV market, *tantai* actresses are most valuable upon their debut. As I discuss in the previous chapter, their market value declines precipitously after.

13. The AV Human Rights Ethics Committee consists of four board members—two co-ed lawyers and two legal scholars. Established as an extension of the Intellectual Property Protection Association (IPPA), its coverage area has extended from intellectual property rights to include AV actresses' human rights. Interestingly, it highlights women's rights only, remaining silent about male actors. The IPPA, which consists of 280 AV makers, as well as the AV Human Rights Ethics Committee, persuaded talent agencies to form their own associations and safeguard their business interests by way of collaborating with the Committee for the survival of the Japanese AV industry. More than 150 agencies became members and organized the Japan Production Guild in 2018.

14. Indeed, in my interviews I found that talent agents customarily took 60 to 70 percent of what the makers paid to them and gave the rest to the *tantai* performer, although they paid nearly half to lower-paid *kikaku tantai* and *kikaku* performers.

15. Director Suzuki, who wished for influential video makers' top-down reforms, also shared that his wife, a former *tantai* actress from the late 1980s, was paid only 300,000 yen per video; he found out later that her full performance guarantee was 2,000,000 yen per video, on average. Even so, his wife was happy about the amount of money she received in hand. She felt she had been exploited far worse while working as an apprentice at a hair salon.

16. Meanwhile, the most powerful players in the AV industry hierarchy—online distribution networks like DMM.com—remain invisible regarding forced AV performance issues. A smart online distribution company can carve out its own AV makers, AV directors, and talent agencies as affiliated yet discrete enterprises, so the parent company remains untainted by the stigma associated with adult entertainment.

17. Rubin 1975.

18. Miriam 2005: 7.

## Chapter 5

1. See Allison 1994; Dasgupta 2013.

2. Both Iijima and Akane died at young ages, of pneumonia in 2008 and an acute asthma attack in 2016, respectively. They were both discovered dead at their apartments, which shocked many fans.

3. This is another example of middle voice in Japanese vernacular language. While *karada ga kosareta* (the body is broken) connotes more a passive voice, *karada wo kowashita* means ([I] let [my] body be broken). In this way, the subject is partially responsible for what happened, meaning neither a mere victim of the event nor a causal subject of it.

4. *Shakai kaiso* (social stratification) tends to be classified *jō* (upper), *chū* (middle), and *ge* (lower) in Japan.

5. This is yet another example of middle voice in Japanese language, which is self-referential and reflexive.

6. *Gendai Yōgojiten* is an encyclopedia of contemporary Japanese language.

7. See Galbraith 2019 for further discussions about *otaku*.

8. The expression *konna koto* (this kind of thing) echoes the sentiment shared by AV actresses like Nakano from chapter 2; as a "thing," AV performance makes them feel guilty and their parents ashamed.

9. Hashimoto 2018: 8.

10. For details, see Sōmushō Tōkēkyoku, chart 9(1).

11. Sōmushō Tōkēkyoku, chart 9(1).

12. Sōmushō Tōkēkyoku, chart 9(1).

13. Hashimoto 2018: 125. According to Hashimoto, underclass men have low social capital in terms of building relationships of mutual trust and struggle to forge harmonious connections and social network support.

14. Kitanaka 2012: 5.

15. Kitanaka 2012: 130.

16. Most men, according to Connell, still "benefit from the patriarchal dividend" and "gain from the overall subordination of women" even though their masculinity may be marginalized in relation to other men (Connell 2005 [1995]: 78–79).

17. By "marginalized masculinities," Connell refers to "not fixed character types but configurations of practice generated in particular situations in a changing structure of relationships" (Connell 2005 [1995]: 81). In relation to "hegemonic masculinity"—which is, as Connell theorizes, a cultural ideal and normative definition of masculinity that not many actually meet—most men nevertheless remain complicit in supporting normative institutions such as marriage, fatherhood, and provider roles so as to gain a patriarchal dividend from the system's hegemony (79).

**Epilogue**

1. Sēfu Kōhō Onrain (Public Relations Office at Government of Japan), 2022, "18-sai de Otona no Igi (Meanings of Reaching the Legal Age of Adulthood at 18)," https://www.gov-online.go.jp/tokusyu/seinen_18/significance.html.

2. Sēfu Kōhō Onrain (Public Relations Office at Government of Japan), 2022, "Tarento, Moderu Kēyaku no Toraburu ni Gochūi wo! (Be Careful about Talent and Model [Management] Contracts!)," https://www.gov-online.go.jp/useful/article/201707/3.html.

3. Kansai Television, RUNNER, May 17, 2022, https://www.ktv.jp/news/keyperson/220517/.

4. Toda Makoto (@toda_makoto), 2022, "AV Shinpō Oyobi AV Shinpō Hantai-suru Kinkyū Akushon o Okonau Hitotachi ni taishite Imagenzai Kanjiteiru koto (What I Feel about New AV Acts and Those Who Are against the Acts)," Twitter, May 15, 8:56 p.m., https://twitter.com/toda_makoto/status/1526020238894309376.

# REFERENCES

Alexy, Allison. 2020. *Intimate Disconnections: Divorce and the Romance of Independence in Contemporary Japan*. Chicago: University of Chicago Press.

Alilunas, Peter. 2016. *Smutty Little Movies: The Creation and Regulation of Adult Video*. Oakland: University of California Press.

Allison, Anne. 1994. *Nightwork: Sexuality, Pleasure, and Corporate Masculinity in a Tokyo Hostess Club*. Chicago: University of Chicago Press.

Allison, Anne. 2013. *Precarious Japan*. Durham, NC: Duke University Press.

Allison, Dorothy. 1984. "Public Silence, Private Terror." In *Pleasure and Danger: Exploring Female Sexuality*, edited by Carole S. Vance, 103–14. Boston: Routledge & K. Paul.

Aoyagi, Hiroshi. 2005. *Islands of Eight Million Smiles: Idol Performance and Symbolic Production in Contemporary Japan*. Cambridge, MA: Harvard University Press.

Appel, Hannah. 2019. *The Licit Life of Capitalism: U.S. Oil in Equatorial Guinea*. Durham, NC: Duke University Press.

Archard, David. 1998. *Sexual Consent*. Oxford: Westview Press.

Asad, Talal. 2003. *Formations of the Secular: Christianity, Islam, Modernity*. Stanford, CA: Stanford University Press.

Assiter, Alison, and Avedon Carol. 1993. *Bad Girls and Dirty Pictures: The Challenge to Reclaim Feminism*. Boulder, CO: Pluto Press.

Bachnik, Jane, and Charles J. Quinn Jr. 1994. *Situated Meaning: Inside and Outside in Japanese Self, Society, and Language*. Princeton, NJ: Princeton University Press.

Barry, Kathleen. 1979. *Female Sexual Slavery*. Englewood Cliffs, NJ: Prentice-Hall.

Benner, Chris. 2002. *Work in the New Economy: Flexible Labor Market in Silicon Valley.* New York: Wiley.

Berg, Heather. 2021. Porn Work: Sex, Labor, and Late Capitalism. Chapel Hill: North Carolina University Press.

Bernstein, Elizabeth. 2018. *Brokered Subjects: Sex, Trafficking, and the Politics of Freedom.* Chicago: University of Chicago Press.

Bourdieu, Pierre. 2001. *Masculine Domination.* Stanford, CA: Stanford University Press.

Bourdieu, Pierre. 2004. "Symbolic Violence." In *Violence in War and Peace,* edited by Nancy Scheper-Hughes and Philippe Bourgois, 272–74. Malden, MA: Blackwell.

Brinton, Mary C. 1992. *Women and the Economic Miracle: Gender and Work in Postwar Japan.* Berkeley: University of California Press.

Brownmiller, Susan. 1975. *Against Our Will: Men, Women, and Rape.* New York: Simon and Schuster.

Bumiller, Kristin. 2008. *In an Abusive State: How Neoliberalism Appropriated the Feminist Movement against Sexual Violence.* Durham, NC: Duke University Press.

Califia-Rice, Patrick. 1980. *Sapphistry: The Book of Lesbian Sexuality.* Tallahassee: Naiad Press.

Califia-Rice, Patrick. 1994. *Public Sex: The Culture of Radical Sex.* San Francisco: Cleis Press.

Carol, Avedon, and Lee Kennedy. 1994. *Nudes, Prudes, and Attitudes: Pornography and Censorship.* Cheltenham: New Clarion Press.

Coates, Jamie. 2014. "Rogue Diva Flows: Aoi Sola's Reception in the Chinese Media and Mobile Celebrity." *Journal of Japanese and Korean Cinema* 6 (1): 89–103.

Collins, Hugh. 1999. *Regulating Contracts.* Oxford: Oxford University Press.

Connell, R. W. 2005 (1995). *Masculinities.* Berkeley: University of California Press.

Cook, Emma E. 2016. *Reconstructing Adult Masculinities: Part-time Work in Contemporary Japan.* New York: Routledge.

Curtin, Michael, and Kevin Sanson. 2016. *Precarious Creativity: Global Media, Local Labor.* Berkeley: University of California Press.

Das, Veena. 2008. "Violence, Gender, and Subjectivity." *Annual Review of Anthropology* 37 (1): 283–99.

Dasgupta, Romit. 2013. *Re-Reading the Salaryman in Japan: Crafting Masculinities.* New York: Routledge.

Derrida, Jacques. 1999. "Hospitality, Justice and Responsibility: A Dialogue with Jacques Derrida." In *Questioning Ethics: Contemporary Debates in Philosophy,* edited by Richard Kearney and Mark Dooley, 65–83. New York: Routledge.

Diet Cabinet Office of Japan. 2017. "Internet Survey on Sexual Violence Targeting Young People." http://www.gender.go.jp/policy/no_violence/e-vaw/chousa/pdf/h29_jakunen_report.pdf.

Dodson, Betty. 1987. *Sex for One: The Joy of Selfloving*. New York: Crown Trade.

Doezema, Jo. 1998. "Forced to Choose: Beyond Voluntary v. Forced Prostitution Dichotomy." In *Global Sex Workers: Rights, Resistance, and Redefinition*, edited by Kamala Kempadoo and Jo Doezema, 34–50. New York: Routledge.

Duggan, Lisa, and Nan D. Hunter. 2006. *Sex Wars: Sexual Dissent and Political Culture*. 10th ann. ed. New York: Routledge.

Dworkin, Andrea. 1981. *Pornography: Men Possessing Women*. New York: Perigee Books.

Dworkin, Andrea, and Catharine A. MacKinnon. 1988. *Pornography and Civil Rights: A New Day for Women's Equality*. Minneapolis: Organizing Against Pornography.

Entwistle, Joanne, and Elizabeth Wissinger. 2006. "Keeping Up Appearances: Aesthetic Labour in the Fashion Modelling Industries of London and New York." *Sociological Review* 54 (4): 774–94.

Fassin, Didier. 2012. *Humanitarian Reason: A Moral History of the Present Times*. Berkeley: University of California Press.

Fischel, Michael J. 2019. *Screw Consent: A Better Politics of Sexual Justice*. Berkeley: University of California Press.

Fried, Charles. 2015 (1981). *Contract as Promise: A Theory of Contractual Obligation*. Oxford: Oxford University Press.

Frug, Mary Joe. 1985. "Re-reading Contracts: A Feminist Analysis of a Contracts Casebook." *American University Law Review* 34 (4): 1065–1140.

Futrelle, David. 2012. "Sex on the Internet: Sizing Up the Online Smut Economy." *Time*, April 4, 2012. https://business.time.com/2012/04/04/sex-on-the-internet-sizing-up-the-online-smut-economy/.

Galbraith, Patrick W. 2019. *Otaku and the Struggle for Imagination in Japan*. Durham, NC: Duke University Press.

Galbraith, Patrick W., and Jason G. Karlin. 2012. *Idols and Celebrity in Japanese Media Culture*. New York: Palgrave Macmillan.

Galtung, Johan. 1969. "Violence, Peace, and Peace Research." *Journal of Peace Research* 6 (3): 167–91.

Gagné, Nana Okura. 2020. *Reworking Japan: Changing Men at Work and Play under Neoliberalism*. Ithaca, NY: ILR Press, an imprint of Cornell University Press.

Gilmore, Grant, and Ronald K. L. Collins. 1995. *The Death of Contract*. Columbus: Ohio State University Press.

Griffin, Susan. 1981. *Pornography and Silence: Culture's Revenge against Nature*. New York: Harper and Row.

Hadfield, Gillian K. 1995. "The Dilemma of Choice: A Feminist Perspective on the Limits of Freedom of Contract." *Osgoode Hall Law Journal* 33 (2): 337–51.

Hambleton, Alexandra. 2016. "When Women Watch: The Subversive Potential of Female-Friendly Pornography in Japan." *Porn Studies* 3 (4): 427–42.

Harris, Cheryl I. 1993. "Whiteness as Property." *Harvard Law Review* 106 (8): 1707–91.

Hashimoto, Kenji. 2018. *Andā Kurasu: Arata na Kasōkaikyu no Shutsugen (Underclass: Emergence of New Lower Class)*. Tokyo: Chikuma Shobo.

Held, Virginia. 1987. "Non-contractual Society: A Feminist View." *Canadian Journal of Philosophy Supplementary Volume* 13: 111–37.

Hendry, Joy. 2019. *Understanding Japanese Society*. 5th ed. New York: Routledge.

Hochschild, Arlie R. 2003 (1983). *The Managed Heart: Commercialization of Human Feeling*. 20th ann. ed. Berkeley: University of California Press.

House of Representatives, Japan. 2016. "Kaigiroku" (Meeting Minutes). For the information in English, see http://hrn.or.jp/eng/news/2016/06/14/coerced-porno graphic-statement/. For Japanese, see http://www.shugiin.go.jp/internet/itdb_kaigirokua/000219020160311005.htm.

Human Rights Now. 2016. "Japan: Coerced Filming of Adult Pornographic Videos." For the information in English, see http://hrn.or.jp/eng/wp-content/uploads/2016 /06/ReportonAVindustry-20160303-tentative-translation.pdf. For the report in Japanese, see http://hrn.or.jp/wpHN/wp-content/uploads/2016/03/c5389134140c 669e3ff6ec9004e4933a.pdf.

Ivy, Marilyn. 1995. *Discourses of the Vanishing: Modernity, Phantasm, Japan*. Chicago: University of Chicago Press.

Kilby, Jane. 2013. "Introduction to Special Issue: Theorizing Violence." *European Journal of Social Theory* 16 (3): 261–72.

Kim, Junghoon, and Naoto Ikegai. 2006. "Sōzō Kēzai ni okeru Kontentsu Sēsaku (Contents Policy in the Creative Economy)." *Keio Media Communications Research* 56 (3): 183–97.

Kitanaka, Junko. 2012. *Depression in Japan: Psychiatric Cures for a Society in Distress*. Princeton, NJ: Princeton University Press.

Koch, Gabriele. 2020. *Healing Labor: Japanese Sex Work in the Gendered Economy*. Stanford, CA: Stanford University Press.

Kokubun, Kōichirō. 2017. *Chūdōtai no Sekai: Ishi to Sekinin no Kōkogaku (The World of Middle Voice: Archaeology of Will and Accountability)*. Tokyo: Igaku Shoin.

Kondo, Dorinne K. 1986. "Dissolution and Reconstitution of Self: Implications for Anthropological Epistemology." *Cultural Anthropology* 1 (1): 74–88.

Kuga, Hiroto. 1999. "Nihonjin no Bunka to Sosharu Wāku: Ukemiteki na Taijink-ankei ni okeru 'Shutaisei' no Haaku (Japanese Culture and Social Work: Grasping 'Subjectivity' in Passive Interpersonal Relationships)." *Shakai Fukushigaku* 41 (1): 113–32.

Larkin, Brian. 2013. "The Politics and Poetics of Infrastructure." *Annual Review of Anthropology* 42 (1): 327–43.

Lebra, Takie Sugiyama. 2004. *The Japanese Self in Cultural Logic*. Honolulu: University of Hawai'i Press.

Lederer, Laura. 1980. *Take Back the Night: Women on Pornography*. New York: Morrow.

Lukács, Gabriella. 2010. *Scripted Affects, Branded Selves: Television, Subjectivity, and Capitalism in 1990s Japan*. Durham, NC: Duke University Press.

Lukács, Gabriella. 2020. *Invisibility by Design: Women and Labor in Japan's Digital Economy*. Durham, NC: Duke University Press.

MacKinnon, Catharine A. 1982. "Feminism, Marxism, Method, and the State: An Agenda for Theory." *Signs: Journal of Women in Culture and Society* 7 (3): 515–44.

MacKinnon, Catharine A. 1983. "Feminism, Marxism, Method, and the State: Toward Feminist Jurisprudence." *Signs: Journal of Women in Culture and Society* 8 (4): 635–58.

MacKinnon, Catharine A. 1984. "Not a Moral Issue." *Yale Law and Policy Review* 2 (2): 321–45.

Macpherson, C. B. 1962. *The Political Theory of Possessive Individualism: Hobbes to Locke*. Oxford: Clarendon Press.

Marx, Karl. 1990 (1976). *Capital: A Critique of Political Economy*. Vol. 1. London; New York: Penguin Books.

McKee, Alan. 2016. "Pornography as a Creative Industry: Challenging the Exceptionalist Approach to Pornography." *Porn Studies* 3 (2): 107–19.

Miriam, Kathy. 2005. "Stopping the Traffic in Women: Power, Agency and Abolition in Feminist Debates over Sex-Trafficking." *Journal of Social Philosophy* 36 (1): 1–17.

Miyamoto, Setsuko. 2016. *AV Shutsuen wo Kyōyō sareta Kanojotachi (Women Who Were Forced to Perform in AV)*. Tokyo: Chikuma Shobo.

Miyamoto, Setsuko. 2016. "Mada Kashika sareteinai Adaruto Bideo Sangyō no Seibōryoku to Wakamono no Hinkon (The Harm of Adult Video: Yet-to-Be-Revealed Sexual Violence in the Adult Video Industry and Poverty among Youth)." *Chingin to Shakaihoshō* (Wages and Social Security) 1649/1650 (January): 18–34.

Morgan, Robin. 1977. *Going Too Far: The Personal Chronicle of a Feminist*. New York: Random House.

Motohashi, Nobuhiro. 2016. *Zenra Kantoku: Muranishi Toru (The Naked Director: Muranishi Toru)*. Tokyo: Ota Shuppan.

Mulcahy, Linda. 2014. "The Limitations of Love and Altruism: Feminist Perspectives on Contract Law." In *Feminist Perspectives on Contract Law*, edited by Linda Mulcahy and Sally Wheeler, 1–20. London: Routledge.

Nakamura, Atsuhiko. 2012. *Syokugyō toshite no AV Joyū (AV [Adult Video] Actress as an Occupation)*. Tokyo: Gentōsya.

Nakamura, Atsuhiko. 2015. *AV Bijinesu no Shōgeki (The Impact of AV [Adult Video] Businesses)*. Tokyo: Syōgakkan.

Neu, Michael. 2018. *Just Liberal Violence: Sweatshops, Torture, War*. London: Rowman and Littlefield International.

Nietzsche, Friedrich Wilhelm, and Horace Barnett Samuel. 2003. *The Genealogy of Morals*. Mineola: Dover.

Osaki, Tomohiro. 2015. "Landmark Ruling in Favor of Victimized Porn Actress Paves Away for Others to Quit, Lawyers Say." *Japan Times*, September 30, 2015. https://www.japantimes.co.jp/news/2015/09/30/national/crime-legal/landmark -ruling-favor-victimized-porn-actress-paves-way-others-quit-say-lawyers/#.XE 3A989KhTY.

Pateman, Carole. 1988. *The Sexual Contract*. Stanford, CA: Stanford University Press.

Popova, Milena. 2019. *Sexual Consent*. Cambridge, MA: MIT Press.

Ramsay, Maureen. 2010. "Liberal Democratic Politics as a Form of Violence." *Democratization* 17 (2): 235–50.

Rich, Adrienne. 1980. "Compulsory Heterosexuality and Lesbian Existence." *Signs: Journal of Women in Culture and Society* 5 (4): 631–60.

Rich, B. Ruby. 1983. "Anti-Porn: Soft Issue, Hard World." *Feminist Review* 13: 56–67.

Rofel, Lisa. 1999. *Other Modernities: Gendered Yearnings in China after Socialism*. Berkeley: University of California Press.

Ronald, Richard, and Allison Alexy, eds. 2011. *Home and Family in Japan: Continuity and Transformation*. New York: Routledge.

Rosenberger, Nancy R. 2001. *Gambling with Virtue: Japanese Women and the Search for Self in a Changing Nation*. Honolulu: University of Hawai'i Press.

Rubin, Gayle. 1975. "The Traffic in Women: Notes on the 'Political Economy' of Sex." In *Toward an Anthropology of Women*, edited by Rayna Reiter, 157–210. New York: Monthly Review Press.

Rubin, Gayle. 1984. "Thinking Sex: Notes for a Radical Theory of the Politics of Sexuality." In *Pleasure and Danger: Exploring Female Sexuality*, edited by Carole S. Vance, 267–319. Boston: Routledge.

Russell, Diana E. H. 1998. *Dangerous Relationships: Pornography, Misogyny, and Rape*. Thousand Oaks, CA: Sage.

Scheper-Hughes, Nancy, and Philippe Bourgois, eds. 2004. *Violence in War and Peace*. Malden, MA: Blackwell.

Scheper-Hughes, Nancy, and Philippe Bourgois. 2004. "Introduction: Making Sense of Violence." In *Violence in War and Peace*, edited by Nancy Scheper-Hughes and Philippe Bourgois, 1–32. Malden, MA: Blackwell.

Spivak, G. 1987. *In Other Worlds: Essays in Cultural Politics*. London: Taylor and Francis.

Stanley, Amy Dru. 1998. *From Bondage to Contract: Wage Labor, Marriage, and the Market in the Age of Slave Emancipation*. Cambridge: Cambridge University Press.

Suchland, Jennifer. 2015. *Economies of Violence: Transnational Feminism, Postsocialism, and the Politics of Sex Trafficking*. Durham, NC: Duke University Press.

Sugimoto, Yoshio. 2010. *An Introduction to Japanese Society.* 3rd ed. Cambridge: Cambridge University Press.

Sullivan, Barbara. 2000. "It's All in the Contract: Rethinking Critiques of Contract." *Law Context: A Socio-Legal Journal* 18 (2): 112–28.

Takeyama, Akiko. 2016. *Staged Seduction: Selling Dreams in a Tokyo Host Club.* Stanford, CA: Stanford University Press.

Tidey, Sylvia. 2013. "Corruption and Adherence to Rules in the Construction Sector: Reading the 'Bidding Books.'" *American Anthropologist* 115 (2): 188–202.

Tsing, Anna. 2000. "Inside the Economy of Appearances." *Public Culture* 12 (1): 115–44.

Ueno, Chizuko. 2021. "Why Do Japanese Women Suffer from the Low Status? The Impact of Neo-liberalist Reform on Gender." *Japanese Political Economy* 47 (1): 9–26.

US Department of State. 2017. *2017 Trafficking in Persons Report.* Washington, DC: US Department of State.

Vance, Carole S., ed. 1984. *Pleasure and Danger: Exploring Female Sexuality.* Boston: Routledge & K. Paul.

Wertheimer, Alan. 2003. *Consent to Sexual Relations.* Cambridge: Cambridge University Press.

Witz, Anne, Chris Warhurst, and Dennis Nickson. 2003. "The Labour of Aesthetics and the Aesthetics of Organization." *Organization* 10 (1): 33–54.

Wong, Heung-Wah, and Hoi-yan Yau. 2014. *Japanese Adult Videos in Taiwan.* New York: Routledge.

Yagi, Tadashi. 2006. "Kontentsu Sangyo no Rōdōshijo: Gējutsu to Rōdō (Labor Market of Content Industry: Arts and Labor)." *Japanese Journal of Labour Studies* 48 (4): 52–57.

Yasuda, Rio. 2018. *AV Joyū, Nochi (After Lives of AV Actresses).* Tokyo: Kadokawa.

# INDEX

adult video. *See* AV
Akane Hotaru, 161
Amatsuka Moe, 1–6, 13, 25, 80, 88–90,
    155, 184, 203n5, 217n2, 218n23
Aoi Sola, 24–25, 211n72
Appel, Hannah, 20, 207n52–n54
Asad, Talal, 16, 21, 206n31
AV (adult video): differences in US
    and Japan, 82, 160; impact of digital
    economy on, 7, 10, 23, 25, 162; as
    intellectual property (copyrighted
    product), 11, 27, 56, 92, 204n10,
    221n13; as masturbation tool, 69, 81,
    84, 160, 166, 177, 184; protection of,
    37–38, 69, 188. *See also* pornography
AV actress: adaptability of, 77, 142–143,
    186; dignity of, 27, 59, 71–72, 74, 83,
    85, 88, 90; 121, 185; emotional state
    and mental health, 6, 89, 188, 194 (*see
    also* AV actress as a career: emo-
    tional labor); excessive supply of, 23,
    26; exploitation of, 153; on fear/risk

of identity reveal, 6, 9, 32, 34, 50, 60,
    62, 64–66, 68, 88, 90, 97, 99, 104–105,
    140, 153, 158, 197, 219n2; "kept in the
    dark," 73, 93, 105, 114–117, 124, 218n12,
    221n15; on relationship issues, 66–68,
    120, 187; sense of self-empowerment,
    7, 87, 143, 196; on silence/secrecy, 15,
    21, 27, 31–33, 60, 67, 69, 80, 81, 89–90,
    188; "wannabe" AV idols, 162–163.
    *See also* AV actress as a career
AV actress as a career: ambivalent status
    of, 80, 105–106, 118, 220n2; becoming
    AV actress, 41, 70, 162; casualization
    of, 25, 161–162; as disposable/valuable
    commodity, 4,7, 48–49, 63, 71, 88, 90,
    110, 114–116, 121, 139, 143, 146, 152–153,
    221n12; earnings/pay of, 77, 97–98,
    119, 162, 193, 211n71; emotional labor
    (*see also* AV actress: emotional state
    and mental health), 4, 27, 42, 60–61,
    82–84, 86–89, 182–183, 188, 215n38;
    fame and success, 24–25, 39,

CPSIA information can be obtained
at www.ICGtesting.com
Printed in the USA
JSHW080316100523
41511JS00001B/1

9 781503 633780